The Castle of Lies

THE CASTLE OF LIES

Why Britain Must Get Out of Europe

Christopher Booker
&
Richard North

Duckworth

First published in 1996 by
Gerald Duckworth & Co. Ltd.
The Old Piano Factory
48 Hoxton Square, London N1 6PB
Tel: 0171 729 5986
Fax: 0171 729 0015

A catalogue record for this book
is available from the British Library

ISBN 0 7156 2693 0

Typeset by Ray Davies
Printed in Great Britain by
Biddles Ltd, Guildford and King's Lynn

Contents

They must be worse than blind who cannot see with what undeviating regularity of system, in this case and in all cases, they pursue their scheme for the destruction of every independent power .... The design is wicked, immoral, impious, oppressive: but it is spirited and daring. It is systematic; it is simple in its principle; it has unity and consistency in perfection. In that country entirely to cut off a branch of commece, to extinguish a manufacture, to destroy the circulation of money, to violate credit, to suspend the course of agriculture ... does not cost them a moment's anxiety. To them the will, the wish, the want, the liberty, the toil, the blood of individuals is nothing. Individuality is left out of their scheme of Government. The state is all in all.

Edmund Burke
Letters on the Regicide Directory 1796

Introduction

As the year 1996 neared its end, it was becoming only too clear that the British people were approaching one of the most critical moments of decision in their history.

As the countries making up the European Union seemed to be moving inexorably towards a far more complete state of economic and political unity than before, Britain had come to look more and more isolated.

The question was no longer whether Britain might suddenly go through a complete change of heart and become an enthusiastic part of that movement.

The question which now presented itself with ever-greater urgency was starkly simple. Would Britain just continue, reluctantly and protestingly, to be carried along on that tide, in a way most of her political leaders still seemed to accept as inevitable?

Or would she soon have to face up to the need to negotiate a wholly new relationship with this immense new unified state emerging in Europe?

The reason why this moment of crisis was approaching was that, in the previous few years, the British people's perception of the entire 'European project' had been going through a historic shift.

For the first 20 years after we joined the Common Market in 1973, we still looked on 'Europe' largely in theoretical terms, as something abstract and remote, not really having much direct impact on people's everyday lives.

But after 1992, when Britain stumbled out of the disastrous experiment of the ERM, we entered on a sharp learning curve. The years when 'Europe' could be perceived simply in theoretical, abstract terms were over. In all sorts of ways, large and small, we began to see how it really operates in practice. And the reality of what was coming to light provided a profound shock.

Although much of the noisier public debate conducted by politicians and the media still managed to obscure the point, what really disturbed a growing number of people in Britain was the recognition that they were now living under what amounted to an entirely new System of government, unlike anything Britain or the world had seen before.

It is that new System of government, in all its ramifications, from the impact it is beginning to have on the lives of ordinary people to the devastating effect it has already had on our political structures, which is the theme of this book.

What this book tries to set out for the first time – on an infinitely larger stage than our previous book, *The Mad Officials* – is just how that new System actually operates in practice, and how it has come about.

The chief reason why it has has taken so long to wake up to the realities of the new System lies in the way it manages to conceal what it is really up to – the extent to which it constantly pretends to be something other than what it is. It operates continually under an immense cloud of plausible-sounding theory, while in practice it turns out to be something totally different.

This smokescreen of pretence is absolutely intrinsic to the way the System works. And one of its greatest assets has been that it is so complex, so riddled with technicalities, so vast in the range of its operations, that it took a long time for those outside the System to begin to crack the riddle, and to see just how far the theory, based on wishful thinking, differed from the practice.

The wishful thinking starts with the desire to build a new, perfect world – safe, hygienic, environmentally clean, devoted to the welfare of people and animals. This little world is Europe, sealed off behind its tariff walls, with a Single Market in which everyone can be prosperous and secure, moving inexorably towards ever closer union – a new nation with its own flag, its own anthem, its own parliament, its own central bank giving central direction to its economy, and eventually its own foreign policy, defence forces, police and all the rest of the apparatus of a single, central government.

This is the dream which is to be brought about partly by a series of treaties which lock each nation ever more irrevocably into a single United State of Europe, the latest of which is under discussion even now.

But beneath that grander vision, the nuts and bolts of building that new world lie in an ever-more elaborate system of regulation and bureaucracy. And this is where the new System impinges directly on people's lives.

What this book shows is how, for reasons peculiar to this country, Britain has been making more of a mess of building this new world than any other country, because of the unique extent to which it has empowered a particular element in society, the bureaucratic machine, to carry out something which by definition cannot be achieved.

This is why in the mid-1990s an ever-growing number of the British people began to sense that something very strange and rather sinister was happening to their society, of which their political leaders had not warned them, and which the politicians now seemed quite powerless to stop.

It was still to take a considerable time for the penny really to drop. And to this day, thanks not least to the extraordinary blindness of much of the media, which have continued to report this revolution in our government with such a relentless combination of superficiality and ignorance, for many the awakening has not even yet begun.

Nevertheless, as the whole System began more and more obviously to part company with reality and to go off the rails, all that was left to the politicians was either to pretend that it wasn't happening it at all, or just to fall back on empty claims that they would strive to get the System reformed. But by now it was out of their hands. This was why in the mid-1990s so many people came to feel more and more alienated from them and from our political system in general, often without really understanding the deeper reasons why.

It might have seemed that there was now nothing which could be done, except to wait for that series of disasters which would mark the dream's eventual collision with reality, and which alone might wake the British people up to the real nature of what was happening.

As the events of 1996 unfolded, particularly in the growing discord between

Introduction

Britain and the rest of the EU over a whole range of issues, including the Single Currency, the fisheries scandal and the unimaginable beef disaster, there were abundant signs that such a moment was at last approaching.

It is to that process of awakening that we hope the story set out in this book, as horrifying in its implications as anything the peoples of Britain and Europe have faced for half a century, may make its own contribution.

Acknowledgements

This book could not have been written without the contribution of what we think of as 'the team', that small but ever-growing network of people who in Britain in the past year or two have been gradually piecing together a proper understanding of how the new System of government we are living under really works.

We have often thought of this process as like the assembling of an enormous jigsaw puzzle, made up of thousands of individual pieces, each contributing to the whole. And our thanks must first go to all those people who have helped supply the pieces, large and small, which have finally been brought together for the first time to make up the picture presented in this book.

If *The Castle of Lies* had a dedication, it would once again – as in our previous, much smaller book, *The Mad Officials* – be, first, to those thousands of readers of the *Sunday* and *Daily Telegraph* and the *Daily Mail*, who have so tirelessly written to us, providing the countless individual stories which have been invaluable in building up the jigsaw. It has simply not been possible, alas, for two hard-pressed journalists, without secretarial help, to answer all those thousands of letters individually. We are hugely grateful to those readers who have merely sent heartening messages of general encouragement. But in particular we are grateful to the many hundreds whose evidence has, in one way or another, whether their names appear or not, contributed to this book.

There is a much smaller team of people, however, who have contributed to building up a more general, in-depth understanding of how this vast, mysterious System works, and how it has come to evolve, often highly secretively, over the years.

Despite the general picture of Britain's politicians given in this book, we would particularly like to single out a tiny group of MPs and peers, both Conservative and Labour, who have upheld the finest traditions of Parliament, in their tireless efforts to penetrate that great protective wall of official concealment which has been the System's greatest ally. In particular we would like to acknowledge Nigel Spearing MP, the Labour backbencher whose painstaking trawls through Hansard have done much to uncover some of the murkier episodes of the past 25 years. Among other MPs on both sides of the House, our thanks for help and inspiration must also go to Iain Duncan-Smith, Austin Mitchell, Sir Richard Body, Christopher Gill, Teresa Gorman, Anthony Steen, Eddie O'Hara, Bill Cash, John Redwood and, by no means least, Norman Lamont. In the House of Lords we are particularly

Acknowledgements

indebted to the indefatigable Lord Pearson of Rannoch; to the Earl of Onslow, Lord Vinson and Lord Buxton; to their Labour colleagues Lord Bruce of Donington and Lord Stoddart; and to George Thomas, now Lord Tonypandy, the ex-Speaker who, in 1995, became so concerned at the threat the new System posed to the sovereignty of Parliament that, in defiance of the traditional discretion surrounding his former office, he could no longer keep silent.

Although it might seem almost a contradiction in terms to mention here a member of the European Parliament, we must also thank Brian Cassidy, the only British MEP who seems aware of the huge problems posed to so many businesses by the explosion in Euro-related bureaucracy.

Others who must be thanked for unflagging help, and for their valiant part in the wider struggle, include Mike Fisher of the Deregulation Task Force; Norman Henry and Margaret Leonard; Charles Wyatt; Vivien Linacre, founder of the Weights and Measures Preservation Society; Keith Pulman; Peter Frankel; Ernest Virgo; Robin Page; Flora Jenner; Idris Francis; Ian Milne and the staff of *Eurofacts* and the *European Journal*. Although they might not necessarily wish to be associated with the more general struggle, we would also like to thank Tim Oliver, Editor of *Fishing News*; Anthony Gibson, South-West Regional Director of the NFU; Roger Eddy; Jules Amis at the *Sunday Telegraph* and Hilary Lowinger at *Private Eye*.

A special tribute is due to those who have waged such a noble fight for the survival of the two industries in Britain most gravely threatened by the new System. It has been exhilarating to work alongside John Ashworth and Tom Hay, twin masterminds of the Save Britain's Fish campaign, who with men like Jim Portus, Chris Venmore, Magni Stewart and Mick Mahon have performed such a heroic feat in exposing the multi-layered outrage of the Common Fisheries Policy, not least in helping to unravel the astonishing political scandal of how this all came about in the first place.

In some ways an even grimmer, because less romantic campaign has been the, at times almost surreal battle fought for the survival of hundreds of expert and professional businesses in the meat trade. Here we owe particular thanks to Don Bennett, Ian Lentern, Toby Baker, Sammy Morphet and Margaret Jones.

For their own inimitable contributions to supplying vital pieces of the jigsaw, we must pay tribute to Bernard Connolly, formerly of DG II in Brussels and author of *The Rotten Heart of Europe*; and to Bill Jamieson, Economics Editor of the *Sunday Telegraph* and author of *Britain Beyond Europe*, who more than anyone lifted our eyes from the suffocating backyard of Europe to show just how well Britain is now performing economically on the wider world stage.

We are indebted to Jim McCue for the quotation from Edmund Burke which stands first in the book, taken from his own forthcoming book *Edmund Burke And Our Present Discontents*; and to Dr Mark Almond for his study *Blundering in the Balkans: the European Community and the Yugoslav crisis*.

A special tribute is due to Brigadier Anthony Cowgill of the British Management Data Foundation, who has fought such a doughty battle for truth, not least by giving the British people a chance to read the consolidated European Treaties when our Government was trying to conceal what it had signed up to at Maastricht; and by first exposing the chicanery involved in the 'European establishment's' use of the CBI as a 'front organisation' for their cause.

Our greatest personal debt, for unfailing help in all sorts of ways, is to Dr Helen Szamuely who, as a Hungarian Jew brought up in the Soviet Union, particularly delights in being dismissed as a 'Little Englander'. The scale of her contribution in bringing to light key facts about the 'Euro-mess' from a thousand Hansards, reports and obscure regulations cannot be overestimated.

We must record our warmest thanks to Michelle Walker and Jennifer Hutton of the European Commission Press Office in London who have given such unfailingly prompt service in supplying us with a mountain of directives and regulations. In this respect at least, and regardless of our wider differences, it is a tribute to the efficiency and 'transparency' of the Commission that its staff should have been unstinting in their help.

We are deeply grateful to Valerie, Mary and our respective families for their patience with our abstraction during the long months when this book was taking shape, and to all those other friends to whom this is relevant.

Finally, we must pay special tribute to the unique contribution of the Rt. Hon. Sir Edward Heath, KG, PC, MP, without whose efforts this book would never have had to be written in the first place.

Prologue

The Binding of Gulliver

One of the more haunting images in English literature is that of Gulliver waking up on the beach on which he has been shipwrecked. He finds to his alarm he cannot move. Gradually he realises that, while he has been asleep, an army of little Lilliputians has tied him down in a mass of silken threads. He is a prisoner.

All over Britain in 1995 and 1996 people began to feel they had been through a not dissimilar experience. They were gradually waking up to the fact that something very strange had happened to their system of government.

*

One morning in April 1995 farmers gathered in the north Yorkshire market town of Malton, as they have done for centuries, to sell their animals. Suddenly from all sides of the market place came a crowd of policemen and officials. Business came to a halt as dozens of farmers were interrogated about the weight of the Land Rovers and trailers in which they had brought their cows and sheep to market. Most were then told, to their astonishment, that they were committing a criminal offence. The combined weight of their vehicles, trailers and the animals in them came to more than 3.5 metric tonnes. This meant, under new regulations, that their farm vehicles should have tachographs, the 'spy in the cab' devices fitted to heavy goods vehicles to record the exact times and distances drivers spend on the road on long journeys. When a farmer who had heard of the new law protested that surely it didn't apply to farmers driving to their nearest market, a policeman asked where he came from. Egton, on the Yorkshire Moors, was the reply. 'Then Malton is not your nearest market' the policeman told him. There was a tiny mart on the moors, at the little village of Ruswarp. The farmer indignantly explained that he didn't use Ruswarp because he could get £60 more for his animals at Malton. This was irrelevant, said the policeman. Under the law Malton was not his nearest market; he would therefore have to spend £700 fitting his Land Rover with a tachograph.

What none of the policemen or officials bothered to explain was that these new rules came from EC Council Regulation 3820/85 on 'the harmonising of certain social legislation relating to road transport'.

*

In Lymington, Hampshire, Rowland Spencer runs Hotbox Heaters, a small firm making specialised gas heaters for use in greenhouses. There are only six such businesses in Europe, all British.

In the early 1990s these firms were told that new regulations were to be issued by the Department of Trade and Industry to implement an EC directive on 'liquid gas appliances', 90/396. This was to make trade easier in the new Single Market by harmonising rules throughout the EC. On 1 January 1996 it would become a criminal offence to sell their heaters without a 'CE' (for 'Communauté Européene') safety mark. This was a system introduced under various Single Market directives to show that products had been tested to comply with EC standards.

As the deadline approached, Mr Spencer spent £20,000 having his heaters tested by a Dutch-owned test house. He imagined the CE mark would now enable his products to be sold anywhere in the EU. To his astonishment, however, he then learned that because different EC countries use no fewer than 37 types of gas, his heaters would have to be tested 37 times, once for each gas. The result of the Single Market legislation was thus to make it uneconomical for Mr Spencer to continue selling his products in Europe at all.

Fortunately, however, his exports to America, Asia and elsewhere in the world, where it was still possible to sell without such prohibitive expense, were rapidly rising.

*

In February 1995, when Joan Tart of Wednesfield, near Wolverhampton, took her Irish setter Monty to the vet, she had a rude shock. A year before, Monty had developed epilepsy. The vet had prescribed a regular dose of phenobarbitone tablets, costing £40 a year, which kept the disease in check.

But now the vet told her this was forbidden, under the new Medicines (Restrictions on the Administration of Veterinary Medicinal Products) Regulations, implementing EC directive 90/676. Phenobarbitone was only licensed for human use, and under the new rules it was a criminal offence, punishable by a fine of up to £5,000, for a vet to administer such drugs unless they had been specially tested for use on animals. Mrs Tart's dog would have to be given a specialist animal product, myaselin, which would cost her £400 a year, ten times as much. This was also considered less effective, and could produce unwelcome side-effects, such as liver damage.

In the early months of 1995 thousands of other pet owners had similar experiences, as they discovered the cost of treatment for their animals had risen by up to 1,000 per cent. Vets too were angered by this restriction on the number of drugs they could prescribe for animals, which originated in the idea that residues from human drugs might be harmful if they somehow got into the human food chain.

This scarcely applied to dogs, cats and budgies. Nevertheless the law was the law, and the impact on costs was so dramatic that animal charities such as the People's Dispensary for Sick Animals had to launch appeals for hundreds of thousands of pounds to cover the astronomic rise in pets' drug bills.

*

In March 1995 near Llantrisant in South Wales dairy farmer Richard Barrett was having to pour hundreds of gallons of perfectly good milk away onto his fields. Although this lost him 23p for every litre he chucked away, if he did not do so he faced paying fines of 28p for every litre he kept, amounting to thousands of pounds.

What particularly angered Mr Barrett was that there were plenty of willing customers for his milk. Indeed only a few months earlier Europe's largest creamery and milk processing plant had closed down in the little South Welsh town of Whitland, with a loss of 400 jobs, because it could not get enough milk.

The reason for all this was that under the EC milk quota system Britain was no longer allowed to produce anything like the amount of milk it needed. The scheme's purpose had been to reduce the 'milk lake' caused by the over-production of subsidised milk in other EC countries. When Brussels came to fix each country's quota, based on past production figures, Britain's dairy farmers were only allocated 85 per cent of the country's needs. But Britain's milk production had already been sharply cut back because, when she joined the Common Market in 1973, a quarter of a million dairy cows were culled on orders from Brussels, and it was on this reduced figure the quota was fixed. Twenty years later this left thousands of farmers like Mr Barrett having to throw away millions of gallons of milk it was illegal for them to produce, while from Somerset to Scotland cheese dairies closed for lack of sufficient milk.

*

Early in July 1995 Brian Nellist, a Hull fruit merchant, was startled to be told by trading standards officials that it would be a criminal offence to sell nectarines worth £3,000 because they were 'too small'. Under an EC regulation it was an offence to sell the nectarines after 30 June because they were under 56 millimetres in diameter. It would have been quite legal to sell them before that date, but as a Ministry of Agriculture spokesman explained, under the Brussels rules, Class D nectarines, between 51mm and 56mm, could not be sold after 30 June, because that was the official date when larger ones became available.

The officials told Mr Nellist he was not allowed to give away the fruit to local pensioners, because they might sell it. It could only be used to feed animals in a zoo, or given to an officially recognised charity. Sixty-nine-year-old Mr Nellist said, 'I am too old to go chasing flamingos around in zoos', but he eventually managed to donate the fruit to a local hospice – at the price, of course, of losing his £3,000.

*

At Ebley near Stroud, Gloucestershire, in October 1995 the little firm of Hooper's, which for 70 years had been turning wood for walking sticks and

3

umbrella handles, closed its doors for the last time, putting nine people out of work. The reason for the closure lay in new DTI regulations, due to come into force on 1 January 1996, implementing the EC's Machinery Directive, 89/392.

Under the new law, it would be a criminal offence for the firm to operate its machines, mostly designed by the firm's managing director Peter Burriss, unless they carried the famous CE mark, introduced to assist trade in the Single Market by ensuring that products were tested to a common safety standard. The problem was the tens of thousands of pounds it would cost to send Mr Burriss's machines away to be tested made it completely uneconomical to keep them running. Yet the machines were not made to be sold in the Single Market or anywhere. Their only function was to provide work for nine people who had now lost their jobs.

*

On a sunny day in January 1996 fisherman Clive Mills stood on an Essex beach watching a mechanical excavator smash his fishing boat, the *Alvic*, to matchwood. It spelled the end of a lifetime's fishing and of a vessel which had earned his family's livelihood for more than 20 years.

The story which led to this sad ending had begun just over a year before when officials of the Ministry of Agriculture, Fisheries and Food (MAFF) carried out a swoop on the tiny Essex fishing port of West Mersea. As the little wooden fishing boats tied up at the quay, the ministry inspectors caught more than a dozen local fishermen trying to land more sole than they were permitted by the quota rules laid down by Brussels under the Common Fisheries Policy.

The reason why the fishermen were breaking the law was quite simple. After successive cuts in their permitted catch, the diktats of the CFP no longer allowed them to catch enough fish to earn a living. Yet what really angered the fishermen was that in the same area of the North Sea, those same Brussels rules were allowing large modern Dutch and Norwegian beam trawlers to catch more sole in a day than the little West Mersea boats could catch in a whole season – in waters which, if Edward Heath had not signed them away in 1972 as 'a common European resource', would still have been British.

For the criminal offence of exceeding their tiny quota, just before Christmas 1995 Clive Mills and another West Mersea fisherman, Roger Free, were fined £12,000 by Colchester magistrates. Ironically, Mr Mills knew his only hope of paying the fine was to go out of business, by applying to MAFF for a share in the £53 million it had allocated to 'decommission' hundreds of British fishing boats. This was to meet targets set by Brussels under another CFP scheme, to cut down EC fishing fleets following the accession of Spain, whose vast fleet was three-quarters the size of the rest of the EC fleet put together. In 1992 Brussels had ordered Britain to cut 'fishing effort' by 19 per cent while Spain, with a fleet many times the size of Britain's, had to reduce by only 4 per cent.

Thanks to the cash he received for giving up his livelihood, Mr Mills was able to pay his fine. Among those watching the *Alvic* being broken up was

Paul Clarke, whose uncle built the vessel in the same year Edward Heath took Britain into the Common Market and the Common Fisheries Policy. The Colne Preservation Society wanted to buy the *Alvic* as a fine example of local craftsmanship, but the officials were adamant. The money could only be paid if the boat was destroyed, so it could never be used for any purpose again.

*

In Southampton in January 1996 Jim Good, a 51-year-old chemical tanker driver, learned from a trade paper that new regulations were to come into force on 1 July implementing an EC directive on driving licences, 91/439. Bespectacled lorry drivers like himself would now have to pass a new eyesight test without glasses or contact lenses, on the grounds that their glasses might fall off in a collision. Visiting his optician, Mr Good was horrified to discover he would not pass the test. The next time his licence came up for renewal he would lose his livelihood.

When Mr Good's case was taken up by his union and the media, some remarkable facts came to light. There was no evidence that any accident had ever been caused by a driver's glasses falling off. Opticians insisted this was not a problem. Yet even the Department of Transport admitted that up to 3,000 drivers would lose their jobs as a result of the new rule (although again they could produce no evidence), while trade sources estimated the true figure might run into tens, even hundreds of thousands.

Finally, it emerged that Britain was planning to implement this directive much more zealously than any other country in the EC, by abolishing a system enjoyed by older drivers called 'grandfather rights'. This meant that only in Britain would such drivers, who take a new eyesight test every five years after the age of 45, lose their licences. Thousands of Britain's safest and most experienced drivers, like Jim Good, would thus lose their livelihoods, while other EC drivers with comparable eyesight would still be free to drive not only on continental roads but in Britain as well.

Yet when his new rule came under fire, a junior transport minister Steven Norris brushed aside all criticism, dismissing the 3,000 drivers who even his own officials admitted would lose their jobs as 'only a small number'.

*

Hampshire farmer Roy Houghton, 72, ran a little dairy in the village of Durley. The business gave work to several members of his family, not least his granddaughter Mary, a multiple sclerosis victim, who was able to drive the milk van serving 500 local customers.

In 1995 Mr Houghton was told by an environmental health official of Winchester City council that, under new regulations implementing the EC's dairy hygiene directive, 92/46, it would on 1 January 1996 become a criminal offence for him to continue capping his milk bottles by hand. He would have to install a fully-mechanised bottling system, costing £50,000. For such a tiny operation this was wholly uneconomical so, very reluctantly, Mr Houghton sold his milk round to the Co-Op and closed the business, putting several people out of work, including Mary.

It then came to light, however, that the directive exempted dairies handling fewer than two million litres a year from the requirement to install bottling machinery. Mr Houghton supplied only 100,000 litres a year, so he should not have been forced out of business.

When Winchester council was questioned, health official Roger Rutty said 'the regulations are not exactly clear'. It also then emerged, however, that the exemption for smaller dairies was specifically drawn to the attention of the officials in a Food Safety Act Code of Practice, which it was their statutory duty to read. But for Mr Houghton and his dairy it was too late.

*

Audrey Waller ran a small business in Carluke, Lanarkshire, making ladies' underwear and other fashion items, which she sold through local shops, including The Sewing Box, owned by her mother Morag. One day in February 1995, finding she had some leftover scraps of material, she made four high-quality teddy bears, which she put in her mother's shop window.

Almost immediately a young trading standards official of Strathclyde council came into the shop to point out that the bears did not conform with the regulations. Under the EC Toy Safety directive, 88/378, any toys manufactured after 1990 had to carry a CE mark to show they had been tested to comply with certain safety standards. By selling her daughter's home-made teddies without the CE mark, Mrs Waller was committing a criminal offence. But to send the bears away for the required testing would cost £200, well over twice their combined sale price.

The young trading standards officer, under a legal obligation to enforce the law, had no alternative but to treat anyone who broke the regulations brought in to implement the Brussels directive as a potential criminal. However so sympathetic was she to Mrs Waller's plight that a few days later she came in to buy one of the bears, so the council could bear the cost of testing it themselves. Indeed a council spokesman pointed out that another set of toy safety regulations had just come into force, under which Audrey Waller should not only be submitting her home-made teddies for testing, but should also have produced a 'technical dossier', listing all parts and materials used in making the toys and 'the method of construction at each stage'. The spokesman did, however, explain that there were exemptions under the regulations for 'folk dolls'. He playfully suggested that Miss Waller might get round the rules by dressing her bears in tartans and marketing them as 'McTeddies'.

The Toy Safety directive was primarily targeted at large-scale toy manufacturers, for whom the cost of safety testing would be a comparatively minor expense. It was never intended to apply to home-made products like Miss Waller's teddy bears. However, in their zeal to implement EC directives to the last iota and beyond, officials of the Department of Trade and Industry could not allow for any exemptions – until trading standards officers themselves could see little sense in the law they were bound to enforce.

*

In February 1995, when Mrs Janet MacLean of Dover gave her son a cheque for £1,000, to mark his 21st birthday, he immediately wrote off to a building society to open an account. But he was told they could not accept his money unless he could prove his identity by means of a passport or driving licence. The society also demanded proof of where he lived, by asking him to send a gas, water or electricity bill addressed to him in his own name.

The MacLeans were among many thousands of people baffled by similar demands after new Bank of England regulations came into force implementing EC directive 91/308, 'on prevention of the use of the financial system for the purpose of money laundering'. The directive's purpose, as its preamble explained, was to help stamp out the international drugs trade. This was why, if someone entered a post office with £100 in cash, asking to open a national savings account, the money now had be refused unless its owner could produce a utility bill to prove his or address.

It was fiendishly clever of Brussels to realise that Colombian drugs barons never pay gas bills. But nor, alas, did Mrs MacLean's son. Since he still lived with his parents he had never received one, which was why, weeks later, he was still sitting on his cheque for £1,000, wondering how on earth he could persuade someone to accept his money.

*

In March 1995 Marian Leak of Yalding, Kent, reported to us how a friend had been passing a local apple orchard and saw the owner uprooting hundreds of healthy trees. She asked whether she could buy some to replace old trees in her own garden, but the farmer said this was not permitted. The trees had first to be counted by an inspector, then burned.

This was part of a scheme to cut down the EC's surplus of apples. Farmers were growing so many that, in 1992/3, more than a million tonnes of apples had to be destroyed at taxpayers' expense, 657,371 tonnes in France alone at a cost of £63 million. The Commission had therefore decided to pay apple growers to grub up their orchards. In 1995 Britain was to lose 14.6 per cent of all its commercial apple trees, including according to one estimate a third of all Cox's Orange trees. Some other countries were losing only 2 per cent. The irony was that there was only a small surplus of apples in Britain, while producers in other countries were over-producing huge quantities precisely because they received EC intervention payments for every tonne destroyed. Yet despite the costly grubbing up scheme, the system which caused the problem still remained in place.

*

One British businessman who welcomed the idea of the Single Market was Peter Maurice, who makes reproduction antique lighting in Hove, Sussex. Although he successfully sells his products in America – one contract was to make a magnificent chandelier for the Virginia State House – he imagined the arrival of the CE mark system, establishing an EC-wide system of standards, would make it easier for him to sell in Europe. Like so many other businessmen, however, he then discovered that the French seemed to take no notice of the CE system. He still had to pay all over again to have his products tested to the French standard.

When Mr Maurice wrote about this to Britain's 'Small Firms Minister' Richard Page at the DTI, he was told his difficulties with selling into the Single Market had nothing to do with trade. He should try 'building regulations' at the Department of the Environment. The official who told him this wrote from the DTI's 'Technology, Standards and Environment Directorate, Standards and Technical Regulations Directorate, 6.3.82, Grey Zone'.

*

Farmer Charles Wyatt was surprised to discover in February 1996 that he could no longer move a single sheep off his farm on Romney Marsh, Kent, without having to fill in an EC form. Under the Sheep and Goats (Records, Identification and Movement) Order 1996, implementing EC directive 92/102, owners now had to give each animal an individual ear tag, with its own set of numbers. Each animal had to be registered with the local Animal Health Office, and whenever it was moved off its own farm, a record giving full details had to be filled in and kept for three years.

As Mr Wyatt explained, 'Even if I move one sheep through the village to a field owned by someone else, I must now complete the form.' At least sheep farmers get EC subsidies – but the officials had decided that the new system must also apply to unsubsidised goats, so even the owner of a single goat now had to comply with the EC's red tape.

*

In the summer of 1995 Harold Grenfell, director of a Swansea building company, discussed with his colleagues the possibility of moving the firm's cement mixers round on trailers. When they asked the Driver and Vehicle Licensing Agency whether this would involve any legal requirements, they were sent a four-page document on 'important' changes to be introduced in 1996 under the EC Driving Licence directive, 91/439.

Mr Grenfell's eye was particularly caught by a section headed 'Upgrading Requirements for Trailers':

> In general an additional driving test will be required for each category or subcategory of entitlement. But there remain certain exceptions to this where drivers have already passed one test which involves trailer entitlements for a larger or equivalent size vehicle. This will mean that passing a test for subcategory C1+E or D1+E will upgrade category B entitlement to B+E. But a test pass for C1+E will upgrade subcategory D1, if held, to D1+E. But a test pass for D1+E will not upgrade C1 to C1+E because the trailer size for D1+E tests is smaller than that required for a C1+E test. Passing a test for category C+E will upgrade category B entitlement to B+E and will also confer entitlement to C1 and C1+E and, if category D1 or D is held, will upgrade this to D1+E or D+E. A test passed for category D+E will upgrade category B and subcategory D1 to B+E and D1+E respectively. But it will not upgrade C1 or C entitlements because the trailer size required for a category D test is smaller than that required for a C+E or C1+E test.

After reading this very carefully, Mr Grenfell decided that perhaps it really wasn't such a brilliant idea to carry those mixers round on trailers after all.

*

Guests at the Drummond Arms Hotel in Albury, Surrey, in the summer of 1995 were surprised to find on the menu a dish described as 'roast beef and Yorkies'. This was because a trading standards official had told the manager that, 'under EC regulations', to use the term 'Yorkshire pudding' was now a criminal offence unless this had been made in Yorkshire.

On further investigation it turned out that there was in existence an EC regulation on 'The Protection of Geographical Indications and Designations of Origin for Agricultural Products and Foodstuffs', whereby locally named foodstuffs could be registered with Brussels and protected against misleading labelling. However, it also seemed the Ministry of Agriculture had not yet got round to implementing the regulation, nor did it intend to register Yorkshire pudding as in need of the EC's protection. The Drummond Arms was thus free to change its menus back again, without committing a criminal offence.

*

In Grimsby John and Celia Smith ran a tiny agency, started by his grandfather in 1936, processing customs documents on imports and exports. In 1991 they processed the paperwork for a large consignment of prawns from the Faroe Islands, on behalf of a Faroese company. It was a straightforward operation, earning the Smiths less than £1,000. The only significant detail was that, under a special European Community arrangement, prawns from the Faroes, Norway and Iceland were accompanied by an official customs document, an EUR1, which showed they could come into the EC duty free, without having to pay the 20 per cent duty which applied to prawns from other parts of the world.

In 1992, however, officials of the Commission's Directorate-General XXI went to the three countries and found that an unspecified quantity of the prawns they exported had been caught by boats whose crews included Russians and Canadians. It was decided that this broke the conditions of the duty-free importing agreement and therefore that all consignments of prawns from the three countries should retrospectively pay full duty. Member state governments, including Britain, Germany and Denmark, were instructed to collect the money. And since the Faroese company for which the Smiths acted had gone into liquidation, UK Customs officials decided the bill should be presented to Mr and Mrs Smith. It was for the staggering sum of £1,280,000.

Under British law Mr and Mrs Smith would have had every reason to challenge this astonishing demand. They had not been trying to defraud anyone. Even HM Customs admitted they had acted in completely good faith, and that any error was certainly not their fault. There was absolutely no reason why they should not have accepted the official EUR1 certificates issued by Faroese customs as valid. But under EC law, none of this counted as a defence.

Furthermore, under UK law, as mere agents, the Smiths would not have been answerable for a debt which, if it was owed by anyone, should only have been paid by the firm they were acting for. But again, under EC law, this too did not apply. Although they were not the importers of the prawns John and Celia Smith were personally liable for every last penny, down to the shoes they stood up in. Their house, their car, their business, all would have to go.

The Smiths were faced with ruin. An appeal to Mario Monti, the European Commissioner in charge of the Single Market, drew from him nothing but the frosty bureaucratic response that as 'importers' they must be liable to pay in full for breaches of the rules (he appeared not to have grasped that the whole point of the Smiths' case was that they were not the 'importers', but merely agents handling the customs papers). Since there was no way the Smiths could begin to pay, they ended up in the High Court, which agreed that their case could be taken to the European Court of Justice in Luxembourg. It seemed that only the British Government was pursuing these debts against prawn importers so ruthlessly. The Danish Government strongly protested to the Commission in Brussels against the injustice of it all. Indeed, when the Smiths' case came before the ECJ in September 1995, the British presiding judge, David Edwards, appeared to have some sympathy for their plight. When he eventually delivered his judgement in May 1996 he carefully picked his way through the thicket of EC law to provide the British Government with a way out. If Customs and Excise supported an application by the Smiths to the European Commission for a waiver, the demand could be dropped. But the Customs officials were not interested. With the support of Treasury minister David Heathcoat Amory, they insisted the case would have to go back to the London High Court for final judgement – even though this might take up to another year and would push Mr and Mrs Smith's already huge legal bills even higher.

*

At Kingsbury Episcopi in south Somerset Julian Temperley spent several years building up the Somerset Cider Brandy Company, making a much-admired English equivalent of the Normandy Calvados. But in November 1995 he was horrified to be informed by the Ministry of Agriculture that, at the end of a meeting in Brussels of something called the Spirit Drinks Implementation Committee, the European Commission had hurriedly introduced a proposal that the term 'cider brandy' should be made illegal. For some reason the Spanish had complained that the term 'brandy' could only be legally used when it was made from wine, and the Commission officials agreed.

For the little Somerset Cider Brandy Company this threatened a disaster. Not only had its reputation been built up entirely round popularising the term 'cider brandy'. It would have to spend up to £100,000 reprinting all its brochures, labels and packaging.

What was odd was that Mr Temperley's company would be the only one in Europe affected. Yet what took the case into the higher realms of the surreal was that the only reason offered for the Commission's proposal was that, in a mention of 'cider brandy' in EC Council Regulation 1576/89, the word 'brandy' was written in italics. Our Ministry of Agriculture apparently accepted that this indicated it was a term 'not possible to translate', and therefore it had to be considered illegal. Yet study of this regulation showed that 'brandy' was also italicised when it referred to wine brandy itself. By the same logic, it would be equally illegal to call cognac a 'brandy'. Why had the officials of our Ministry not pointed this out?

*

In the summer of 1996 Richard Bowden of Appledore, north Devon, was just one of hundreds of Britain's shellfishermen facing disaster because of an astonishing contradiction in the Government's approach to two Brussels directives. Mr Bowden earned much of his income catching mussels on the estuary of the rivers Taw and Torridge, but he and dozens of other local shellfishermen had now been told that they could no longer sell their mussels because the estuary was polluted by discharges of sewage. This was under the Food Safety (Live Bivalve Molluscs and Other Shellfish) Regulations 1992, implementing the EU's Shellfish Hygiene directive, 91/492, which made it illegal to sell shellfish except from waters officially designated as free of pollution.

What angered the fishermen, however, was that, if the British Government had obeyed an earlier Brussels directive, the Taw-Torridge estuary would no longer be polluted. The Shellfish Waters directive, 79/923, laid down that, after 1987, it would no longer be legal to allow pollution of waters containing shellfish. But when the Department of the Environment estimated that to comply with this directive in full would cost £6 billion, it was decided this was more than Britain could afford. The DoE officials therefore decided to ignore the terms of the directive, allowing sewage discharges into most of Britain's shellfish waters to continue.

As a result, by 1996, only 18 of England's 242 recognised shellfish waters, 7 per cent, had been designated under the directive as safe. In the South West Water area, covering Devon and Cornwall, only three of 23 areas meet the new EU standards, and it was this which faced fishermen like Mr Bowden with disaster. Although they were being forced out of business because the Government insisted on the strictest compliance with one directive, this was only because of the Government's refusal to comply with the earlier directive. The officials' hidden agenda seemed to be that, to avoid having to spend that £6 billion, it was worth sacrificing much of Britain's shellfish industry and the livelihoods of hundreds of men and their families. This was done in such a hole-in-corner fashion that they were offered no compensation.

Among those who did benefit, however, were the privatised water companies, which were saved huge amounts by not having to comply with the Brussels legislation, and none more than South West Water, of which Richard Bowden and his fellow Taw-Torridge fishermen are customers. In February 1996, when SWW's managing director Bill Fraser lost his job, after the company had been responsible for several pollution incidents, the shellfishermen were scarcely consoled to see him given £800,000 severance pay and retained as an SWW consultant on £50,000 a year.

In the summer of 1996 lawyers acting for Mr Bowden were preparing to sue both South West Water and the Government for full compensation for loss of his livelihood. Furthermore they lodged a formal complaint with the

European Commission about Britain's failure to implement the Shellfish Waters directive, and it seemed likely that action would follow in an effort to force Britain to comply.

So in the end, it seemed, Britain might not make those savings after all. But meanwhile much of her shellfish industry would have been closed down. The shellfish market would then be opened up to other EU countries such as Holland, where all oyster beds had been designated as meeting the EC's top 'Class A' standards, even though most are around the estuary of the Rhine, the most polluted waterway in Europe.

*

At Benington Boston, Lincolnshire, Roger White ran a large plant nursery, selling around 40 million vegetable plants a year, mainly to local farmers. In 1993, under the Plants Health Regulations, implementing EC directive 77/93, it became a criminal offence for him to sell any plants unless they were accompanied by a document known as a 'plant passport', showing exactly which garden and bed they were first grown in. The purpose of this was to prevent the spread of plant diseases in the new Single Market. Even when not being sold to other EC countries, each batch of vegetables now had to carry its own passport, and was invoiced with the firm's individual 'EEC plant number'.

The number originally given Mr White's nursery by the Plant Health and Seeds Inspectorate in 1993 was 'UK-21576'. But in 1995 the local inspector came to tell him his invoices would have to be reprinted. They should now read 'UK-E/W 21576', because Scotland was now separate and the E/W stood for England and Wales. For making his visit to instruct the firm about this change, the inspector charged £30. In May 1996 the plant health and seeds inspector made another visit to tell Mr White that he must reprint his invoices all over again. They should now read 'UK-E/W 21576 EEC Quality'. For being told to add those further two vital words, Mr White awaited another bill for £30.

*

In April 1995 Graham Brand, who ran a large poultry packing plant near Ipswich, Suffolk, was awaiting a first visit from the veterinary inspector assigned to supervise operations in his plant by a new government agency, the Meat Hygiene Service. This had begun work on 1 April to enforce a series of EC hygiene directives on Britain's meat industry. Not the least extraordinary feature of the new agency was that, among its team of 950 highly-paid officials, it had recruited 22 Spanish vets to enforce the new regulations, even though some of them could barely speak English, and Spain itself had ignored the directives.

One of these Spanish officials, Senor Tabuenca, had been assigned to Mr Brand's poultry plant, and before the MHS started operations, its officials told Mr Brand he would have to employ Sr Tabuenca for ten hours a week, at a cost of £18,000 a year. Mr Brand was not best pleased by this because the Spaniard's predecessor, a vet employed by the local authority, had only needed two hours a week to carry out exactly the same job. He had therefore written to the £78,000-a-year head of the new agency, Mr Johnston McNeil, suggesting that this 500 per cent increase in charges must represent 'a clerical error'. The agency had replied that the new charges were 'consistent' with its national policy.

Nevertheless, on 3 April, when the Spanish official arrived at the plant, he was told the firm would expect him to complete his work in two hours, as this was 'consistent' with the time his predecessor had taken to carry out the same duties. Sr Tabuenca's response, on 13 April, was to issue a statutory notice, under the Fresh Meat (Hygiene and Inspection) Regulations 1995, ordering the firm to cease its operations immediately. Without notice, he was thus proposing to close down a successful, long-established business, putting 80 people out of work.

When Mr Brand's solicitor rang the MHS to discuss the matter, he was told they would not speak to him. He should talk to a particular official at the legal department of the Ministry of Agriculture. Repeated attempts to contact this official were in vain. In fact the disaster facing Mr Brand and his 80 employees was only one example of similar problems confronting scores of other meat businesses at the same time, as they faced increases in charges of up to £80,000 and more a year. Yet junior agriculture ministers like Mrs Angela Browning and Earl Howe had constantly reiterated that the new agency, operating from plush new headquarters in York, would be more 'cost-efficient' than the old system, and that charges to individual firms would 'on average' be lower.

After we publicised Mr Brand's plight he was summoned to the ministry in London where the first thing officials told him was that he must not speak to the press. He was then, as a compromise, offered a dramatic reduction in the charges for Sr Tabuenca's services. Although these were still considerably higher than what he was paying before, rather than see his firm closed down and his 80 employees thrown out of a job, he accepted.

*

In November 1995 the media gleefully reported how Prince Charles had spent the morning after the Princess of Wales's notorious Panorama interview wandering round a pilchard factory in Newlyn, Cornwall, which had been turned into a museum recording the history of the pilchard industry. What none of the journalists bothered to enquire into was the rather odd story behind this 'museum'. In *The Mad Officials* we reported how in 1992 the business had been almost forced to close when, under the EC's fish hygiene directive, 91/493, it had to stop exporting £100,000-worth of pilchards a year to Italy in the traditional boxes used for centuries, and pack them instead in plastic containers. When the Italians complained that the fish arrived covered in mould, owner Nick Howell discovered through scientific analysis that the fault lay entirely with the failure of the Brussels officials to grasp the basic laws of hygiene. It was their beloved plastic, causing the fish to sweat, which was causing the problem. But the ingenious Mr Howell discovered a way round. Under a 'derogation' or exemption from the rules, if he turned his entire operation into a 'working museum', he could return to using wooden boxes. As soon as he did so, the pilchards once again arrived in Italy in perfect condition.

*

Despite all his years serving in the South Yorkshire police force, Ralph Pike had never witnessed anything like the 'raid' carried out in August 1996 on the health shop he now ran in Sheffield. Just before closing time at 5 pm, two officials entered his shop, Nature's Trail, accompanied by a uniformed policeman. They waved a search warrant from Bow Street Magistrates Court in London, and peremptorily explained, in front of customers still in the shop, that they were looking for 'unlicensed medicines'.

The officials were from the Medicines Control Agency, the body now responsible for licensing drugs in Britain, and what they were looking for, it turned out, was a dietary supplement called melatonin. This astonished Mr Pike because melatonin is a product which he and thousands of other shops had sold without any problems for years. It was a harmless, natural substance, found in tomatoes, porridge, corn flakes and countless other foods. It had never been sold as a medicine, but was valued by millions of users as a supplement because it cleans the body of toxic substances, and has been found to help sufferers from insomnia and jet lag.

But what surprised Mr Pike even more was to discover why the Medicines Control Agency had suddenly decided to rule that melatonin was a medicine after all. The officials were relying on their interpretation of a 30-year-old Brussels directive, 65/65, which requires anything which can be defined as a medicine to be licensed. The crucial wording in the directive was that anything which can be used for 'restoring, correcting or modifying physiological function in human beings' must be regarded as a 'medicinal product'. Typically with EU directives, this definition was so vague that, strictly speaking, it meant that a glass of brandy or even a glass of water to a thirsty person should require a licence, because these 'restore' or 'modify' the 'physiological function' of the person drinking them. But the MCA officials' decision to classify melatonin in this way meant that it had to be withdrawn from health shops all over Britain, because no one has ever considered it a medicine before and therefore it has no licence.

In fact the bureaucratic catch-22 was that melatonin could not be licensed anyway, because it is a naturally-occurring substance and would therefore be impossible to patent. This would make it virtually impossible to licence, since any company which made it, like Pharma Nord of Denmark which supplied Mr Pike's shop, would have to pay hundreds of thousands of pounds for the licensing procedure, and any other company would then be able to sell it. Nevertheless the reason why the MCA had suddenly taken an interest in melatonin was that two big pharmaceutical companies were spending millions of pounds developing a chemical equivalent of this substance, which they were hoping to market, licensed by the MCA, at around ten times the price of the natural version.

For companies like Pharma Nord the officials' ruling, which was banishing their natural melatonin from the shops, had come as a devastating blow. The previous year the Danish company had sold £1 million-worth of its product, and later in August 1996 MCA officials raided a company warehouse and confiscated £10,000-worth of the stock. Pharma Nord's lawyers planned to seek a judicial review of the MCA's decision in the London High Court, arguing that the officials were quite wrong to use the woolly wording of the EC directive in this way, when melatonin could not be classified as a medicine under more precise British law.

As for Mr Pike, when the MCA raided his shop, it just happened he was out of stock of melatonin anyway, so the officials had to leave empty-handed. But, along with thousands of other health shop owners, he awaited the High Court's decision with keen interest. If the Court upheld the officials' right to interpret the directive in this way, then not just melatonin but hundreds of other natural products might soon disappear from health shop shelves.

*

In the summer of 1995 Margaret Reichlin, the retired head of a London school art department, came across an alarming new problem when she wanted to buy paint for the stonework of her Hampshire cottage. Seven years earlier she had suffered irreparable damage to her health from highly toxic chemicals which had been used to treat the timbers in her house. It had cost her £25,000 to make her home habitable again (she had received no compensation from the builders who applied the chemicals and officials of the Health and Safety Executive showed no interest in following up her case). But she had also become so acutely sensitised to a wide range of chemicals that it was now vital to her to know precisely what were the chemical ingredients in any product she used. Otherwise she risked a recurrence of severe health problems, even physical collapse.

During those seven years it had been easy for her to identify these chemicals because under the HSE's COSHH (Control of Substances Hazardous to Health) Regulations 1988, she could ask for a brief data sheet listing all chemical components. But now, when she asked for her paint, no COSHH sheets were available. So essential was it that she should know whether she could use the paint safely that she asked her supplier to make enquiries. Three weeks later the manufacturers, ICI, sent 22 sheets covered in small print. But these did not answer the one point she needed to know: which chemical the paint used as a fungicide.

She rang the HSE to ask why she could no longer obtain the information she needed. She was told that what ICI had sent were 'the new Chip data sheets', which unlike the old COSHH sheets did 'not have to list dangerous substances'. 'Chip' the official went on, 'comes from the EU and we have no control over it'. It turned out that 'Chip', the Chemicals Hazard Information and Packaging for Supply Regulations 1994 did indeed derive from no fewer than three EC directives. But the COSHH regulations had also derived from an EC directive, 80/1107. So the net result of moving from one EC system to another was that vital information previously mandatory was no longer available. What surprised Miss Reichlin even more was to read two glossy booklets from the HSE entitled *Chip 2 For Everyone* and *The Complete Idiot's Guide to Chip*. These clearly stated that 'the objective of Chip 2 is to help protect people and the environment from the ill effects of chemicals'. To Miss

15

Reichlin it seemed the only obvious result of this noble objective was to ensure that people were no longer protected at all.

*

Also in the summer of 1995 John Gardner, a crime analyst for the Surrey police, drew our attention to the remarkable complications imposed on the police force by an official diktat that all information held on police computers should be metricated. Official descriptions of potential suspects included heights, weights and shoe sizes which now had to be translated into metric equivalents, although it was natural for everyone engaged in police work to use British imperial measures. As a result, wrote Mr Gardner, they constantly now found themselves having to wrestle with details which they could not immediately understand. 'Referring to a suspect as 1.8m tall, weighing 60kg and having a shoe size of 38 doesn't mean much to the average policeman. Although there are computer keys which can be pressed to translate the measures, they are not convenient and have to be used each time for each separate measurement, quite a burden if I have to trawl through 20 or 30 suspects.'

The reason for the change was that it was part of the massive new switch to metrication being pushed through by the British Government in 1995 to comply with two EC directives, 80/181 and 89/617, which were intended to force Britain and Ireland into line with the continental metric system. Later in this book we shall cover this episode in greater detail. But what Mr Gardner highlighted was one of countless curious anomalies thrown up by the way the British Government chose to do this.

Not only uniquely in Europe did Britain make it a criminal offence not to use the metric system for a whole range of trading transactions; the DTI officials responsible for the changeover went much further. They took the EC legislation as an excuse to enforce metrication over the widest possible area of national life, including the metrication of all public administration, such as court proceedings and police work. An instruction even went out to all government departments that official contracts would not in future be allowed to refer to $3\frac{1}{2}$" floppy discs. These would have to be described as '88.9 millimetre floppy discs' (even though continental computer firms like Escom naturally label their products as 3.5" discs, the international standard).

*

One of the handful of non-metric measures Britain was allowed to retain, for cosmetic reasons, was the use of miles for road signs and speed limits. Although the DTI officials were thus forced to leave these untouched, nevertheless they observed that the legislation only referred to 'roads'. Therefore they decided that speed limits on waterways would now have to be metricated. What this led to in practice could be seen from a letter sent to the DTI in January 1996 by Nicholas Hancox, director of legal services for Norfolk County Council, which as the authority administering the Norfolk Broads was responsible for the largest complex of navigable waters in Britain. He pointed out the consequences of metricating Broads speed limits.

16

For a start it would mean replacing 700 speed limit signs, only renewed three years earlier. Since many were in 'remote riverside areas and difficult to access', the cost would be 'extremely high'. Almost all the 5,000 motor boats and cruisers on the Broads had speedometers calibrated in mph only. Re-calibration or replacement 'would be extremely onerous and time-consuming'. The radar speed guns used by river inspectors would have to be replaced at a cost of many thousands of pounds. The same would be true of all the Broads Authority's existing literature, explaining how crucial speed limits were to protecting the Broads' very fragile environment.

Because the risk of damage caused by boat wash, speed limits had been worked out very precisely at 3, 4, 5 and 6 miles an hour. Simply to metricate these by rounding upwards or downwards to a whole number would defeat their purpose. It would only be possible therefore to give exact translations, such as 4.8 kilometres per hour, 6.4 kph etc., which would be not only absurd but unworkable (not least since most Broads users instinctively understood British measures, but would be all at sea with metric). In the council's view this would simply result in causing 'significantly increased damage' to the environment.

Such would be just one consequence of the DTI's insistence on metricating every area of 'public administration' in Britain. What made this still odder, however, was that the authority claimed for doing this was those same EC directives. The preamble to the directives showed they were only authorised under Article 100 of the European Treaty, which is solely concerned with matters of trade and the Single Market. In fact, in claiming these directives as legal justification to enforce metrication in matters which had nothing to do with trade, the DTI officials were acting in breach of EC law.

*

In High Wycombe in August 1995 David Ealand, one of the most successful of the new breed of English winemakers, faced a bizarre court case. It was only six years since Mr Ealand, formerly a senior partner in a City law firm, began making top-quality dessert wine at his vineyard near Henley. His 'Noble Bacchus' immediately began winning a stream of awards. It was compared by connoisseurs with the finest dessert wines of France, and sold – at nearly £10 a bottle – to top restaurants and many countries in Europe.

However, under the complex rules covering wine production in the EC, wine made in Britain can only be classified in the lowest category as 'table wine'. But sugar-rich dessert wines unavoidably contain more alcohol than the EC rules allow in table wine. In February 1994 the Wine Standards Board, which administers the EC rules on behalf of the Ministry of Agriculture, informed Mr Ealand that, under 'EC Regulation 822/87', his wine was not a wine, and 'is not subject to the EC Wine Regulations'. Mr Ealand had to stop calling his product a wine and relabel it as 'a fermented grape dessert drink'.

But already the tale had taken an even more bizarre twist. One day in 1993 Mr Ealand's winemaker, Peter Arguile, had drawn off five litres of the 1992 vintage to experiment with a tiny bottle of peach flavouring essence they had been sent as a sample by a manufacturer. When he had concluded his

17

experiment, he without thinking poured the wine back into the tank. The amount of flavouring was so minute that it was months before the mistake came to light. But as soon as it did, Mr Ealand informed the Wine Standards Board, which in November 1993 placed a temporary restriction order on the entire batch, losing Christmas sales worth over £10,000.

It was three months later that the Wine Standards Board confirmed to Mr Ealand that, under the EC wine regulations, his product was not a wine. Under the law, therefore, there was nothing to stop him adding any flavouring to the drink he liked, and it might have been expected this was the end of the matter. But in June 1994 Mr Ealand and Mr Arguile were astonished to receive summonses on six criminal charges. These were that they had added an 'unauthorised flavouring' to their 'wine', in breach of 'Council Regulation 822/87', the 'Common Agricultural Policy (Wine) Regulations 1993' and the 'European Communities Act 1972'. In other words, the two men were being prosecuted by the ministry for offences against the same regulations which it had confirmed they were 'not subject to'.

When their case came up before Mr Alan Ormerod, a stipendiary magistrate at High Wycombe, they were confident there could only be one verdict. The prosecution tried to argue that the adding of the flavouring had been 'premeditated', although Mr Ealand explained how angry he had been when the mistake came to light, since there was no way it could have improved his award-winning wine. However, the court was told, all this was irrelevant. The real point was that his wine was not covered by the regulations anyway.

But to general amazement the magistrate found the men guilty on four out of six charges, imposing fines of £8,500 with £8,000 costs. The verdict prompted a flood of unfavourable media coverage, under headlines such as 'Vineyard Fined for Adding Artificial Flavour to Wine'. But not one report picked up the central point that the two men had been charged under laws which the ministry itself had ruled did not apply to them.

*

In March 1995 Geoff Richardson, chairman of a small Yorkshire firm Aquaspersions, was so angry about a disaster which had befallen his company that he reported his story to a Select Committee of MPs.

The story began some years before with a young laboratory technician named Robert Pickford. His speciality was devising ways to keep crops free of pests through biological controls, environmentally-friendly methods which can drastically reduce the need for chemical poisons. Pickford was so successful he eventually became research director for Humber Growers, Britain's leading cucumber growers.

One of his early triumphs back in 1980 was devising a way to deal with tiny insects called thrips. Instead of drenching the plants with poisons, Pickford suggested simply spraying the greenhouse floor with harmless sticky stuff on which the insects would be trapped. Thanks to 'Thripstick' the problem was solved. But in 1987 the company faced an even worse problem, a plague of whitefly – and this inspired Pickford to his finest brainwave.

Watching his wife ironing one day, he saw her using starch to stiffen the clothes. What if he could somehow apply starch to the whitefly pupae? Might this not stiffen the casing so that the tiny insects couldn't struggle out? His wife's spray-on starch didn't do the trick. But Pickford's mother then suggested he try her old-fashioned potato starch, which worked a treat.

Everyone was so excited about this extraordinarily ingenious new answer to the whitefly menace that another company, Aquaspersions, was brought in to help transform it into a saleable product. The two companies spent £400,000 on developing and patenting what they called Hugtite. It passed all the necessary tests by the Pesticides Safety Directorate and attracted interest from across the world. Finally plans were in place for a major chemical company, Levington Horticulture (formerly Fisons) to launch Hugtite on the international market in January 1995. Sales in the first year alone were projected at £1 million.

Then the blow fell. The companies were told that under new rules to comply with an EC directive 'on the placing on the market of plant protection products', 91/414, they would have to submit their product to a hugely complex and expensive series of new safety tests. These would cost at least another £250,000 and take three years.

This was because, under the EC rules, potato starch was considered to be a new and hitherto untested 'active substance'. It therefore had to be tested just as if it was some dangerous new chemical. In fact potato starch is something so harmless and familiar that we eat it everyday in soups, sauces, pie glazes and hundreds of other food products. It is even used in the glue on envelopes, so we may lick it every time we send a letter. Nevertheless the EC rules said the starch had to go through this bizarre rigmarole, at a cost so prohibitive that Levington's pulled out. This left the two small companies with their colossal £400,000 bill, for a product which everyone wanted but which could now never be sold.

So angry was Aquaspersions' chairman Geoff Richardson that, when he heard the Agriculture Committee of the House of Commons was conducting an enquiry into the licensing of pesticides, he sent in the details of what had happened. The MPs were impressed enough to include this horror story in their printed volume of evidence. But when it came to writing their report they made no mention of it. The problem was this insanity came from the EC. And when it came to laws from Brussels, the MPs knew they were powerless to do anything, even though they had caused an ingenious British product, with the potential to earn tens of millions of pounds on the world market, to be chucked on the scrapheap.

*

For 25 years customers of the Dolphin Centre shopping complex in Poole, Dorset, were delighted by three large wooden sculptures of dolphins outside the entrance. Generations of children clambered happily over the low, polished-wood models without incident. In March 1996 the dolphins vanished, and everyone assumed they had gone for cleaning. But eventually the real explanation came to light. Peter Dixon, the Dolphin Centre's safety manager, had been studying new regulations introduced to implement the EC's Health and Safety in the Workplace directive, 89/654. Under these, safety officers were required to assess their workplace for any potential risks, and Mr Dixon reported that the dolphins might pose a risk to a child playing on them. Terrified of compensation claims, the store's owners ordered the dolphins to be taken into storage.

When the true reason for the dolphins' disappearance emerged, there was considerable local anger that the store could have done anything so silly. As one young mother told the local paper: 'I'm just furious – they haven't caused an accident in 25 years, so why should they have to go? I can't believe it.' But Mr Dixon's response was: 'It is irrelevant there haven't been any injuries. Under the directive, you have to consider the risk of what might happen.'

*

In May 1996 the organisers of the 10th Woolpit Steam Rally near Bury St Edmunds, Suffolk, were infuriated. After months of work, they had been forced at the last minute to cancel a popular annual event which raised up to £4,000 a year for local charities. The farmer who was lending some of his fields to provide free parking for the hundreds of cars expected at the rally had been told by the Ministry of Agriculture that this was not possible. The reason why the fields were available was because the farmer had been ordered not to grow anything on them under the EC's set-aside scheme. This was the system by which, to reduce crop surpluses, EC farmers received £340 a hectare, or a total of £1 billion of taxpayers' money each year, not to grow crops on 10 per cent of their land.

Under the EC's Commission Regulation, 762/94, subsidies could only be paid if the set aside land was not put to any 'lucrative use incompatible with the growing of an arable crop'. When the British Government checked this with Brussels, Commission officials confirmed that set-aside land could therefore not be used for parking for charitable fundraising events, even though no money would be made from the fields themselves because the parking was free. Any farmer who allowed even one of his set-aside fields to be used for an afternoon's parking for a village fête would lose not only all his set-aside subsidies, but all his other subsidies as well, possibly amounting to hundreds of thousands of pounds. With 1,294,000 acres of land in England and Wales taken out of use in 1996, an area the size of Lincolnshire, dozens of charity events were thus affected all over the country.

A particularly significant phrase in the regulation was that 'lucrative use' was only ruled out so long as this was 'incompatible with the growing of an arable crop'. By one of those curious anomalies the EC system was so good at throwing up, although farmers could only receive subsidies if they did not grow food crops, there were in fact some arable crops which they *were* permitted to grow on their set-aside land. These were crops for 'industrial use', such as oilseed rape used for fuel oil (which was why large tracts of the English countryside sprouted a garish yellow) or hemp for industrial fibre (although this could not be grown without obtaining a special Home Office certificate to show it was not the kind of hemp used for smoking). In such cases, the farmer not only continued to receive a part of his subsidy for not growing crops; he could then make even more by selling the crops he did grow.

As an absurdity, however, even this paled when the set-aside system was measured against its original purpose, which was to cut down the notorious

EC 'grain mountain'. This had only arisen in the first place because farmers were paid huge subsidies to grow more grain than the EC needed. Typically, the EC's answer was not just to cut the subsidies, but to pay the farmers further subsidies not to grow the grain. In 1992, the year before compulsory set aside came in, the EC grain harvest was 166 million tonnes. In 1996, thanks to farmers throwing even more chemicals at their fields to intensify yields, it was estimated the harvest would be 184 million tonnes. Thus the net result of a scheme to cut EC grain production would be an increase of 18 million tonnes – plus of course the cancellation of the Woolpit Steam Rally.

*

In 1995 Allan Lloyd wanted to paint the window frames of his family's 18th-century, Grade 2 listed house at Colwall, on the Malvern hills. His view was that the job could only be effectively done with traditional lead-based paint, as had been used on the house for 250 years. But Mr Lloyd was told by his local council that he could not now use lead paint without a special licence from English Heritage. This was laid down under the Environmental Protection (Control of Injurious Substances) Regulations 1992, implementing EC directive 89/677 restricting 'the use of certain dangerous substances'.

After many months English Heritage told Mr Lloyd he could not be given a licence because his house was only listed Grade II. Lead paint was only permissible on historic buildings listed Grade I or Grade II*. For him to use lead paint on his own home would therefore be a criminal offence.

But here arose a puzzle. When the directive banning lead paint was consulted, it clearly stated, among the exemptions (in Euro-speak 'derogations') from the rule, that lead paint should be allowed for 'the restoration and maintenance of historic buildings'. Why then was Mr Lloyd being told it would be a criminal offence to use lead paint on his historic building? Reporting this, we predicted that, when the point was put to the Department of the Environment, back would come 'the usual weaselly, self-justifying letter from the ministerial word-processor, signed by a supposedly Conservative minister who, as usual, will not have a clue what is going on'.

Sure enough, back came a letter signed by junior minister Lord Inglewood. It admitted the existence of the derogation, but his officials curiously described this as only permitting 'the use of lead paints in Grade I and Grade II* listed buildings'. Indeed weasel words, for the directive clearly referred to all 'historic buildings'. Even more surprisingly, however, the letter explained that the derogation had actually been asked for by the British Government itself. But the DoE officials had then taken the view that to include Britain's 437,500 buildings listed Grade II 'would amplify the administrative burden and could lead to improper use of lead-based paints'. They had thus quite arbitrarily decided to exclude most of the historic buildings in the country. Not exactly a case of 'the Lord giveth, then the Lord taketh away' – but it certainly seemed odd first to plead with Brussels to give an exemption for historic buildings, then to be the only country in the EC largely to ignore it.

*

When the 7th Earl of Onslow, a keen horseman, read through the leaflet he was sent by the British Horse Society in May 1996 he could scarcely believe his eyes. Members were advised that, under new EC rules, every time they loaded a horse into a horse box they should now fill in a form called an Animal Transport Certificate. The information required on the form came under eleven separate headings, including the full name and address of the horse's owner; exact date and time when horse enters horse box; registration number of towing vehicle; transporter's fax number; and date and time when journey ends.

'What really made me hit the roof', as Lord Onslow put it at his home at Clandon Park, near Guildford, Surrey, 'was that I even had to give the postcode of the horse's final destination – so next time I go hunting in Leicestershire, I have to find out the postcode of the field where we park the trailer.'

Could it really be true that Brussels was now ordering horse-lovers to fill in a form every time they take a pony to the local gymkhana? Further research showed that directive 95/29, on 'the welfare of animals in transport', did indeed cover the transporting of 'domestic solipeds' (Euro-speak for horses), not to mention 'domestic animals of the bovine, ovine, caprine and porcine species' (cattle, sheep, goats and pigs, to the rest of us). It was true the directive laid down that each time such animals are transported, they must be accompanied by 'the documentation required by the European Community', including the details listed above (although no mention of the postcodes of fields). But 95/29 also clearly stated that this did not apply to 'the transport of pet animals accompanying their owner on a private journey'. So why was the British Horse Society advising its members to the contrary?

The noble earl did more digging, to uncover a situation only too familiar. It was not just Brussels which did not intend the directive to apply to private owners; the British Government's own regulations said the same. But as was happening only too often with the plethora of new regulations pouring out of the machine, somewhere down the line a fog of confusion had set in. Lord Onslow discovered the British Horse Society was far from alone in misreading the rules. The previous month Lancashire police had actually flagged down several horse boxes to warn owners they were committing a criminal offence by not carrying their certificates. This idea that horse owners should fill in a form every time they put a 'domestic soliped' into a horse box was a complete fantasy. But bureaucracy in contemporary Britain was now proliferating so fast that such confusions had become all too common.

*

We were first put on the trail of what turned out to be one of the most devastating instances of such confusion in July 1995, when we had a message from a retired doctor working for a community health council in Bexhill, Sussex. He had a fearful problem on his hands. He had been trying to discover why he could no longer get help from social services with the vital task of giving baths to elderly and infirm people living at home. As he pointed out, there was no more effective a way to keep old people healthy than to ensure they were regularly bathed. Yet suddenly he could not get his usual assistance, and this was blamed on mysterious 'EC regulations'. All his attempts to discover what this was about, from the BMA to the Royal College of Nursing and the DTI, had got nowhere. Could we help?

We replied that the problem might have something to do with EC directive 90/269 'on the minimum health and safety requirements for the manual handling of loads where there is a risk particularly of back injury to workers', the so-called 'manual handling' or 'back ache' directive. But we didn't enquire further until, over the next few months, we came across more examples from all over the country, where it seemed, because of 'new EC regulations', social services or 'carers' were now refusing to help with lifting infirm or disabled people.

In Bristol, for instance, 68-year-old businessmen Peter May was no longer able to get help with bathing his wife Ursula, incapacitated by a stroke. He was told his usual nurses were no longer permitted to lift more than '16.6 kilograms', or two and a half stone; so Mr May, not in the best of health himself, had to lift his wife on his own, while a fit young nurse stood watching, forbidden to assist.

When we then examined the directive the mystery only deepened, because it only laid down, in the most general way, that care should be taken to ensure that workers were not asked to lift loads which might cause injury. No exact weights were cited. The directive merely suggested that loads might pose a risk if they were 'too heavy or too large'. The Health and Safety Executive's Manual Handling Operations Regulations 1992, implementing the directive, were no more specific. So where on earth had that ludicrously precise figure of '16.6 kilograms' come from? The clue came from the guidelines, put out as usual to help in interpretation of the regulations. Here a diagram showed the sort of weights where it might be worth assessing whether a load could cause injury. For a man lifting from the waist, 25 kilograms was suggested, while a note indicated that a load for a woman might be two thirds of that – in other words 16.6 kilograms. Although it was underlined in bold that these 'guide-line figures are not limits', here was what we were looking for.

Somewhere down the line, it seemed, officials of the Department of Health and the National Health Service Executive, completely ignoring the instruction that these figures were not to be taken as 'limits', had done just that. They had translated the guidance figures into firm instructions, with the result that, all over the country, countless thousands of infirm and disabled people were no longer being given the help they needed. One touching example we were sent was that of Katherine Bissett, whose incapacity was so serious that she had lived in various homes for 30 years, but who still loved to come home to visit her parents at such times as Christmas and Easter. But this was no longer possible because the staff at the home where she lived in Cambridgeshire had been told they could no longer help lifting her and her wheelchair into the specially-fitted van to travel. No one was more frustrated by this than the staff themselves, who longed to help, but had been ordered not to in case they incurred injury and might use the regulations to support a claim for compensation.

When Katherine's mother Rosemary Bissett wrote to her MP, a reply came from the Department of the Environment signed by junior minister Sir Paul Beresford. After expressing perfunctory sympathy that 'the withdrawal of services' had caused 'problems' for 'Kathy', the letter went on to say that Mrs Bissett had been 'wrongly advised' that the problems came from 'European Community legislation'. 'Neither the Directive nor the Regulations impose the type of arbitrary weight lifting limit described by Mrs Bissett.' It was almost as if Mrs Bissett herself was to blame for making such an error. But the letter went on at length to emphasise that 'over 48,000 serious manual handling accidents were reported to the Health and Safety Executive and local authorities in 1994/5'. This was a really serious national problem, and the minister was 'sure Mrs Bissett would agree that it would not be right for health care employers to try to increase the mobility of clients at the cost of an unnecessary injury to employees'. In other words, there was a perfectly good reason why Katherine could no longer receive help with the lifting of her wheelchair, and if anyone was in the wrong it was Mrs Bissett herself, for foolishly suggesting that this had anything to do with regulations, European or otherwise.

*

As we were aware from hundreds of examples we were sent by readers, the ministerial word processors of Whitehall were churning out huge numbers of letters like this in 1995 and 1996.

Usually they were sent in reply to some MP who had written to a minister about some constituent's problem. And the odd thing about them was that, whatever their subject, the condescending tone and style of these letters was always the same. Their most striking feature was that, whatever absurdity the system had thrown up, however damaging its consequences, the officials could always find words to justify it. Whatever it did, the system was always in the right; particularly when it came to justifying the consequences of the ever-growing avalanche of legislation stemming from Europe. And anyone who dared suggest otherwise, like Mrs Bissett, could be dismissed as completely in the wrong.

But increasingly the British people were beginning to think otherwise. In fact, as more and more of them became directly affected by the workings of this new system of government they were living under, they began to recognise there was something about it which had gone very wrong indeed.

Part I

Understanding a Monster

1. We Enter the Castle

'This is the first mention I've heard of these Control Officials,' said K., 'and naturally I don't understand them yet. But I fancy that two things must be distinguished here: firstly what is transacted in the offices and can be construed officially, this way or that; and secondly, my own actual person, me myself ... threatened by their encroachments, which are so meaningless that I can't even yet believe in the seriousness of the danger.'

Franz Kafka, The Castle, Chapter 5.

One of the more haunting novels of our century is Kafka's *The Castle*. The hero K. comes to a strange village, where he has been summoned to take up a new job. He enters an apparently ordinary village inn. In conversation he soon begins to pick up hints that there is something very odd about this place. Life is by no means as normal as it at first appears. The inhabitants are subdued. They have an air of apprehension, even fear, and he discovers that this indefinable sense of menace all emanates from a vast castle on a hill overshadowing the village. It is the very place where he has been summoned to take up his post.

This is no ordinary castle. It is more like a town, a warren of buildings. And it is swarming with a vast army of mysterious, largely unseen officials. K. gradually learns that, although the village's inhabitants know very little about the officials, almost everything about their lives has passed under the castle's control. Eventually K. penetrates the bureaucratic twilight world within the castle, to try to locate the official who has sent him the letter. No one seems to know anything about him. But, in conversation with a middle ranking official, a 'Superintendent', K. tries to unravel what is going on.

K. learns that everything about this shadowy organisation, made up of endless departments, such as 'Department A' and 'Department X', each with their own hierarchies of officials, seems to be shrouded in mystery. It is a System so labyrinthine that no one ever takes direct responsibility for anything. But the one point K. establishes very clearly is that, whatever the System does, it can never be admitted that it has made a mistake. The Superintendent emphasises at one point, 'It is a working principle of the Head Bureau that the very possibility of error must be ruled out of account.' And when he then mentions a 'Control Authority', K. asks what this does. What happens if the Control Authority fails? 'Only a total stranger could ask a question like yours', the Superintendent condescendingly explains. 'Is there a Control Authority? There are only control authorities. Frankly it isn't their function to hunt out errors in the vulgar sense, for errors don't happen, and even when once in a while an error does happen, as in your case, who can finally say that it is an error?'

*

The stories recounted in our prologue of life in Britain in 1995 and 1996 all had one thing in common. Obviously all were examples of nonsensical bureaucracy. Some were relatively trivial. Others, like those where businesses were forced to close for no reason at all, were much more serious. But all were brought about by this same curious new System of government, part-European, part-British, which was now so rapidly extending its tentacles into almost every area of British life.

The purpose of this chapter, as we enter the Castle, is to set out some of the more general principles by which this System operates, which will help to illuminate everything which follows in the rest of the book.

*

One of the most disconcerting things about the debate which began to rage over Britain's membership of the European Union in 1995 and 1996 was the way the two sides to the argument never really seemed to engage. On one side, the supporters of membership talked about the huge benefits Europe had brought to Britain, in particular the freedom to trade in the Single Market. But this claim was almost invariably made in general, abstract terms, unsupported by much practical evidence. When the other side responded with examples of how the system did operate in practice, like those quoted in the last chapter, these naturally showed the impact of the EC on British life in a much more negative light. But they were invariably waved aside by the EC's supporters as mere 'Euro-myths', either fictitious scare stories or freakish exceptions, far outweighed by all those wondrous, if not too carefully specified benefits.

In the past few years, through our journalistic and other investigations, we have perhaps taken a more detailed look at how this new System of government actually operates than anyone. Certainly no enquiries have covered such a wide range of its activities. And something which has struck us with particular force is that wherever one examines this System closely, one sees it going wrong. And the more one understands how it works, the more obvious it becomes that the System is invariably going wrong for the same basic reasons and in the same fundamental ways.

In recent years we have investigated hundreds of individual case histories like those reported in the previous chapter. And as the rest of this book will show, they are far from being just atypical exceptions. The anomalies and absurdities those stories exemplify turn up wherever one looks. They are endemic to the entire System.

The examples in our last chapter all had certain things in common. They began with some directive or law being passed in Brussels. This was turned into British law by officials in Whitehall. This was then enforced by lesser officials. And finally we see some business or private individual ending up as the victim of what seems to be a completely indefensible, absurd, often highly damaging nonsense. But often the puzzle with individual examples like these is to work out precisely at which stage in the System the really damaging element in the nonsense has crept in. Is it the fault of the original directive or regulation from Brussels? Or the way in which that has been 'transposed' into British law? Or the over-zealous manner in which has been enforced? It may be any of these. Or more likely it will be a combination of them working together.

In many of the examples we cited in the last chapter the nonsense undoubtedly began in Brussels, as in the stories of the fish quotas which did not enable small British fishermen to earn a living, or the decision to impose retrospective fines on innocent importers of prawns. But in each case the ending of the story was made far worse by the astonishingly rigid and blinkered way in which these rules were interpreted and enforced in Britain. So that, by the time Clive Mills had to watch his fishing boat being smashed up or Mr and Mrs Smith faced their crazy fine of £1,280,000, far more money than they had ever made in their lives, a large part of the absurdity involved was the fault of British officialdom for the blindly remorseless way in which it had carried out Brussels' original instructions.

In other examples, like the supposed ban on 'carers' being allowed to help lifting infirm or disabled people, it could be argued that the fault did not lie with Brussels at all. The Manual Handling directive never imposed specific weight limits on what nurses could lift, any more than the Animal Welfare directive ordered private horse owners to fill in a form every time they put their 'domestic soliped' in a horse-box. In each of these cases, the problem did not even arise from the British regulations, which simply echoed the provisions of the directive. The real nonsense crept in lower down the chain of command, with officials who had not read the rules properly.

But the point is that these nonsenses would never have had the chance to creep in if the whole process had not been kicked into motion by Brussels in the first place. And wherever the nonsense arises, the ultimate effect is the same. Ordinary people find themselves in the grip of some monstrous absurdity which becomes so firmly embedded in the System that nothing can be done about it.

The one thing that is certain about the impact of EC legislation on Britain is that, as it passes down the line of command from its origin in Brussels, it never along the way becomes more sensible, more rational, more efficient. Invariably the process is precisely the opposite. The effects of the nonsense are ratcheted up at every stage down the line. Even if the process begins innocently enough, as with that provision of the Manual Handling directive, sooner or later the nonsense will creep in; because that is how Britain operates the System. That is how, compared with other Community states, Britain is making a unique mess of this new form of government, whose centre is no longer London but Brussels.

This is why in the end it does not really matter at which stage of the process the madness first shows itself. The whole process must be taken as one continuum. And that is why trying to unravel the workings of this System we refer to it as the Brussels/Whitehall/enforcement triangle.

Part I. Understanding a Monster

The Brussels/Whitehall/enforcement triangle

1. Europe – the wellspring

The start of the process is Brussels, the European Commission and the Council of Ministers, churning out the ever-swelling torrent of directives and regulations necessary to shape and administer the Single Market, the Common Agricultural Policy, the Common Fisheries Policy and the rest of the abstractions which make up the onward march of the 'European Union'.

2. The Whitehall version

Stage two lies in the way these directives and regulations then have to be translated by Whitehall officials into British law. This is done in the shape of those official diktats known as statutory instruments or regulations. Notoriously often (as we reported in our earlier book, *The Mad Officials*) these compound the problem by turning the original Brussels version into something much more prescriptive and onerous, adding requirements not contained in the original EC directive. This particularly contrasts with the more relaxed approach adopted by many other EC countries, so that a five-page directive from Brussels may be translated into just two pages of regulations in France or Portugal, while Whitehall turns it into 50.

In Britain, as we saw in the story of the Manual Handling directive, this may be further compounded by the 'guidelines problem'. Ministries and agencies issue guidelines, intended merely to assist in interpreting the regulations; but these may include suggestions going beyond what the regulations themselves require, which then come to be applied as if they are law.

3. Overzealous enforcement

Stage three, compounding the problem further, lies in the striking change which in recent years has come over the attitude of many of the petty officials empowered to enforce all this mass of new legislation, such as environmental health officers, trading standards officers, pollution inspectors, MAFF officials and the rest. As we described in *The Mad Officials*, a new regulatory ethos emerged in Britain in the late 1980s and early 1990s which was particularly evident in such fields as hygiene, safety and environmental protection. This fired many of the officials involved with a new self-importance, an almost puritanical zeal about their work, which led them to adopt a new, much more confrontational approach to those they were regulating. Almost routinely they came to treat even the most responsible and law-abiding people trying to run any kind of business as if they were potential criminals.

A final problem often makes the situation worse still. Such has been the quantity and complexity of legislation pouring out of the machine that even those who have to enforce it may not be clear as to just what the law requires. But so oppressive has been the ethos created by all this welter of new lawmaking, and so draconian are the new powers it often gives to the officials, that this creates what we call 'the climate of fear and confusion'. People become simply bewildered and overawed, too frightened to question the System.

We saw an instance of this in the story of the little Hampshire dairy forced to close down when officials threatened it with criminal prosecution if it did not spend prohibitive sums of money installing a mechanised bottling plant. Only when it was too late did it come to light that the law made no such requirement.

A final measure of the confusion inspired by all this mass of new legislation derived from Europe was the way even the courts could lose their way in the thicket, as we saw in the story of the judge who found a Henley winemaking firm guilty of criminal offences under regulations which the firm had already been ruled by the officials it was not subject to.

Such is the basic outline of how the system works. But for an explanation of why it so often ends up producing such absurdities, we must now look at what it is trying to achieve.

The shibboleths

One of the most striking features of the System of government centred on the European Union is how frequently the net effect of its frenzy of bureaucratic and legislative activity is to produce results opposite to those intended.

If we consider the avalanche of new legislation introduced in Britain in recent years, we can see how how much of it has been inspired by certain central concerns. We have called these 'the shibboleths', the holy causes of our age.

One of these is hygiene.
A second is safety.
A third is protection of the environment.
A fourth is protection of the consumer.
A fifth is to promote a fairer society by opposing discrimination against any groups which can be seen as exploited or discriminated against, particularly women, racial minorities or the disabled.

It is remarkable how much of the legislation handed down from Europe in recent years has been produced to promote these causes. What they all have in common is that they can inspire in people a desire to build a perfect, protected, just, secure world. And here we must very much add to the list the inspiration of building a unified Europe itself, the almost religious vision of different countries being brought together into a harmonised union, with its Single Market, its Single Currency, its 'common policies' on agriculture and fisheries, a common purpose in everything.

Who could question this desire to bring about a safer, more hygienic, less polluted, fairer, more unified world? In theory it sounds fine. The only trouble is that we have more and more come to see what it means in practice. We come to see how the very desire to realise such a Utopian vision can engender in people a strange combination of self-righteousness and blindness, which justifies almost any means to realise that vision through imposing laws and regulations.

Yet most curious of all, as we came to see as we investigated this pheno-menon in detail, was the extent to which all this frenzy of regulatory activity was simply not, in practice, achieving any of the high-minded ends it was intended to achieve, even sometimes the very reverse. Legislation intended to regulate hygiene was not improving the safety standards of food. Most of the vast sums having to be spent on complying with new safety rules were doing very little to make the world safer, and could even make it more dangerous. Enormously costly new rules to promote a cleaner environment were having remarkably little impact on genuine environmental problems, and might even increase pollution.

Even more did this apply to the particular dreams associated with building a European Union itself. The Single Market, far from being just a liberation of trade, seemed to centre on weaving a mighty spider's web of bureaucratic rules, a mountain of directives and regulations, which all too often ended up making trade within the EC not easier but harder. The Common Agricultural Policy, originally intended to provide Europe with cheap food and to protect the livelihoods of the largest number of farmers, ended up making food much more expensive, making rich farmers richer and driving hundreds of thou-sands of others off the land.

Perhaps the most glaring example of all was the Common Fisheries Policy. In the name of 'conserving Europe's fish stocks', Brussels attempts to do this by imposing such a crazy system of bureaucratic rules that these inevitably lead to the pointless destruction of billions of fish a year and have created one of the worst man-made conservation disasters in the world.

This same holds true in every area one examines. And the fundamental reason is invariably the same. The only way the system knows to try to bring all these things about is through bureaucracy, involving ever more regula-tions, ever more paperwork, ever more armies of inspectors. This gradually builds up a vast, ramshackle regulatory machine which loses all contact with practical reality. The ends it is meant to achieve and the problems it is intended to solve become almost irrelevant. The system becomes almost wholly self-referential, concerned only with enforcing compliance with its own procedures. It is this which becomes the real purpose of the exercise, an end in itself.

Thus, while this frenzy of regulation imposes ever-growing burdens on those affected, the real problems are left almost completely untouched. This is the phenomenon we call 'taking a sledgehammer to miss the nut'. And no country in the European Union has learnt how to operate this system more conspicuously to its disadvantage than Britain.

Politicians as puppets

A particular reason why Britain has made such a unique mess of its mem-bership of the European Union – again this is a theme which will run through the rest of this book – has been the very curious part played in this new system of government by our elected politicians.

As we shall later consider in detail, perhaps the most alarming consequence of Europe has been its profoundly corrupting effect on our democratic system of government. The injection of the European dimension has been the most powerful single factor in making our political system so labyrinthine, so infested with bureaucratic technicalities, that the politicians themselves simply cannot grasp it all any longer. At every level of government it is no longer the elected politicians who are in charge of the machine. It is the officials, who are themselves just creatures of a System which has run out of anyone's control.

During the course of our investigations in the past four years there is nothing we have found more shocking than to discover just how far this new System has reduced the ministers who are supposedly in charge of government to puppets. This applies even on the most personal level. They are like ghosts. It is impossible even talk to them about these problems any more. It is as if they are imprisoned behind a glass wall, almost wholly uncomprehending of the disaster this new System of government is bringing about, either its scale or its nature.

Of course the illusion is still given us, through our television screens and shots of ministers appearing in the House of Commons, or disappearing through glass doors into one of those interminable meetings of the Council of Ministers, that our democratically elected politicians are still somehow in charge, able to make decisions on our behalf. But it is no longer the politicians who are even nominally in control. It is not even those shadowy armies of officials who, behind the scenes, at least go through the motions of formulating those decisions, preparing the diktats and regulations which the ministers then dutifully sign into law.

What is in control is the System itself. And, with accelerating momentum, it has been turning into a very odd System indeed.

Uusually it is only when, like all those we described in the first chapter, people experience at first hand what it is like to fall under the shadow of this weird mutation of bureaucracy we are seeing in our time, that they really begin to appreciate that what we are faced with here is a real monster. A monster with many different heads, but which are all ultimately parts of the same creature.

One reason why many people have not yet fully recognised this monster is that they have not yet fallen personally into its clutches. But another is that, in the climate of our time, it is so peculiarly persuasive. One might think that anyone could recognise some of the more extreme absurdities it perpetrates, like the sort of examples we included in the first chapter. But if one questions the reasoning behind such lunacies, it is never long before one is back in that suffocating twilight world where the mighty shibboleths hold sway. No sooner are these holy causes invoked – the need for hygiene, for safety, for environmental protection, the Single Market – than it is remarkable how the System can make even the most glaring insanities sound quite reasonable. The ends come to justify the means, even if those ends are not in practice being realised at all.

As we remarked at the end of the previous chapter, nothing demonstrates this more vividly than what happens when someone embroiled in some crazy battle with bureaucracy, then writes in desperation to his or her MP. The MP writes to the minister. Back comes that letter of self-justifying gobbledygook, drafted by the same officials who were probably responsible for the nonsense in the first place. Yet however indefensible that nonsense is, the letter always makes it sound like the most reasonable thing in the world. It usually ends 'I hope you will find this helpful'. The minister, having not of course read the letter, tops and tails it – 'Dear Jim, yours ever Angela' – and sends it back to the MP, who sends it on to his constituent.

It is a perfect example of a closed system, which has not touched reality at any point. Nothing at all has been achieved. The constituent is still in his awful mess. The only lesson he has learned, if he didn't know it already, is that the System, the bureaucracy, the monster, is always right.

We must now look at this monster in more detail.

2. Brussels – Heart of the Monster

> I found myself corresponding with the Chancellor, Denis Healey, about import levels of apricot halves and canned fruit salad, and ... I recall one low point when nine Foreign Ministers from the major countries of Europe solemnly assembled in Brussels to spend several hours discussing how to resolve our differences on standardising a fixed position of rear-view mirrors on agricultural tractors.
>
> *Time and Chance*, the memoirs of James Callaghan, 1987

One document reveals the true nature of this strange phenomenon, the 'European Union', more clearly than anything else. Anyone who wants to understand what the EU is about should forget the cloudy abstractions of the Treaty of Rome or its most recent outgrowth, the so-called 'Treaty on European Union' signed at Maastricht. No publication more clearly reveals the true character of the EU in practice than something called the *Directory of Community Legislation In Force and Other Acts of the Community Institutions*.

Few outside the inner reaches of the System have even heard of this hefty volume, costing 110 ecus (over £90). Certainly few members of parliament have ever even seen a copy. But it is a vital guide to picking one's way through the EC labyrinth because above all Brussels is a law factory, a vast machine churning out directives and regulations. And here in these 1,000-plus pages of small print in double-columns are listed the tens of thousands of directives, regulations, decisions and resolutions which show us the essential nature of that lawmaking, what really makes the EU tick.

At first glance, the volume's 20 general subject headings might lead one into thinking that the dominant theme was 'liberalisation'. There are sections, for instance, on

'Customs Union and Free Movement of Goods'
'Freedom of Movement for Workers and Social Policy'
'Right of Establishment and Freedom To Provide Services'
'Economic and Monetary Policy and Free Movement of Capital'

Then there is that beguiling emphasis on common purpose in the 'Common Agricultural Policy' (the longest section of all with 350 pages, each containing up to 100 items of legislation); the 'Common Fisheries Policy'; 'Common Foreign and Security Policy'. This follows 'Environment, Consumers and Health Protection' as the Directory moves towards its close, with a final section headed 'People's Europe'.

But penetrate below those general headings to the laws themselves, and here we catch the real flavour of what all this lawmaking is about. Here is the type of thing of which the Directory lists many thousands of examples (the numbers give the year each law was passed, with its reference number):

93/431 Commission Decision establishing the ecological criteria for the award of the Community eco-label to dishwashers

94/924 Commission Decision establishing the ecological criteria for the award of the Community eco-label to toilet paper

1640/79 Council Regulation limiting the granting of production aid for Williams Pears preserved in syrup

90/357 Commission Decision on the setting up of an Advisory Committee on Cork

74/409 Council Directive on the harmonisation of the laws of Member States relating to honey

70/772 Commission Recommendation addressed to the Member States concerning the tights and stockings sector of the textile industry

1054/73 Commission Regulation on the detailed rules for aid in respect of silkworms

489 Y O 7269(01) Council Resolution on banning smoking in places open to the public

83/129 Council Directive concerning the importation into Member States of certain seal pups and the products derive therefrom

3664/93 Council Regulation imposing a definitive anti-dumping duty on imports into the Community of photo-albums in book form originating in the People's Republic of China

3945/89 Commission Regulation fixing certain indicative ceilings and certain additional detailed rules for the application of the supplementary trade mechanism to fruit and vegetables, as regards broad-leaved endives

3715/91 Council Regulation establishing for 1992 the list of vessels exceeding 8 metres length overall and permitted to fish for sole within certain sectors of the Community using beam trawls whose aggregate length exceeds 9 metres

1601/91 Council Regulation laying down general rules on the definition, description and presentation of aromatised wines, aromatised wine-based drinks and aromatised wine-product cocktails

79/693 Council Directive on the approximation of the laws of Member States relating to fruit jams, jellies and marmalades and fruit purees

This last is one of hundreds of directives concerned with 'harmonising' or standardising the laws of the different EC countries on almost every conceivable type of product. These include page after page of such items as:

84/538 Council Directive on the approximation of the laws of the Member States relating to the permissible sound level of lawn mowers

69/493 Council Directive on the approximation of the laws of the Member States relating to crystal glass

73/361 Council Directive on the approximation of the laws of the Member

States relating to the certification and marking of wire ropes, chains and hooks

84/527 Council Directive on the approximation of the laws of the Member States relating to seamless, unalloyed aluminium and aluminium alloy gas cylinders

75/107 Council Directive on the approximation of the laws of the Member States relating to bottles used as measuring containers

One of the largest groups of such directives, regulations and decisions, nearly 450 of them, concerns 'harmonisation' of laws concerning the production of motor vehicles, such as:

74/60 Council Directive on the approximation of the laws of the Member States relating to the interior fittings of motor vehicles (interior parts of the passenger compartment other than the interior rear view mirrors, layout of controls, the roof or sliding roof, the backrest and rear part of the seats)

or the famous 'windscreen wiper directive':

94/68 Commission Directive on the approximation of the laws of the Member States relating to the windscreen wipers and washer systems of motor vehicles

But other activities are not far behind, such as more than 400 pieces of legislation imposing rules on the permissible varieties of plants and seeds; while the most regulated industry of all is milk production, subject to over 1,100 separate items of legislation, such as

690/92 Commission Regulation establishing a reference method for the detection of cows' milk casein in cheese made from ewes' milk

and this is not to mention scores of additional laws affecting cheesemaking, butter production and other activities relating to milk.

So it goes on for hundreds of pages, listing directives, regulations, decisions and recommendations for almost everything under the sun, from subsidies for a sewage works in some small town in Greece to aid for breeding rabbits in the Canary Islands, from rules on 'school provision for gypsy and traveller children' to the 'transfer of rights to replant vines', from the setting up of special bus services between France and Luxembourg to the importing of 'sheepmeat and goatmeat from Bulgaria', from rules laying down the sizes and dimensions of wine bottles to 'the preferential tariff charged to glasshouse growers for natural gas in the Netherlands'. There is even a Council Recommendation concerning 'the promotion of books and reading'.

No one actually knows how many pieces of legislation have been produced by this machine. The directives and regulations mentioned in the index alone number more than 20,000, but this is a very substantial underestimate of the total, because the Directory's indexing system lists only the first entry under any particular item. This may later have been subject to dozens more directives or other forms of amendment which do not appear in the index, and which cannot therefore be looked up without knowledge of the reference number of the initial entry.

Does this not all tell its own story? One cannot read through these pages without getting one overwhelming impression, of how the driving force behind all this lawmaking seems to be a compulsion to impose a bizarre legalistic framework on almost every area of economic and even social activity imaginable, with a desire to regulate it in the minutest detail. How could such a gargantuan enterprise possibly hope to work? How could it have any connection with the real world? One might even be reminded of that other section of Swift's *Gulliver's Travels*, in which the hero visits the Academy of Lagado, where teams of legislators and projectors 'fell into schemes of putting all arts, sciences, languages and mechanics upon a new foot'. The professors engaged on building this Utopia were constantly contriving 'new rules and methods of agriculture and building, and new instruments and tools for all trades and manufactures ... with innumerable other happy proposals. The only inconvenience is that none of these projects are yet brought to perfection, and in the meantime the whole country lies miserably waste.'

Brussels – the nexus

How are these laws produced? A widespread misconception about 'the Euro-bureaucracy' is that it is only limited to the permanent officials of the European Commission and its satellite bodies, such as the European Parliament, the Committee of the Regions, the European Court of Justice and the rest. As enthusiasts for the System love to point out, there are only 'a mere' 18,000 officials in the Commission itself, with its 26 'Directorates General', though in recent years this number has been growing with remarkable speed.

But this is completely to misunderstand the true role Brussels plays in our new System of government, as can be seen when one explores the way the European Community generates its laws. Any particular item of legislation may in the first place be proposed by officials of one of the Directorates General of the Commission, known in shorthand by Roman numerals, such as 'DG III' concerned with the 'internal market' or 'DG XIV' in charge of fisheries. But the proposal is just as likely to originate with government officials of one of the 15 Member States. It may then go through a long process, beginning in technical committees which draw together officials representing ministries from all those 15 governments. Every working day of every week thousands of those officials are converging on Brussels from all over the Community, from Helsinki, Lisbon, Vienna, Athens, Madrid, Copenhagen, Paris, London and all the rest. Brussels and the Commission itself merely act as a nexus, providing a link between all the bureaucracies of all the governments.

Indeed when we speak of the 'Brussels bureaucracy' we are not just talking about the permanent officials of the Commission, as if they were a breed apart. Thousands of those officials are on temporary secondment from the bureaucracies of the Member States. An absolutely crucial part of the System is the practice by which each Government sends its 'high-flying' civil servants to Brussels for tours of duty, so that they can return home after a year or two, not only familiar with the way the Commission works, but firmly imbued with 'the ethos of Brussels'. It is hoped they will have gained a 'belief in the European construction' which will stand them and the European cause well as they subsequently rise to ever more senior positions in their own departments. In all these ways Brussels is merely the centre of a mighty anthill, connecting and locking ever closer together all the bureaucratic machines working for all the governments, employing millions of officials. Such is the true size of the bureaucracy behind the making of all this Euro-legislation, on a scale the world has never before seen.

The mass of technical committees co-ordinated by the Directorates General may eventually feed their proposals up to the next layer in the hierarchy, the Economic and Social Committee (ECOSOC), which again joins together officials representing all the governments with officially accredited experts and other representatives from the various countries. From there they go to another body of officials, COREPER, or the Committee of Permanent Representatives of each member state, where the directive or regulation is agreed in its final form. Only then may there finally be a chance for elected politicians to pronounce on what has emerged from all these layers of bureaucracy, if a particular proposal is so contentious that it needs to be argued over in one of the endless meetings of the Council of Ministers.

But even here we are only talking about those types of legislation which in theory at least are decided by the Council of Ministers, such as Council Directives which must then be implemented or 'transposed' by each goverment into the law of its own country. The Council also issues Regulations, which differ from directives in that they immediately become law throughout the Community and have to be enforced as they stand. There are also Council Decisions which apply as law only to some specific local situation; and other lesser varieties of law-making such as Council Recommendations, Opinions and Resolutions.

On the other hand, the same categories of legislation can also be produced by the Commission itself. At least Commission Directives again have to be implemented individually by each state. But Commission Regulations, which as regulations pass immediately into law binding throughout the Community, are produced by committees of officials meeting in Brussels and may not require any involvement by elected politicians at all. These official edicts represent the purest distillation of rule by bureaucracy imaginable. And in recent years, as we shall see, the Commission Regulation has become the largest and fastest growing of all the types of legislation the System employs.

The yellow banana

Of course the real measure of this System is the nature of the laws it produces. In the rest of this book we shall see many examples, but for a specific flavour of the kind of thing this anthill is up to we may pick out just two.

The first is Commission Directive 95/10, issued in April 1995, on 'the method of calculating the energy value of dog and cat food intended for particular nutritional purposes'. This, the Commission decreed, must be done according to a specific formula based on 'the percentages of certain analytical constituents of the food: this value is expressed in megajoules (MJ) of the metabolic energy (ME) per kilogram of compound feeding stuff'. The formula is as follows:

(a) Dog and cat food, with the exception of cat food with a moisture content exceeding 14 per cent: MJ/Kg of ME – (0.1464 x percentage crude protein + 0.3556 x percentage crude oils and fats + 0.1464 x percentage nitrogen-free extracts); (b) Cat food with a moisture content exceeding 14 per cent: MJ/Kg of ME – (1.1632 x percentage crude protein + 0.3222 x percentage crude oils and fats + 0.1255 x percentage nitrogen-free extract) – 1.2092; where the percentage of nitrogen-free extract is calculated by taking the difference between 100 and the percentage of moisture, crude salt, crude protein, crude oils and fats and crude fibre.

A second example is that Commission Regulation 2931/94 'fixing the aid for the supply of breeding rabbits on the Canary Islands'. It is of course notoriously difficult to get rabbits to breed. But in all human history perhaps only the European Commission could have devised a scheme where taxpayers could be compelled to subsidise rabbit-breeding, in this case by handing over to anyone wishing to breed rabbits on the Canaries the sum of 26 ecus, or £21, for each 'pure-bred or grandparent' rabbit, and 20 ecus, or £16.80, for each 'parent' rabbit.

In the rest of this chapter we shall look more generally at six further instances of laws produced by that Brussels anthill, each inspired by that shibboleth of our time, the great god 'safety'.

*

Our first example emerged to view in 1994 when the producers of the EC's 300 million liquid gas cylinders were much agitated by a proposal, under the Liquid Gas Appliances directive, that these should each carry a 'tactile' safety warning which could be read by blind people. The industry claimed this would be hugely expensive, to achieve no gain in safety. But Commission officials then came up with a proposal for how it should be put into practice. The tactile warnings should be printed into the metal of the cylinders. The industry pointed out that this would not only cost £2 billion but could also be highly dangerous, as it would weaken the cylinders and make them liable to explode.

At a Brussels committee meeting the official representing Britain, a Mr Walker of the DTI, forcefully argued that these safety warnings were unnecessary, winning unanimous support from officials of other governments. But the Commission officials pointed out that, under the Council directive, tactile warnings were now a mandatory requirement. So a compromise was proposed by a Dr Hart, a Commission official who also happened to be British (although he now lived in some style in Italy, was married to a Dane and liked to call himself 'an international'). This was for a 'tactile label' to be tied to each cylinder, called from its shape and colour the 'yellow banana'. Thus was approved a scheme which no member state government wanted or thought necessary, threatening a cost to the industry estimated at £500 million.

*

2. Brussels – Heart of the Monster

Our second example concerns rosin, the sap from pine trees, one of the unsung heroes of our civilisation. It is a vital ingredient in paper manufacture, chewing gum, truck tyres, surface coatings, depilatory wax, retsina and countless other products. Despite the fact that it has been used for thousands of years with almost no known risk – one or two people are mildly allergic to it – in 1990 officials of DG XI, concerned with the environment, became convinced that rosin should be added to the list of 'hazardous substances' under Council Directive 67/548 on 'the Classification and Labelling of Dangerous Substances'.

So little did the officials know about rosin that their first paper opened with the claim that it could be obtained from 'dried pine'. Dry pine is of course wood from which the resin has dried out. Yet for the next five years the international rosin trade was plunged into a nightmare. New proposals for regulating and labelling rosin poured from Directorate XI like some crazed fountain which could not be turned off.

When Britain's largest rosin importer Francis Pound approached his MP Ian Talor he was told 'this is solely a matter for the European Parliament'. When he wrote to his MEP Tom Spencer, he was told he should be addressing queries 'not to me but to London'. The civil servant of the Health and Safety Executive responsible for trying to make sense of all this gobbledygook became so worn down she took early retirement. As instructions and counter-instructions about the wording of safety warnings now required for every rosin consignment followed each other in bewildering succession, confusion spread across the globe to all the countries where rosin originates.

Eventually in 1995 the regulation was dropped, but only after costing the trade 'millions of pounds'. By now however the rosin importers had a new problem on their hands. Under Commission Regulation 793/93 they were informed that if they imported into the EC more than ten tonnes of 'any of the 110,000 substances listed on the European Inventory of Existing Commercial Substances (EINECS)', which had been brought in 'to protect health, safety and the environment', it was now mandatory to supply details of all such imports on a 3.5" disc to ISPRA, an EC monitoring unit in Italy.

*

Our third example concerns another highly 'dangerous substance' according to the officials of DG XI, Scotch whisky. In 1994 whisky distillers were alarmed to hear that their product was included under a new directive, targeted at dangerous chemicals, which would make it illegal to carry 'flammable liquid' by road in containers of more than 250 litres. This would have involved replacing more than six million casks, at a cost of hundreds of millions of pounds, in which whisky has for years been safely carried by lorry during two stages of its manufacturing process. After a fierce battle, they won a temporary 'derogation', exempting whisky from classification as a 'dangerous substance' for five years. Nevertheless they were forced to spend £2 million putting an EC 'hazard' sign on each cask, even though these already carried warning labels and British officials conceded any benefit from the new labels would be 'extremely small'.

Scarcely was this battle concluded than the whisky men were faced with a further directive on the Control of Major Accident Hazards Involving Dangerous Substances. Its aim was to prevent any repetition of the notorious chemical disasters at Seveso and Flixborough. But by raising the 'flashpoint' of 'flammable liquids', whisky was again rated as a 'hazardous chemical'. In fact since a fire in 1960 the whisky industry had already brought its fire safety measures up to the highest standards, not least since if a company loses a warehouse full of maturing Scotch it has lost its most valuable asset.

Brussels was reluctant to accept that the fumes from burning whisky would not create a Bhopal-type chemical disaster. Nevertheless after lengthy negotiations the officials made a concession, exempting the whisky men from some of the more onerous requirements of the directive. But only on condition that they presented an individual 'safety case' for each of their 68 maturation warehouses, costing £50,000 a time.

*

Our fourth example concerns Emtryl, a wonder drug used by Britain's pheasant breeders, who annually rear 20 million birds, two-thirds of the EC total. Pheasant rearing in Britain employs 13,000 people and generates around £600 million a year. But to an astonishing extent this is only made possible by Emtryl, which eliminates diseases which could kill up to half those birds. In 1995 the officials of DG VI, concerned with agriculture, issued Commission Regulation 1798/95 which made the use of Emtryl for game birds illegal. This was because a single American study 20 years before had shown that Emtryl could cause mutations in protozoa. Hence, it was argued, it might conceivably cause cancer in humans eating the pheasants, although by the time the birds were shot and eaten any possible effects of a drug administered months before would long since have disappeared.

British officials fought in vain against a regulation which would wipe out an industry and condemn up to ten million birds to a lingering death. Although Emtryl was now banned for game birds, by Brussels' customary sublime logic its use was still permitted for turkeys and pigs up to the time they were killed and eaten.

So transparently crazy was this Commission Regulation, which became EC law as soon as it was issued, that for once British ministers decided to dig in their heels. In the House of Lords, a government spokesman, Lord Lucas, described the situation as 'completely illogical', although curiously he hastened to add that the decision was 'in no way unreasonable'. Asked what effect this 'completely illogical' though not 'unreasonable' law would have, Lord Lucas stated 'we have no knowledge whatever of game-breeders who intend to use Emtryl during this breeding season' (as he well knew, there wasn't a breeder in Britain who wasn't gagging to use the stuff), 'but we have no plans to police the matter'. In other words, for the very first time, the British Government openly admitted it was quite happy to allow thousands of people to get away with breaking EC law.

*

Our fifth example was DG XI's so-called nitrates directive, 91/676. This was introduced to impose strict limits on the run-off of nitrates from farms, because of a fear that if these got into drinking water they might cause 'blue baby syndrome' in young children and stomach cancer in adults.

In fact there have been only 20 'blue baby' cases in Britain in 35 years and the last recorded fatality was in 1950. Stomach cancer is highest in north Wales, where nitrate levels are lowest, and lowest in the south-east, where nitrate levels are highest. In 1995 a research team from Aberdeen University's medical school even confirmed that, far from nitrates causing stomach cancer, the disease may actually be caused by lack of them, while it is impossible for nitrates to cause 'blue baby syndrome' at all.

Nevertheless British officials in the Department of the Environment diligently set about implementing the directive. 1.6 million acres of farmland were designated as 'Nitrate Vulnerable Zones' or NVZs. And in April 1996 the DoE imposed drastic new rules on the 8,000 farmers in these NVZs, which completely transformed the way they ran their farms. For a farmer like Mark Horvath of Woodbridge, Suffolk, the new rules affected almost every aspect of his farm management. It now became illegal for him at certain times of year to manure his fields. He could no longer grow nitrogen-rich crops like peas and beans. He would have to spend tens of thousands of pounds a year storing manure from his pigs, or having it removed by tanker.

All this would have such a devastating effect that Mr Horvath feared he might have to give up his farm altogether. Yet tests showed that nitrate discharges from his farm into the nearby River Waveney were quite acceptable. The problem was that nitrate levels in the river exceeded EC limits only because of discharges from a gravel pit upstream, over which the directive had no control. Similar absurdities came to light all over Britain. Yet a leading firm of agricultural estate agents, Humbert's, estimated the new Brussels rules could cut the value of farmland now in NVZs by up to £300 an acre, or a total of up to £480 million.

*

Our last example, also centred on the fear of nitrates, was a measure which became notorious for its threat to close down a complete British industry.

The commercial growing of lettuces in greenhouses in Britain is centred in Lancashire, Lincolnshire and the south-east, providing a livelihood for 12,000 people and turning over £65 million a year. But in 1994 word came from Brussels of a new Commission Regulation being drafted under Council Regulation 315/93 on 'contaminants in food'. This proposed a drastic limit on the level of nitrates permissible in certain vegetables, including lettuce. These nitrates are not produced by fertiliser, but relate to the effect of sunlight on the natural chemistry of the plant. Plants directly exposed to sunlight in the open have a low level, in those grown under glass it is much higher, and the British growers realised there was no way their produce could meet the proposed requirements. It would be impossible for most to survive.

The way this proposal arose provided a revealing insight into how laws can emerge through the Brussels system. The nitrate scare originated in Germany and Holland, whose health ministries were persuaded that nitrates in vegetables could cause cancer. The two governments therefore proposed new laws to limit nitrate levels in vegetables sold in their own countries. However, under the rules of the Single Market, this automatically aroused the involvement of Brussels, since any such restrictions on trade must be considered on an EC-wide basis. The matter therefore passed into the hands of the Commission's Standing Committee on Food.

In fact the scientific grounds for restricting nitrates in vegetables were so flimsy as to be non-existent. Eminent scientists such as Sir Richard Doll testified that, far from nitrates being carcinogenic, the incidence of cancer was significantly lower in people who eat vegetables containing nitrates. But the German and Dutch officials were unshakeable in their view, and they soon found curious allies. The vegetable growers of southern Europe realised the regulation would give them a huge commercial advantage, because it would devastate their competitors in Britain, Belgium and Holland, growing lettuces under glass, while their own lettuces, grown in the open, would easily meet the new limits. The southern European countries therefore joined in support of the proposal.

In the end Britain was alone in opposing the new regulation. The Belgian and Dutch growers only woke up to the threat to their own industries belatedly, because of concern in Britain, by which time their governments had already pledged support to the proposal. And as a Commission Regulation the issue was to be decided by officials, without politicians being involved. Although Britain was totally opposed to what it regarded as a ludicrous and highly damaging measure, MAFF admitted that, as soon as the proposal became law, the British Government would have to enforce it. Thus, in the name of Single Market rules intended to promote trade between EC countries, a British industry selling its produce almost entirely within Britain would be wiped out.

After we publicised this story in October 1994 it became something of a cause célèbre. The decision was postponed and the eventual outcome in 1996 was a typical EC fudge. The limits were to stay, but glasshouse lettuce growers were given a reprieve for five years, during which time they were supposed to find ways of complying with the new requirements.

This episode shone a devastating light into some of the murkier corners of how the Brussels system of law-making can operate.

First, it was a typical example of how all too frequently some bogus scientific notion gets inserted into the system and then, like a computer virus, becomes almost impossible to eliminate.

Secondly, it was an example of how particular interests can use the cover of such high-minded causes such as hygiene, safety or the environment to manipulate the regulatory system to their own commercial advantage.

Thirdly, it exemplified just what a powerful role was now being played in the Brussels system of law-making by the Commission Regulation, using powers delegated to the officials by the Council of Ministers to produce a form of legislation which for bureaucrats is absolutely ideal because it requires no involvement by elected politicians at all.

As a result of our exposing this, the British Government was asked in the House of Lords in what circumstances the Council of Ministers might recall for political decision proposals made under powers which had been delegated to Commission officials. So perfectly does the resulting explanation capture the essential ethos of the Brussels system of government that it may be quoted in full:

> Article 145 of the Treaty, which deals with the delegation of implementing powers to the Commission, allows the Council to impose procedural requirements on the way the Commission exercises such powers and also provides for those procedures to be codified in advance in a Council Decision. The Decision in question (No 87.373 known as the Comitology Decision) lays down three types of procedure, each involving Committees composed of representatives of Member States – Advisory Committee, Management Committee and Regulatory Committee – chaired by the Commission, which delivers opinions on proposals for Commission legislation.
>
> Both the Management Committee and the Regulatory Committee procedures, but not the Advisory Committee procedures, require proposals to be referred to the Council in certain circumstances. Under the Management Committee procedure, a proposal must be referred to the Coucil where the Committee votes against it by qualified majority, while the Regulatory Committee procedures requires the proposal to be submitted to the Council if the Committee does not approve the measure by qualified majority. The Management Committee and Regulatory Committee procedures come in two variants, but in each case the Council has a period of time in which to take a different decision. In addition, the Comitology Decision sets out a further procedure which may be applied when the Council confers powers on the Commission to take safeguard measures. This does not include a specific provision for a procedure involving a Committee; instead any Member State may appeal to the Council.
>
> The Comitology Decision does not specify which procedure should apply to particular subjects. However, for important matters, including the management of the agricultural commodities and fisheries markets, food law, animal and plant health, the Council has in delegating implementing powers to the Commission specified one of the procedures, usually either the Management or Regulatory Committee, which provide for recourse to the Council. The Commission's proposal on nitrates in lettuce is, for example, subject to the Regulatory Committee procedure.
>
> I hope you find this information helpful.

This masterpiece of bureaucratic prose has only one real, underlying message. What in effect the officials who drafted it are saying is that the whole system is so complicated precisely because we don't want any outsider to understand it. We, the officials, are in charge.

And this is just the credo of the officials in Brussels. We must now see what happens when all this avalanche of legislation passes to the next stage down the line, when it lands on the desks of those other officials in Whitehall whose job is to turn it into local law for the people of Britain.

3. Whitehall Makes it Worse

That is known in the jargon as 'Bookerism', after the journalist who identified the ill. Christopher Booker is strongly against the European Community, but being an honest journalist he has spotted that much of the regulation is derived not from the Community but from the itch of Whitehall to insert its own bureaucratic instincts into the process.

Foreign Secretary Douglas Hurd, House of Commons, 24 November 1992

In the late summer of 1992 press reports appeared of a curious row over a new set of fire regulations about to be passed into law by the Home Office. Ministry officials had said their Fire Safety in the Workplace Regulations, implementing two EC health and safety directives, would impose costs on Britain's businesses amounting over ten years to £1.7 billion. This in itself was a colossal sum. But when trade and professional organisations such as the District Surveyors Association examined the actual requirements of the new regulations, they estimated that the true cost to businesses would be far higher, up to £8,000,000,000.

It then turned out the situation was odder still. The directives in question were among six on health and safety at work, the so-called 'six pack', about to be brought into law in Britain to coincide with the start of the Single Market on 1 January 1993. Two of these mentioned fire safety, although one – the so-called 'framework directive' 89/391 – only in the most general terms. The other, the Workplace directive 89/654, contained essentially just 34 lines relating to fire. How had the Whitehall officials managed to turn those few sentences into what promised to be the most costly set of regulations Britain had ever seen?

The answer was that the officials had added all sorts of requirements not contained in the original directives. They had translated those original 34 lines from Brussels into nearly 20 pages of regulations, plus more than 100 pages of explanatory 'guidance'. This came to a total of over 3,500 lines, or more than 100 times the length of the original Brussels text. The guidance included many recommendations which went much further than the regulations, such as that any hotel must be able to evacuate all its guests in less than two minutes in the middle of the night. The biggest single innovation was that the new British regulations were to apply not just to all normal businesses but also to the self-employed, who under the directives were exempted. This meant the new rules would cover more than three million businesses. Many people working at home would have to instal fire doors, fire alarms and other expensive safety measures. The new regulations would apply to churches, stately homes and other types of building exempted under

46

the directives; while further additions by Whitehall included requirements to hold regular fire drills and to keep extensive written records.

What was particularly odd was that Britain already had its own well-tried and very successful system to promote fire safety in the workplace. Industry accounted for only 2 per cent of all fire deaths, while more than 40 times as many took place in private homes which were completely unaffected by the new regulations. Other EC countries such as Ireland argued that the directives added nothing to their own existing fire safety measures and therefore saw no need for any new rules. Only in Britain did it seem that civil servants wanted to use the directive as an excuse to introduce a host of new rules which independent experts insisted would do nothing to improve safety, yet would impose costs running into billions of pounds.

*

So glaring was this instance of Whitehall officials proposing to go completely over the top in the way they turned an EC directive into UK law that when public attention was drawn to what was happening, by ourselves and others, it provoked something of a furore. The Home Secretary Kenneth Clarke acted just in the nick of time to prevent his junior minister Earl Ferrers signing the regulation into law, and it was sent back to the officials to be redrafted. But, as we reported in *The Mad Officials*, in the autumn of 1992 we were discovering so many similar instances of how, in translating EC directives into UK law, the Whitehall officials were inserting onerous requirements not mentioned in the original directives that it was obvious this had become almost routine practice.

There was, for instance, the curious way in which DTI officials chose to implement the EC's Toy Safety directive, 88/378. This specifically stated that toys made from 1990 onwards had to carry the 'CE' safety mark, showing they had been tested as complying with EC safety standards. But when the officials issued their British version, the Toy Safety Regulations, they inexplicably ruled that the CE requirement applied to all toys, regardless of the date when they were made. This came as a particularly devastating blow to charity shops like those run by Oxfam, which had to stop selling the second-hand toys which raised millions of pounds a year.

Another instance was the blindly cumbersome way the DTI officials were proposing to implement the EC's Electromagnetic Compatibility (EMC) directive, 89/336. The directive stated that, as from 1996, all electronic or electrical goods would have to carry a CE mark to show they had been tested as not interfering with any other electronic equipment. But the original directive contained just five pages. The DTI version enlarged this to 84 pages of detailed regulations and guidance notes; and Britain's mass of small specialist electronics firms were horrified to discover that, under the British version, they would have to send every assemblage for testing at an approved test house at a cost of £1,000 a day. One electronics engineer, Colman Twohig of Rochester, Kent, who supplied dredging vessels with specialised assemblies which might cost no more than £50, rang up the DTI to point out that this requirement would probably close down thousands of small firms like his. The officials frankly admitted they had not realised this when drafting the regulations. It was scarcely consoling then to discover that the French version of the directive ran to just two pages, and that other EC countries had no plans to implement the directive at all.

We were then approached by various scrap metal dealers, horrified by a peculiar disaster which seemed to be threatening their industry, worth £3 billion a year, as a result of the very odd way in which officials of the Department of the Environment were proposing to implement two EC environmental directives on waste disposal and vehicle batteries. The officials were proposing to treat scrap yards exactly as if they were landfill sites, imposing draconian rules which would make it difficult for many scrap businesses to survive. Yet when the relevant directive 91/156 was examined, it turned out its real aim was in fact to encourage the type of recycling which was the basis of the scrap metal industry. It had therefore drawn a clear distinction between businesses based on recycling, and those based on the final disposal of waste in landfill sites. But this distinction the British officials seemed quite wilfully to be ignoring. Similarly the officials intended to impose such cumbersome rules on the disposal of vehicle batteries that this threatened to bring Britain's highly efficient system of battery recycling to a complete halt. Again it turned out that the whole purpose of directive 91/157 was actually to encourage the recycling of batteries, for which Britain already had a record second to none in Europe.

*

In the autumn of 1992, our first reports on this extraordinary compulsion of Whitehall to elaborate on the contents of Brussels directives caused some stir. They played a considerable part in John Major's decision, at that year's Conservative Party Conference, to launch with considerable fanfare his Government's 'deregulation' policy. A special 'Scrutiny' unit was set up in the DTI to investigate the phenomenon of what came to be known as the 'gold plating' of directives. Attempts, not always successful, were made to have all the examples we have so far mentioned modified or withdrawn for further consideration. But we continued to come across other examples, where either the policy remained unchanged or where the damage had already been done.

One small, sad example was the fate of Andrew Fairweather, who during the 1980s built up the second-largest quail farm in Britain on the edge of the New Forest. In 1991 he received a booklet from the Ministry of Agriculture entitled 'Food Sense – 1992 and You' on how to compete in the forthcoming Single Market. He discovered that, although quail had previously been regarded as 'game', they were now officially 'poultry' and therefore his premises came under a proposed new EC Poultry Hygiene directive. Mr Fairweather gradually realised that his modest quail farm was now being treated as if it was an industrial poultry plant – and that to stay in in business would involve large-scale rebuilding, costing him more than his annual turnover. Among lesser requirements, he would have to instal showers so that he and his six employees could wash every time they moved from one shed to another, which was dozens of times a day. Mr Fairweather attempted to contact MAFF to discuss his problem but, despite months of telephoning, he could find no one to answer his queries. He was now being told by customers all over the country, from Plymouth to Glasgow, that, unless he complied with the regulations, they would no longer be legally permitted to buy his quails. He finally accepted there was no way he could afford to stay in business and closed down the Long Reach Quail Farm, putting six people on the dole. It later emerged the EC directive was not even issued until a year after he closed, and the UK regulations were only published six months after that. Mr Fairweather therefore raised the matter with his MP. Back came a letter signed by food minister Nicholas Soames confirming that, under the EC legislation, his closure had been unavoidable. Nevertheless Mr Soames thought it might be 'helpful' to know that, under a subsequent directive, quail were no longer classified as 'poultry' but had once again been reinstated as 'game'.

*

An example with rather wider implications we first came across when we we learned from an undertaker of the curious situation which had arisen over the importing of coffins from Spain. Every year some 300 British people die in Spain, and their relatives wish to have them returned home for burial. Under UK regulations implementing an EC environmental directive, 84/360, on 'the combatting of pollution from industrial plants', it was illegal to burn Spanish coffins in a British crematorium. This was because Spain had not complied with the directive, and there was therefore no guarantee that Spanish coffins did not contain forbidden pollutants. On arrival in Britain therefore the corpse had to be 'decoffined', then 'recoffined' in a British box complying with the regulations. It could then be legally incinerated without polluting the environment. As for the disused Spanish coffin, the undertaker explained that he would quite legally 'take it out the back and put it on a bonfire'.

However, what this eventually brought to light was that EC directive 84/360 made no mention of coffins or crematoria. It was entirely the decision of officials of the DoE to extend the application of the directive. Nor had the officials even issued any UK regulations on the matter. They had simply issued Guidance Note 52, instructing the British funeral industry to comply with the pollution standards set by the directive, even though these had never been directed at crematoria in the first place. The result was that Britain's crematoria had to embark on a hugely expensive rebuilding programme, at an eventual cost of £100 million (adding £65 to the cost of the average cremation), so that they did not emit more than 'one billionth of a gram per cubic metre' of dioxins, chemicals which are given off from any domestic bonfire. In 1993 the government's own Warren Spring Laboratory tested the only three British crematoria which supposedly complied with the DoE's guidance, and found they were still emitting between 25 and 46 times the permitted limits of dioxins. In theory therefore, when the £100 million had been spent, it seemed possible that every crematorium in the country would still be illegal. The only way relatives could then legally cremate their loved ones would be to take them abroad to a country like Spain, where the directive had not been applied in such a ludicrously unnecessary draconian fashion.

*

The real question, of course, was why was Whitehall 'gold plating' Brussels directives in this remarkably damaging way? One answer commonly offered was simply that the British tradition of making laws was completely different from that on the continent. The drafting of legislation coming out of Brussels was often quite general and woolly in its phraseology, whereas the tradition of the British civil service was to be much more precise. It was therefore inevitable, the theory ran, that the Whitehall version would often be much longer than the original directive, because it was important to 'dot every i and cross every t' so there could be no misunderstanding as to exactly what a regulation was meant to mean.

But this did not explain why the Whitehall officials so often seemed to add requirements which were not in the directive at all, and always in a way which made its impact much more damaging. Why, for instance, had those DTI officials chosen to draft the Toy Safety Regulations to include older and second-hand toys, when the directive was so specifically targeted at new toys made after 1990? Why had the DoE officials insisted on applying those pollution standards to crematoria when the original directive made no mention of crematoria? Obviously the real reason why the practice of 'gold plating' had become so widespread went much further than just a matter of ensuring that the British versions were more precise.

A second explanation offered was the generally agreed policy of Whitehall, led by the Foreign Office, that when it came to implementing Brussels legislation the British Government must be seen as 'the good boys of Europe'. Even Mrs Thatcher, in the closing years of her premiership, had often wished to emphasise how dutiful Britain was in this respect. When she was under fire for being at odds with the rest of the EC over some issue, she would delight in reeling off to the House of Commons how Britain led the field in the amount of Single Market legislation she had implemented, whereas other countries, which liked to be thought more 'Europe-minded', lagged behind.

It was certainly true the Foreign Office was particularly insistent that other ministries should comply with EC legislation. But even this did not explain the remarkable lengths to which it was prepared to go to further this cause. A revealing instance of this was the curious story of how its officials were on one occasion actually pressuring a ministry to close down almost an entire British industry, for reasons which even the European Commission itself found incomprehensible.

*

Britain's herbal medicines industry employed 3,000 people, turning over £300 million a year supplying five million customers, and under the 1968 Medicines Act its products were specifically exempted from licensing requirements. But in the summer of 1994 officials of the Medicines Control Agency, a new body set up to license all drugs sold in Britain, observed that in a 30-year-old EC directive, 65/65, on drug licensing there was no mention of herbal medicines being exempted. The MCA's lawyers therefore took the view that EC law and

British law were in conflict; in which case, under the rules of the European Community, EC law must take precedence. Herbal medicines would have to be subjected to licensing procedures, just like any other medicine.

However, this presented a procedural problem. Under British law it would be impossible to repeal that section of the Medicines Act which gave herbal remedies an exemption without going through all the time-consuming complications of passing a new Act of Parliament. Fortunately for the officials, however, there was a short cut to hand. Under Section 2 (2) of the European Communities Act 1972, there was a simple procedure whereby, if a British statute was found to be in conflict with EC law, the British version could simply be repealed by a 'statutory statement', up to 30 of which might go through parliament on the nod in a day. Therefore the officials of the MCA and the Department of Health drafted the necessary instrument, the Medicines for Human Use (Marketing Authorisations, Pharmacovigilance and related matters) Regulations 1994, whereby the relevant section of the Medicines Act exempting herbal remedies could be struck from the statute book without parliament even having to discuss the matter.

The result was that the herbal medicines industry was suddenly faced with the threat of a complete disaster. To license each of its 3,000 products, at the standard fee of £84,000 to the MCA, would cost a minimum of £250 million, far more than it could afford. The industry estimated, around 2,700 of the products would have to be withdrawn. At least four-fifths of its firms would close altogether.

Immediately the industry launched a powerful lobbying campaign, calling on its millions of loyal customers to pressure their MPs. And in November 1994, when we reported on the crisis in the *Daily Telegraph*, some very odd facts came to light. Not only did it appear that no other country in the EC was applying the directives to herbal remedies in this way. Still more remarkably, even the Commission itself expressed surprise at the way the British Government had chosen to interpret them.

As the crisis facing the industry came to its height, its representatives and attended a meeting at the Department of Health where junior minister Tom Sackville made a remarkable admission. The real pressure on his officials to pass the new regulation, he confessed, was coming from the Foreign Office, in its desire for Britain to be 'the good boys of Europe'; and it seemed this rule applied even when the Commission itself was opposed to what Britain was doing. Just for once, so great was the political embarrassment building up over the issue that the Cabinet instructed the Department of Health to climb down. The proposed regulation was withdrawn and, for the time being at least, the industry was saved.

*

This episode provided a remarkable insight into the lengths to which Whitehall officialdom now seemed prepared to go to carry out what it believed to be the edicts of Brussels. And what was particularly striking about it was the way the officials seemed to be going so much further than Brussels required or even wanted.

A not dissimilar example was the remarkable threat which emerged in

1995, as we described in the first chapter, to the livelihood of thousands of older lorry drivers. Officials of the Department of Transport issued regulations, implementing an EC directive on driving licences, 91/439, requiring all lorry drivers to pass a new eyesight test with uncorrected sight. So far, the British law merely echoed the directive. But what then emerged was that Britain was the only country in the EC which was quite arbitrarily proposing to withdraw from older drivers what were known as 'grandfather rights', giving exemption from the new licensing requirements to those who had been driving safely since before 1983. It was this which provoked the row, because it would deprive countless older British drivers of their licences and jobs when their continental counterparts were not being treated in the same way. Again the European Commission expressed surprise that Whitehall seemed so determined to act on its own in such a damaging fashion. But again the Foreign Office officials pressed the DoT officials to stand firm – until the issue provoked such political embarrassment that transport minister Steven Norris was forced by colleagues to withdraw the proposal. He did this with very bad grace, blaming the media for having 'exaggerated' the number of lorry drivers who would lose their jobs, and his officials insisted all along that the drivers would have little difficulty in finding new ones. In fact one colleague who pointed out particularly forcefully how unlikely it was that older drivers would easily find new employment was a Foreign Office minister who had himself run a truck company, and who knew from experience just how callously unrealistic this argument was. As with the herbal medicines, however, this episode did at least provide another rare instance of how political embarrassment might occasionally lead to politicians overriding the officials. Much more usually, however, the officials got their way completely unchallenged, as we shall see in the next chapter.

*

What these examples show is that the desire for Britain to show itself as dutiful in complying with Brussels legislation could by no means be the full explanation why these Whitehall officials were using Britain's membership of the EC to inflict such unique and unnecessary damage on their own country. So what was the real reason?

One cannot answer this question without appreciating the profound change of culture which has been taking place all through Britain's bureaucracy in recent years. And of this there was no better illustration than the desperate battle for survival which hundreds of businesses in one industry had to fight against a Whitehall department which seemed prepared to stop at nothing to close them down. So much did this reveal of the curious change in attitude in the ranks of Whitehall officialdom that it merits a chapter to itself.

4. MAFF Declares War on the Abattoirs

> One of the most striking features of the passage of Directive 91/497 was the extent to which the negotiations – which were ostensibly solely about hygiene standards – were driven by other, wider issues.
>
> Review of The Implementation and Enforcement of
> EC Law in the UK Scrutiny Report by DTI, 1993

Two industries in Britain faced a more desperate battle for survival under the impact of Euro-legislation in the early 1990s than any others. One, the fishing industry, we shall come to in a later chapter. The other was the meat industry, or more precisely the majority of Britain's abattoirs, as they grappled with the consequences of an EC directive on meat hygiene, 91/497. But what was odd about this battle was, firstly, how little it genuinely related to any concern for hygiene; and, secondly, how far it was centred not so much on the directive itself as on the very peculiar way in which it was implemented by officials of the Ministry of Agriculture, Fisheries and Food.

Some years before Britain joined the Common Market, Brussels had issued a directive, 64/433, to ensure that abattoirs producing meat to be traded across national frontiers complied with conditions which met the so-called 'EC export standard'. After Britain joined, the directive was implemented in new UK regulations which over several years resulted in a general two-tier restructuring of the industry. On one hand were the large 'industrial' abattoirs which, albeit with the aid of many millions of pounds in grants, spent huge sums on rebuilding their premises to comply with the 'EC export standard'. On the other were hundreds of medium-size and small 'craft' slaughterhouses, most of which sold their meat only for local consumption, but which was often of a quality higher than that mass-produced by the large firms.

With the approach of the Single Market, Brussels issued a new directive, 91/497, almost identical with the previous one. But the intention now was that this should apply to all except the very smallest slaughterhouses, and its provisions were to hit Britain peculiarly hard in two respects.

Firstly, for historical reasons, Britain had a much higher proportion of medium-size slaughterhouses than most EC countries. These would now all have to spend up to £1 million rebuilding their premises to comply with the 'export standard', even if, as in most cases, they had no intention of exporting their meat. And, unlike the larger abattoirs, they would not be given any help from public funds.

Secondly, they would also now have to pay for a new system of hygiene supervision carried out by vets. This in fact provided yet another striking example of how British and continental traditions differed. In Britain slaughterhouses had for decades been inspected by qualified meat inspectors and health officials employed by local authorities, under a system deriving from the great 19th-century hygiene revolution centred on local medical officers. This system had given Britain meat as safe as any in the world. But in most continental countries a quite different system had evolved centred on vets, although those responsible for meat safety usually had qualifications specific to the task, unlike British vets who had little or no training of this kind. Now, however, thanks to directive 91/497, it was decided to impose on British abattoirs a clumsy two-tier combination of both systems. Not only would they continue to use the existing inspectors, but on top of this would also have to pay for supervision by vets without experience in public health inspection – which meant that charges to Britain's abattoirs would suddenly become much higher than anywhere else in the Community.

There were two reasons why the MAFF officials were determined to implement this directive with maximum rigour. First, it provided them with the opportunity to realise a project they had been discussing for years, to centralise bureaucratic control of Britain's meat industry. The directive would give them the excuse to replace the inspectors working for hundreds of different local authorities with a central inspection system, run by a new agency under the aegis of the ministry itself. Secondly, they were strongly supported by the larger abattoirs which, in the 1980s, had spent enormous sums on rebuilding to comply with the earlier directive. In many cases this had left them with under-used capacity, and with outgoings their output could not justify. For unabashedly commercial reasons, they therefore now welcomed the prospect of their smaller competitors also being made to spend huge sums on rebuilding, and if many were actually forced out of business by the prohibitive cost, so much the better.

*

The shadow of this revolution began falling over the meat industry even before the new directive was published. In 1990 Britain still had more than 800 abattoirs. But already ministry officials were warning them of the big changes on the way, and in 1991, even before the directive was finalised, and long before the regulations appeared to show what the law would actually be, abattoir owners were supplied with a hefty guidance pack, 'Food Sense – 1992 and You'. This purported to anticipate all the expensive changes required to obtain a licence to stay in business after the Single Market arrived on 1 January 1993. The owners did their sums to see what it would cost them to comply, and this was a major reason why, between 1990 and the end of 1992, more than a quarter of all Britain's abattoirs, 205 in all, shut their doors. These included small traditional slaughterhouses producing some of the best-quality meat in the country.

With the approach of the January 1993 deadline, it became clear that a disaster was in the making. Large areas of rural Britain would soon have no local slaughterhouse left, robbing farmers, auctioneers and butchers of a crucial link in their local economy. But when this concern was voiced to ministers, the line from the officials was unwavering. Minister of Agriculture

54

4. MAFF Declares War on the Abattoirs

John Gummer and his food minister Nicholas Soames repeatedly denied any suggestion that the wholesale closure of slaughterhouses was any consequence of the directive. The official explanation, constantly repeated in ministerial speeches and letters, was twofold. First, it was claimed that closures were inevitable because there were more slaughterhouses than the market could justify. 'The industry', the officials repeatedly intoned, 'is suffering from 45 per cent overcapacity.' This figure in itself was deliberately misleading, because it was based on the maximum capacity available throughout the year, whereas the meat trade is highly seasonal; even the most successful abattoir might well only operate at 100 per cent capacity around Christmas. What the official figure more seriously concealed, however, was that the only sector of the industry suffering from a genuine problem of overcapacity was those large new industrial plants rebuilt to 'EC production standards' in the 1980s, using millions of pounds of public subsidies. Most of the smaller craft slaughterhouses being forced out of business by the cost of the new regulations had been working to full economic capacity, until the ministry's new rules knocked their budgets haywire. But this then enabled Messrs Gummer and Soames to deploy their ultimate weasel claim. Owners who shut down, they on several occasions chillingly explained, had 'taken a commercial decision not to invest in the future of their business'.

What the officials also never fully admitted, however, even to their ministers, was the extent to which many of the more costly demands they were making of these businesses were not included in the directive or even in the regulations. The conditions the officials had been imposing as necessary to obtain a ministry licence were based only on their own ministry 'guidance' which had no force in law. But since this had been issued well over a year before the regulations were published, no one had the information available to challenge the officials' demands. One 'requirement' which particularly baffled abattoir owners was that vehicles carrying live animals and those carrying meat must enter and leave the premises by separate entrances. In many instances owners were thus ordered to spend tens of thousands of pounds on building a new entrance, even though trucks leaving and entering would, within a few yards, pass each other on the road. Another 'requirement' causing problems was for loading bays to be completely sealed from the outside air, even though meat leaving the slaughterhouse might soon quite legally be wheeled on a barrow across the road. The new veterinary officials also had to be looked after, provided with a shower and an office which might not be used for more than ten minutes a week. All these were being insisted on as conditions for a licence to operate after 1 January 1993, although it only later emerged that many were not actually required by law. Yet so horrendous were the costs involved that many owners gave up in despair.

*

In fact a much greater disaster was only averted at this time because, under a 'derogation' in the directive, abattoirs would still be permitted to hold a temporary licence to continue operating, so long as they pledged their intention to complete the necessary rebuilding works within three years. More than 200 took advantage of this, hoping they could somehow raise the money to survive.

But on 1 January 1993 came the second half of MAFF 's double whammy – the arrival of the new ministry vets, for whose services owners had to pay up to £65 an hour. Stories abounded in the industry as to how unfamiliar many of these vets were with the technicalities of the meat business. Some could not even distinguish between the carcase of a pig and a sheep. Yet as officials they had been given extraordinary new powers over the running of each slaughterhouse, even down to the right to decide when work should begin and finish. Despite their frequent ignorance of the trade, they expected to be treated with deference and were not slow to show who was now in charge of operations.

The atmosphere of the meat trade changed dramatically. In the first week of the new system we reported on one abattoir in Farnborough, Hampshire, where no fewer than six officials were gathered to supervise the work of three slaughtermen. Larger firms were facing additional costs of thousands of pounds a week, and it was not long before the cost of paying for these new officials was driving a whole new swathe of abattoirs out of business. In February 1993, when Nigel Batts had to tell his 17 employees that the Reading Abattoir was closing and that they were out of a job, he told us it was 'the worst thing I have ever done in my life'. In the first year of the new system, 104 more firms closed their doors, a sixth of those remaining, reducing the national total to 543. The following year another 47 closed, bringing the total below 500.

Typical of many smaller firms disappearing at this time was Wyndham Lewis's slaughterhouse and butchery business, run by his family for six generations in the south Welsh village of Bedwas. It was a perfect example of the traditional rural economy, involving several families of the Lewis clan, who reared their own sheep and pedigree cattle, took them to the family abattoir and then, through their own butchers' shops, sold beef and Welsh lamb of as good quality as any in the country. But the exorbitant costs of the new veterinary supervision were more than the business could afford. As Mr Lewis said the day he closed his doors in August 1994, 'The Government have been saying that they were going to step back from people's lives. But the burden of bureaucracy has increased. I am a lifelong Conservative supporter, but I could never bring myself to vote Conservative again.'

Mr Lewis certainly put his finger on one notable feature of this devastation the officials had unleashed on hundreds of responsible, efficient businesses; that it was being so compliantly supported by Conservative ministers, representing a party which had traditionally stood for small businesses and against increasing the powers of bureaucracy and the state.

Even more remarkable, however, was that this destruction was being carried out in the name of a Brussels directive, when no other meat industry in Europe was being treated in the same way. Even Whitehall officials frankly admitted that hygiene requirements had not been a central concern when the directive was drafted. As the Government's Review of the Implementation and Enforcement of EC Law in the UK put it, this lack of genuine concern for hygiene was 'one of the most striking features' of the negotiations behind Directive 91/497, which were 'driven by other, wider issues'. The report's authors noted, for instance, how 'Germany had already begun to use public health arguments to try to restrict access to its market', and how sensitive the French were to the growing impact on their home market of imports of British lamb. Undoubtedly such commercial considerations played a part in ensuring that, because of the peculiar structure of Britain's meat industry, it would be more seriously affected by the directive than any other in the Community.

But this in itself did not explain why Britain's own officials were then apparently so uniquely ruthless in the way they implemented the directive, first by adding so many requirements not called for by Brussels, then in the way they seemed determined to close down so many of Britain's abattoirs for reasons which appeared to have nothing to do with hygiene. This was startlingly confirmed by a case in which we became directly involved in 1995.

*

In Bacup, Lancashire, pig farmer Jim Law ran a small slaughterhouse, killing not only his own pigs but those from other farmers nearby, to supply more than 40 butchers in the area with pork of the highest quality.

As early as 1990 Mr Law had been told by MAFF officials that, with the new Brussels directive on the way, his slaughterhouse fell far short of what would be required to achieve the 'EC export standard' necessary to stay in business after January 1993. Not of course that Mr Law wished to export his meat anywhere except locally, nor that his premises were in any way unhygienic. They simply were not constructed according to the 'standard' the ministry required. So, after conversations with the ministry, Mr Law spent £200,000 rebuilding his little slaughterhouse in the way he thought the officials wanted. Only then was he told that he still would not qualify for a licence simply because his abattoir was 'too small'.

At this point he asked for our assistance. Inspection of his immaculate premises confirmed that here was a perfect test case to demonstrate that the ministry's policy was not motivated by a genuine concern for hygiene. An appeal was lodged against MAFF's refusal to give Mr Law his licence, and the result in the summer of 1995 was easily the longest case ever heard by the three ministry nominees on its supposedly independent meat tribunal.

Thanks to pressure brought on ministers by our allies in both Houses of Parliament, it was agreed that the MAFF officials directly responsible for Mr Law's case would be available to be subjected to cross-examination. Over many days, in a Manchester hotel room in that stiflingly hot summer, the three officials, Mr Hewson, Mr Cartwright and Mr Wild, were taken in minute detail through their reasons why Mr Law should be driven out of business. What the interrogation demonstrated, in a way which even the officials eventually found it hard to deny, was that, in wanting to refuse Mr Law his licence, they were not actually enforcing the provisions of the directive or the regulations. They were picking out points almost at random from a guidance document originating in Brussels known as the *Vade Mecum*, which had no force in law, to find arguments to justify a decision they had already taken, that Mr Law's abattoir should be closed down.

What gave away the officials' game more than anything was their suggestion that, under the Brussels rules, Mr Law might be allowed to stay in business, but only on what was known as a 'low throughput licence', which would so reduce his output as to make it impossible for the business to survive. This was based on the number of 'livestock units' which a slaughter-house killed each week. Originally Brussels had ruled that each pig counted as 'three livestock units', which would have reduced Mr Law's output to barely a tenth of what he needed. Admittedly now, after pressure from the Germans, Brussels had ruled that a pig counted as 'seven LUs', which would at least allow Mr Law to kill pigs on three days of each week. But as the MAFF officials knew, this still would not be enough to keep his business viable and to justify employing twelve men. And the officials were absolutely determined that Mr Law should not be given a full licence, entitling him to work the five days a week he wanted. In other words, they were prepared to admit his premises were perfectly hygienic enough for him to kill pigs for three days. But if he repeated precisely the same exercise on two more days, his abattoir suddenly became unhygienic and he could not be given a licence.

Faced with this Alice in Wonderland reasoning, the tribunal conceded that the regulations appeared to be 'extremely complex', and that there were 'inexplicable divergences' between the regulations and the directive. It agreed there was no 'logical reason' why Mr Law should be allowed to kill pigs on three days but not on five. Most tellingly of all, the tribunal even conceded that if the case was being heard under British hygiene law, it would have been necessary for the officials to prove that Mr Law's meat posed a genuine risk to public health, and that they had made no such case. But under EC law, the chairman pointed out, this principle did not apply. All that mattered was how the officials themselves chose to interpret the law. And although the tribunal agreed that the officials had not been able to justify most of their case, it still concluded that, on three tiny technical points, Mr Law should be refused his licence.

The face of the ministry officials had been saved. The case had aroused embarrassing public attention, and a few weeks later, after Mr Law had carried out minor works to deal with the three outstanding points, his licence was quietly granted. But the main point was that the right of the officials to interpret the law in virtually any way they chose had been upheld. And by this time those same officials had also pulled off the masterstroke which had been the underlying objective of their policy all along.

*

Throughout this whole saga, the real aim of the MAFF officials, going back well over a decade, had been to bring about a complete revolution in Britain's meat trade, by vesting unprecedented power over the industry in a new centralised agency under the ministry's own control. This they finally achieved in April 1995 when they set up the Meat Hygiene Service, with its national headquarters in York. The task of inspecting meat businesses was taken away from local authorities, and placed in the hands of 1,000 officials employed by the ministry's new agency, which would eventually be funded entirely from charges on the industry amounting to over £50 million a year. Proportionately these charges had already doubled in just three years.

4. MAFF Declares War on the Abattoirs

The MAFF officials managed to set up their new agency, armed with draconian new powers, without any debate in parliament. They did this simply by issuing a series of regulations or statutory instruments. Furthermore, they had long held that the meat industry would be much easier to administer if it could be reduced to a comparatively small number of large industrial abattoirs and poultry plants. With hundreds of smaller businesses already closed, and more to come, they were well on the way to achieving their ultimate goal. And in this they were actively supported at every stage by the 80 or so large companies which dominated the meat trade, which hoped to benefit enormously from the massive reduction of competition in the industry, and which eventually might be the only ones remaining.

Such all along had been the real hidden agenda of both the groups which would benefit from the new system, the officials and the big firms. They had only been able to achieve it with the aid of that Brussels directive, providing cover for every move they made, and of course by invoking the shibboleth of 'hygiene' which appeared to give moral justification to everything they had done. But in reality, as the Law case so vividly demonstrated, the whole story had nothing to do with hygiene at all. If anything, British meat would actually be less safe as a result of the whole exercise, since the quality of the meat produced in many of those small craft slaughterhouses was better than much of that produced in the large factory abattoirs, and the risk of cross-contamination in the industrial-scale mass-production plants was higher. In fact the only serious food poisoning incident connected with British meat in recent years had been in Lancashire in 1991. It came from *E.coli* in beefburgers made for a multi-national fast food chain from meat produced at a large industrial plant which met all the ministry's 'hygiene' requirements, and was the proud possessor of an 'EC export licence'.

5. The Officials versus the People

We must do more to lighten the burden of government regulation ... now is the time to mount a new offensive. We're already on the march against the Euro-crat. But you know it isn't just Brussels that relies on red tape. It's Whitehall. It's the town hall. I say again, this sort of thing must stop. I have asked Michael Heseltine to take responsibility for cutting through this burgeoning maze of regulations – who better for hacking back the jungle. Come on Michael, out with your club, on with your loin cloth, swing into action ....

Prime Minister John Major, launching his deregulation policy
at Conservative Party Conference, Brighton, October 1992

It was commonly observed by people who ran almost any kind of business in Britain in the 1990s that a striking change had in recent years come over the nature of their day-to-day dealings with bureaucracy. Gone were the days, they said, when most officials behaved like polite public servants, capable of sorting out problems in a friendly and practical manner. What they had noticed creeping in at all levels was a hard, aggressive new officiousness. Of course there were still shining exceptions to this rule. But nowhere was this confrontational, nit-picking attitude more evident than in the conduct of many of those petty officials on the ground who had the task of directly enforcing the avalanche of new regulations.

In the Britain of the mid-1990s, as we reported in *The Mad Officials*, this showed in many areas other than those related to legislation originating from Brussels. There was, for instance, the bizarre fashion in which young social workers used their newfound powers under the 1989 Children Act to close down hundreds of well-run nursery schools and playgroups; or the 'hygiene blitz' launched by environmental health officials, under the 1990 Food Safety Act, against thousands of pubs, restaurants, cheesemakers, butchers, bakers and other food businesses. But nothing gave greater impetus to this tendency than the explosion of regulations stemming from the EC.

We come now to the third leg of the Brussels/Whitehall/enforcement triangle, to what was in effect the front line of the battle. We remarked earlier how it was part of the pattern that, as legislation passed down through the system, its effect never became more innocuous or more rational. At each stage down the line its damaging effects were ratcheted up, and what here became even more obvious was that chilling arrogance now so common that it sometimes seemed as if British officialdom had declared war on all those with whom it had to deal. In this chapter we look at a few cases which exemplify this new attitude, all related to those three great shibboleths, safety, the environment and hygiene.

5. The Officials versus the People

*

We begin with what might be called 'The Strange Tale of the Pipecleaners and the Pig's Eye'.

In Ringwood, Hampshire, Acorn-Hobbycraft was a fast-growing little company which made children's model kits. It was run by two enterprising young model designers, Simon Hadden and Chris Newby, who raised the capital against the value of their homes. They were soon selling through major outlets like W.H. Smith and Woolworths, and in 1993 they anticipated their turnover would be more than £600,000. But on the run-up to Christmas in 1992 their kits attracted the attention of trading standards officials of the London borough of Barking and Dagenham. The officials took the view that various items in the kits might be dangerous to children, such as paper balls and those very familiar modelmakers' soft 'pipecleaners' which can be bent into animals and figures.

The officials' view was that these might be in breach of the DTI's new Toy Safety Regulations, implementing the EC's directive on toy safety, 88/315. Although the kits had already been approved as safe by Acorn's local trading standards department in Hampshire, the officials sent the pipecleaners for testing. The conclusion was that they were potentially so dangerous that the officials imposed suspension orders, forcing Acorn kits to be withdrawn from sale all over the country. Just before Christmas this dealt the little firm a tremendous blow, and both they and W.H. Smith appealed against the orders. Magistrates at Wootton Bassett in Wiltshire found in their favour. The orders were lifted, the kits went back on sale, and the court gave an order for the council to pay £30,000 in compensation for lost sales.

The Barking and Dagenham officials then appealed, and sent the pipecleaners for further tests. One of these involved obtaining the eye of a dead pig from a nearby abattoir, placing it in a vice and then poking a pipecleaner into it. The tests established that if you prod a pipecleaner into the eye of a pig often enough, it may cause damage. Translate that into a child's eye and the same obviously is true, although it is equally true that a child's eye might well be damaged by poking a pencil into it, a knitting needle or any one of a hundred other objects commonly found around the home.

Armed with this devastating evidence, in the autumn of 1993 the council appeared in Swindon Crown Court, before Mr Justice Peter Fanner. Expensive lawyers including QCs appeared for both sides. Acorn produced expert evidence of their own, supported by Hampshire trading standards department, that the pipecleaners presented no risk. After a week's solemn discussion of pigs' eyes everyone on the defence side believed the whole case was so ludicrous the judge could come to only one conclusion. But Judge Fanner ruled in favour of Barking and Dagenham. To sell the pipecleaners was a criminal offence.

The consequences to Acorn Hobbycraft were devastating. Faced with legal costs amounting to some £350,000, the company was forced into liquidation. Six full-time and eight part-time workers lost their jobs. The directors were saddled with crippling debts, and all for some pipecleaners, 260 million of which according to DTI records had been sold without any known accident, except to a gentleman who had pricked his thumb, and which continued to be legally sold in shops all over the UK. Not long after Acorn went bust, the BBC's Blue Peter was showing children how to make Jurassic Park animals out of exactly the same pipecleaners.

In 1996 it came to light that officials in Brussels were drafting new European toy safety standards. These sensibly accepted that 'sharp points' are often involved in assembling toys, that account should be taken of the genuine risk involved and that eye tests should not be considered sufficient evidence on their own, precisely because many other objects can injure eyes if improperly used. However it also emerged that these new standards had already been in draft in 1990, two years before the Acorn case began. Had they been adopted then, the case might never have happened. But so long had it taken for them to grind through the relevant committees that they were not due to become law until 1997. This knowledge was scarcely of much comfort to Acorn's young directors as they attempted to rebuild their lives, after their ordeal at the hands of those aptly named Barking officials, abetted by the ineffable wisdom of Judge 'Pipecleaner' Fanner.

*

Our next examples reflect the extraordinary confusion resulting from the new regulations which showered out of the Department of the Environment as it implemented a plethora of EC environmental directives. In *The Mad Officials* we reported on various insanities which arose from the complex new regulations relating to 'emissions to air'. Companies were faced with closure or immense costs, because their industrial processes emitted minute quantities of chemicals such as acetic acid (vinegar) or alcohol, which failed to meet the ludicrously exacting new pollution standards laid down by Brussels, while many major pollution sources, such a car exhausts, went virtually unchecked. We told, for instance, the story of the Teesside chemical company tied up in a nightmare of paperwork and losing hundreds of thousands of pounds, simply because one of its plants was emitting a tiny amount of acetic acid. This, the company worked out, amounted to far less pollution in a year than was emitted by the car belonging to the inspector from Her Majesty's Inspectorate of Pollution (HMIP) on his almost daily visits to their works.

Another major source of confusion and absurdity was the extraordinarily cumbersome new system of waste regulation, under which any materials which counted as 'waste' had to be disposed off according to rigid and often expensive procedures. These frequently gave rise to crazy anomalies, such as the case of the Midlands road-tanker factory which had a trench for a major oil pipeline dug over its land. When the owner Mike Fisher asked if he could keep the excavated earth for landscaping – his own soil – he was told this now counted as 'controlled waste'. Under the new 'EC rules' it must be removed in lorries and buried in an 'authorised' landfill site.

*

Equally crazy was the sad little story of the 'pets' cemetery' created on a grassy slope looking out over the sea of the Moray Firth by Steve Findlay, a street cleaner for Moray District Council. The occupants of the little grave-yard, only a few yards across, included 14 dogs, five cats, two hamsters and a dead dolphin which had been washed up on the shore below. But in the summer of 1994 Mr Findlay was informed by the council he worked for that, under the new Waste Management Regulations, implementing two EC waste directives, the contents of his cemetery constituted 'controlled waste'. He must pay £200 to license the cemetery as a 'waste disposal site', plus £50 a year 'subsistence fee'.

It was true the regulations officially classified dead pets as 'waste', al-though they gave exemption to people who bury pets in their own gardens. But the directives themselves, 75/442 and 91/156, also exempted 'animal carcases'. The DoE loftily explained to us that this did not mean dead pets but only 'agricultural animals'. Of course we should have known that a dead pussy cat was not an 'animal carcase' in the Euro-sense of the word. But the DoE also pointed out that, under the 'guidelines', enforcement officials were instructed not to impose 'an unjustifiable or disproportionate burden on those regulated'. When we drew this to the council's attention, the response from no less a dignitary than Moray's Chief Executive Mr Summers was to inform Mr Findlay that he not only required a 'Waste Management Licence' to operate his cemetery. He must now get 'Planning Approval' as well.

*

Rather more serious was the problem faced in 1994 by the Shillingstone Lime and Stone Co. which owned a chalk quarry looking down over the Stour valley in Dorset. This included a unique survival of an industry which once dotted the downlands of England, Britain's only remaining traditional small-scale lime works. But the 850 tonnes of lime it burned from the chalk each year in three 70-year old kilns were not just some quaint, historical relic. The lime was prized as invaluable by many of the country's leading experts in restoring historic buildings, because it had a colour and a range of subtle properties which could not be rivalled by the mass-produced stuff made in modern industrial plants.

In 1991 the plant's manager Paul Simmonds received an invitation from a Mr Leslie Stuffins, head of 'Division West' of Her Majesty's Inspectorate of Pollution, to pay £45 to attend a conference on 'Integrated Pollution Control'. Here Mr Simmonds learnt that, because the lime works emitted small quantities of lime dust, it would now, under regulations implementing EC directive 84/360 on 'the combating of pollution from industrial plants', have to pay an authorisation fee of £9,150 to stay in business, plus an annual subsistence fee of £4,500. Because the plant only made profits of £7,000 a year – it was owned as a sideline by two London marketing men who had bought it to save it from closure – this would make it virtually uneconomic to keep operating. In fact it emerged the new charges had already played a significant part in closing down the only three other craft lime works in the country.

Immediately the Head of Architectural Conservation at English Heritage appealed to officials of the DoE's 'Directorate of Air, Climate and Toxic Substances', for help in avoiding what, to historic buildings experts like himself, would be a disaster. But Mr Simmonds's problems now worsened. Not only was he reminded that failure to apply for authorisation from HMIP was a criminal offence, punishable by an unlimited fine and/or imprisonment. He was ordered by another HMIP inspector to measure the 'emissions to air' from the works. These amounted to two tonnes of lime dust a year. Even though most of this immediately settled in the surrounding quarry, he was therefore told he would have to spend £15,000 on scrubbing equipment, to prevent the two tonnes of lime dust reaching the air. This was particularly illogical since the firm also supplied Dorset farmers with no less than 18,000 tonnes of chalk dust a year to chuck over their fields. Yet this practice was completely unaffected by the regulations.

When Mr Simmonds protested the company simply could not afford to spend £15,000 to prevent what was only a 'trivial' amount of pollution, he was sternly informed by the inspector Mr Koshti that the emissions could not be 'deemed trivial'. They exceeded the amount permitted under the Environmental Protection (Prescribed Processes and Substances) Regulations 1991 by no less than 200 per cent. On a visit from a third HMIP inspector, Mr Simmonds was therefore told he would now have to instal yet more preventive measures, at a cost of £100,000.

At this point protests began to flow in from leading architects and conservationists all over the country. The threat posed to Shillingstone by HMIP's heavy-handed enforcement was publicised, and the response of the officials was to rush out an amendment to the regulations, transferring responsibility for 'small lime-slaking processes' from HMIP to local authorities. We also drew attention to the fact that the EC directive laid down, under Article 13, that enforcement should not entail 'excessive costs for the plant concerned'. This was quoted in the HMIP Chief Inspector's own Guidance to Inspectors on Lime Manufacture and Associated Processes, which should have been familiar to all the inspectors involved.

Only thanks to thousands of hours of work spent fighting this madness, it seemed the battle was at last over. Two years later Shillingstone lime works was still making its unique contribution to the restoration of Britain's historic buildings, having had no further interference from officialdom.

*

A rather less fortunate victim of the HMIP officials was Chris Pilkinton, who ran a firm making high-tech optical fibre for telecommunications equipment in east London. Launched in 1980 as part of GEC, the firm had been through two further ownerships and in 1992 temporarily closed. But it was then bought by a large Turkish manufacturing group, HES, and established a fast-growing export business, worth £5 million a year and employing 30 people.

In July 1994, however, Mr Pilkinton had a visit from an HMIP inspector, Mr Hudson, who pointed out that, under the Environmental Protection (Prescribed Processes and Substances) Regulations 1991 implementing EC directive 84/360, the firm should have been 'authorised' to operate by HMIP, because its process generated small quantities of 'prescribed substances'. The problem was not that the factory was actually giving off pollution. It already had all the required scrubbing equipment. The trouble was only that the firm did not have the necessary authorisation. And here the officials lighted on a technicality which was truly bizarre. Because at the precise date the new regulations came into effect the firm's process had been temporarily shut down, the HMIP officials decided it would have to go through all the complex procedures required to authorise a wholly new process, even though it had been operating for 14 years. This might take anything up to four months. Meanwhile Mr Pilkinton was ordered, on threat of criminal prosecution, to stop production.

This was disaster. Even when the authorisation came through, it would still take three months more to bring the process back into full production. He was thus faced with losing half a year's trading and probably some of his overseas customers. He immediately had to lay off half his workforce, and the company's Turkish owners informed him that, unless he was able to fulfil existing contracts, they would have to close down the factory altogether and transfer production to Turkey.

At this point, with £5 million-a-year's worth of exports and 30 jobs in jeopardy, Mr Pilkinton sent off a desperate appeal to Michael Heseltine, both as President of the Board of Trade and as the minister Mr Major had put in personal charge of eliminating unnecessary red tape. The politician who had said that he was prepared to intervene on behalf of British industry 'before breakfast, before lunch and before dinner', did not respond for several weeks, until Pilkinton eventually received a mis-spelt letter, signed by the Great Intervener but obviously written by the officials, saying there was nothing he could do. According to the minister in charge of 'deregulation', the HMIP officials had acted perfectly properly.

At the same time Mr Pilkinton also approached us for help. We advised him that, since the directive clearly stated that implementation should not impose 'excessive cost', HMIP might well be in breach of EC law. We suggested he should simply resume production, which he did. We later, however, heard that HES Fibres' Turkish owners had become so frustrated by 'excessive British bureaucracy' they had shut the factory and moved production abroad.

*

Very occasionally the over-zealous bureaucrats could be outsmarted and worn down by a determined opponent who knew the rules better than they did. One such was David Gardiner, a former High Sheriff living in an old rectory high on the Berkshire Downs. Living alone in a bungalow next door was his employee Mr McGee. Both properties drew their water from a borehole drilled into the chalk. As Mr Gardiner put it, the water was 'as God made it, hard as nails but water I can put in my whisky, not the chlorine-stinking fluid many people have to put up with from their taps. My well is very precious to me, and I look after it very carefully.'

In 1992 Mr Gardiner had a letter from Newbury District Council to say that under the Private Water Supplies Regulations 1991, implementing the EC's 'drinking water' directive, 80/778, he would now have to pay £752 to have his water tested. This struck Mr Gardiner as somewhat excessive, since he had already paid to have his water tested twice in 1992. The latest report from Odstock Hospital pathological laboratory had shown, as usual, that it was free of any harmful impurities. Charge for the test £6.

Mr Gardiner then discovered that he was only required to pay for his water to be tested because of Mr McGee living next door. If only one house was involved, no testing was needed. He therefore suggested to the council that, rather than pay £752 'simply for the privilege of supplying one man with water', it would be better if Mr McGee only used his water 'for washing and flushing the loo and I kept him supplied with bottled water for drinking'. The official, Mrs Stevenson, shot back that, if he did this, she would have to report that Mr McGee's house had no 'potable water' and was thus 'unfit for human habitation'.

Mr Gardiner now suggested there was nothing in the law to prevent him having the water tested himself. Mrs Stevenson agreed, so long as he met certain conditions. These covered a page of A4 paper, but one was that Mr Gardiner's tests should meet all the requirements set out in four weighty technical treatises, titles supplied. Mr Gardiner pointed out it might take him many 'hours of study and research to find out just what you are getting at'. Could Mrs Stevenson not just supply extracts of the relevant passages? Mrs Stevenson replied that, while she would not expect Mr Gardiner to acknowledge 'the vast amount of work' devoted by her department to protecting public health, they had not been given any additional resources to cover this work. Nevertheless he was free to come into the council offices to consult the books for himself.

So the battle continued for several months. By diligent study of the regulations, Mr Gardiner eventually beat down the council into revising its proposed regime. Instead of testing his water under '44 parameters' it would now only need to test for six, reducing the charge from £752 to only £141. But even this, Mr Gardiner pointed out under Para 4.7 of the DoE's guidelines, was more than the law allowed. After several more exchanges, including a tense public meeting and a threat from Mr Gardiner to raise Newbury's misinterpretation of the guidelines with the DoE, even the indefatigable Mrs Stevenson finally wearied. The Newbury officials abandoned their efforts to test Mr Gardiner's water, and he heard no more.

In other parts of the country, however, attempts by local authorities to enforce the Private Water Supplies Regulations continued to cause serious problems. At the top of the Kirkstone Pass in Cumbria, Pat Yates, owner of Britain's third highest inn, was faced with bills for nearly £1,000 a year to test the pure rainwater she collected from the mountainside. If her pub had stood only a few yards away in the next council district, the council would have tested her water for nothing. In the spa town of Llandrindod Wells, the council even prohibited the drinking of the town's famous water, precisely because it contained the very minerals such as iron and magnesium which had drawn health-conscious visitors to the resort for 150 years. Eventually, after local officials visited Brussels, along with those from other English spa towns, Commission officials graciously agreed to a 'derogation', allowing the spa waters a special exemption from the standards prescribed in directive 80/778.

5. The Officials versus the People

*

One victim who might have envied Mr Gardiner's success was John Margesson, who in the 1980s built up a successful trout-rearing business near Chepstow in Gwent. By 1993 this was turning over £200,000 a year, mainly supplying fish to other trout farms, and providing a livelihood for twelve people. But one February day he had a visit from MAFF officials. They told him they were checking for diseases under new Fish Health Regulations, implementing EC directive 91/67 'concerning the animal health conditions governing the placing on the market of aquaculture animals and products'.

They took away 30 trout from his fish ponds, to be tested at the ministry's fish diseases laboratory at Weymouth, and he was then informed that an unspecified number had tested positive for something called BKD, or bacterial kidney disease. Despite its alarming name, this is a relatively mild condition, widely found in Britain's rivers. Mr Margesson was therefore horrified to be told that he was immediately prohibited from selling any live fish from his farm, although since BKD is harmless to man, he could continue to sell them for eating. Since his business was mainly supplying other trout farms, he had to lay off his workforce, his income dried up and he faced the loss of his family home, on which he had a large mortgage.

Faced with such a disaster, Mr Margesson decided to consult the EC directive supposedly the cause of all the trouble. He was surprised to find that, although it listed two fish diseases so serious that they required governments to take action, BKD was listed as among less serious conditions on which governments could only take action if they first had approval from the European Commission. The UK regulations echoed this, giving ministry officials no power to test for BKD – even though this was the authority they had cited for testing his fish.

When we publicised this curious case as yet another where the officials appeared to be misusing EC law, eventually a full reply was issued under the name of food minister Nicholas Soames. This first denied that BKD was a 'mild' condition. Regardless that the directive suggested otherwise, it posed a 'real threat' to fish health. It was quite wrong to say that the ministry had gone beyond its statutory powers by not first obtaining permission from Brussels, as the directive laid down. Two years earlier the ministry had notified Brussels of its intention to take action against BKD. The fact that EC officials had not yet replied was taken to be approval. Furthermore, the letter pointed out, the officials had not acted under the EC directive at all. They had simply been using 'general powers' under the Diseases of Fish Act 1937.

Although this was not what the officials had claimed earlier, and the 1937 Act made no reference to BKD, at that time scarcely known, it seemed their only concern was to find what looked like legal authorisation for what they done. But for Mr Margesson it no longer mattered which powers they thought they were acting under. His business was ruined, he and his young family were living on income support and any day now the building society would be coming in to repossess their home.

Part I. Understanding a Monster

*

The plight of John Margesson was that of countless others who, in John Major's Britain of the mid-1990s, found themselves falling into that strange new shadowy underworld which was being created in all directions by the dark synergy of the Brussels/Whitehall/enforcement triangle. It had conjured into being a fantastic twilit realm, where no one could any longer be certain what the law was or quite where it originated from. For bewildered victims like Mr Margesson or Mr Pilkinton or the young directors of Acorn-Hobby-craft there was only one thing they did know: that the officials at the heart of this mysterious new System seemed determined to destroy them at any cost.

The case of one such victim we managed to turn into such a cause célèbre in this curious new war between the officials and the people that it deserves a chapter to itself.

6. Lanark Blue – The Officials versus the Cheesemaker

> I have felt at various points in these lengthy proceedings that it would be so much more satisfactory if the Applicants and the staff of their Environmental Health Department fulfilled their statutory functions in a less combative and confrontational manner ... such ... a dogmatic and unduly rigid 'policing' approach and philosophy ... seems out of place, out of date and unhelpful.
>
> Sheriff Douglas Allan giving judgement against Clydesdale District Council in the Lanark Blue case, 5 December 1995

Humphrey Errington is hardly the sort of man you might expect to find in the front line of a vicious battle with officialdom. His father Sir Lancelot Errington was Permanent Secretary in the Department of Health and Social Security, and he was brought up in the genteel setting of Weybridge and educated at Wellington public school.

Even less would one expect to find such a man making cheese from sheep's milk, on a windswept farm 1,000 feet up on the hills of Lanarkshire. But in the 1980s Errington's superb Lanark Blue cheese – hailed as 'the Scottish Roquefort' – established itself at the forefront of the renaissance in Britain's farmhouse cheesemaking. Praised by French cheese experts, it won numerous awards, was said to be enjoyed by the Queen, and was sold in every top cheese shop in London.

However, in December 1994 Mr Errington suddenly found himself plunged into a nightmare. Environmental health officials in Edinburgh had discovered that some of his Lanark Blue contained bacteria called *Listeria monocytogenes*. It could scarcely have sounded nastier. One of the most celebrated food scares of recent years was the great 'listeria hysteria' of 1989. This had begun on the continent with several outbreaks of a very unpleasant disease called listeriosis, leading to several dozen deaths, which had been traced back to listeria in Swiss soft cheese and Belgian pâté. And it was perhaps not surprising that the environmental health officials of Errington's own local council, Clydesdale, decided to ask the local magistrates court to order that all his remaining 1994 Lanark Blue, with a retail value of £54,000, should be destroyed. With it would go his business on which more than a dozen people relied for their livelihood.

Just before the case was due to be heard Mr Errington despairingly appealed to us for help. As we began to assess his situation, the first point which needed to be made was that, despite its lurid reputation, listeria is a much more complex organism than most people are aware. There are scores, possibly thousands of different strains of *Listeria monocytogenes*, the vast majority quite harmless to human health. They are often found in the rich bacterial flora which is essential to the ripening of blue and soft cheeses. As a leading cheese wholesaler told us, 'in our routine tests for listeria, counts of 10-20,000 are common. We only get worried when the counts are much higher'. In fact only a tiny handful of strains have been associated with the rare and potentially fatal disease known as listeriosis; and even these are only likely to prove harmful, or pathogenic, to certain 'high risk groups', such as pregnant mothers, the very old, babies and those who are immuno-compromised, such as HIV sufferers. This was why, since the listeria scare of 1989, a wide range of foods had carried a warning from the Chief Medical Officer advising those at risk not to eat them.

The only thing which really mattered in the case of Errington's Lanark Blue was whether its listeria belonged to one of that handful of strains which had been shown to be pathogenic. As we soon discovered, the strains the EHOs claimed to have found had never been associated with human illness of any kind. Indeed, during the four months it had already been on sale, the equivalent of 63,000 portions of the cheese the Clydesdale officials wanted to destroy had already been sold to the public without any sign of ill-health.

This was not, however, how the officials saw it, as became obvious when the court hearing took place in Lanark before a local justice, Mrs Wilson. The council's young Principal Environmental Health Officer, Robert Steenson, made it clear that, in their eyes, all forms of listeria were equally dangerous. And what Steenson then revealed was that the EHOs had taken their cue from some forthcoming regulations, implementing EC directive 92/46, on 'the hygiene of dairy products'. This ruled, astonishingly, that it would be illegal to sell cheese containing even the tiniest amount of listeria, irrespective of its strain.

This was a bombshell. Its implications ran far beyond the immediate case. If these regulations were enforced, it would sooner or later bring an end to the selling of Stilton, Brie or any soft or blue cheeses. When we publicised this in the *Sunday Telegraph* and the *Daily Mail*, it provoked uproar. As a spokesman for the National Dairy Council trenchantly put it, 'Silly, silly Brussels. If we didn't have any Listeria in blue cheese we wouldn't have any blue cheese. It effectively rules out cheese production in this country.'

It was impossible to believe that the French and Italian cheesemakers would allow such ludicrous Euro-nonsense to halt the production of Camembert and Dolcelatte. Sure enough, a few days after our first article appeared, we received a remarkable fax from the Ministry of Agriculture, Fisheries and Food. The officials had discovered a 'derogation' in the directive, under which 'cheese made in a traditional manner' could be given an exemption from the 'listeria standard'. The continentals had of course applied for this exemption. But until that moment MAFF had remained oblivious to the derogation. Only now, in the nick of time, were they taking steps to ensure that British cheesemakers could take advantage of it.

*

Back in the courtroom, this still left Clydesdale's EHOs locked in their determination to destroy Mr Errington's cheese. They openly boasted that it was an open-and-shut case which would take only an hour or two to settle. But when Errington's defence team argued that the council had not completed carrying out its tests properly and that anyway the type of listeria found was harmless, the justice Mrs Wilson invited the two sides to hold further discussions, in the hope that the matter could be resolved outside the courtroom.

When the council completed its tests, however, these showed every batch of the Lanark Blue to be contaminated with levels of listeria so high as to be barely credible. A second court hearing was inevitable, and here a new player entered the drama. Clydesdale had called for help to Dr Jim McLauchlin of the Public Health Laboratory Service, supposedly the top official listeria expert in the country. He was considered so grand a figure in the Scottish courtroom that, by arrangement with Clydesdale's lawyers, the justice ruled that, when McLauchlin had given his evidence, Errington's defence team, now led by a top Edinburgh advocate Michael Jones, would not be allowed to cross-examine him. Questions could only be put to the great man through Mrs Wilson. She would then deliver her judgement in writing, promising to give reasons for her decision.

A week later Mr Errington first learned that Mrs Wilson had issued her verdict when he was rung by the local paper. She had simply ruled that the cheese should be destroyed, without any explanation. Fortunately for Mr Errington, her conduct of the case had been so unusual that his lawyers asked Scotland's highest civil court for judicial review. In April at the Edinburgh Court of Sessions Lord Justice Weir handed down a damning judgement. The refusal to allow Dr McLauchlin to be cross-examined had been 'in breach of natural justice'. He recommended that the case should be heard again by a sheriff. Clydesdale immediately appealed, but in June Weir's judgement was upheld in even more trenchant terms by the Lord President, who ruled the case must be heard again properly by a sheriff, not by an 'inexperienced lay justice'.

*

By this time, as the two sides prepared to resume battle later in the summer, the Lanark Blue case was attracting increasingly widespread attention. Our allies, led by Lord Pearson of Rannoch, had already made it something of a cause célèbre in the House of Lords. Media coverage was growing. A well-known Scottish gourmet, Arthur Bell, appeared on Scottish television eating what looked like a hunk of Lanark Blue. He immediately received an angry letter from the Clydesdale officials threatening criminal prosecution unless he revealed where he had obtained the cheese (in fact he had not been eating Lanark Blue, but Mr Errington's other blue cheese, Dunsyre Blue).

By August, nine months after the story began, the two sides had assembled their expert teams. The star witness for Clydesdale was still Dr McLauchlin, retained at a fee of £500 a day, plus lodging in a first-class hotel. But Errington's advocate could now call on a whole array of expert witnesses. These ranged from one of Britain's leading authorities on food safety policy, Professor Verner Wheelock, to M. Jean-Jacques Devoyod, a splendid moustachioed figure from France, agreed to be the greatest living expert on the microbiology of Roquefort. The defence was to be argued under two main heads: that the strain of listeria found in Lanark Blue presented no risk to public health, and that the levels of listeria the council claimed to have found were, scientifically, impossible to achieve anyway.

With only two days to go before the trial, Clydesdale threw another, potentially devastating punch. They handed over the evidence they intended to call, including more than 1,500 pages of technical scientific papers trawled from all over the world. Errington's defence team had just 48 hours to absorb this mountain of documents, even though it was clear that most had been available to the prosecution months before. When these were combed, however, it also seemed that even the prosecution could not have read them through in much detail. Study after study appeared to confirm the defence case, that most forms of listeria were not pathogenic and that the strains found had never been associated with human illness.

The hearings began unfolding through three weeks of September, before Sheriff Douglas Allan. For Clydesdale Dr McLauchlin had not moved an inch from his earlier argument, echoing the EC directive, that all forms of Listeria monocytogenes are potentially dangerous. In a brilliant cross-examination, Mr Jones showed how Dr McLauchlin contradicted himself and could produce no credible evidence for his case. Errington's witnesses, including Dr North, pressed home that Clydesdale had completely avoided the central issue. Did the particular form of listeria found in the Lanark Blue pose a genuine health risk? In the end, with many days of adjournment, it took until November to complete the hearings. Clydesdale made a prolonged effort to blacken Dr North's character, having trawled through MAFF and other official files for any personal evidence which might discredit him (just before North began his evidence they submitted another 31 documents in evidence). As their last star witness, Errington's team produced Professor Hugh Pennington of Aberdeen, a microbiologist of world standing. At another point the officials went back to the Sheriff for leave to test Errington's 1995 Lanark Blue as well, which would have cost him a further £3,000 in lost cheeses, which the sheriff brusquely dismissed as 'harassment'.

In fact the costs of the case, rising to thousands of pounds a day, had already become of serious concern to Errington. Because of the technicality that this was an 'administrative hearing', the sheriff had made clear that, even if Errington won, he could not claim his own costs, though these already amounted to more than £120,000, enough to bankrupt his business. So critical was the situation that a national competition was launched to raise money, under the patronage of Lord Tonypandy, formerly George Thomas, Speaker of the House of Commons, now an outspoken Euro-sceptic, and the well-known cookery writer Sophie Grigson. This was supported by other leading food experts and by an array of cheese shops, hotels, restaurants and food firms.

For the Clydesdale officials, of course, money was of no concern. Even if they lost the case, they were secure in the knowledge that the taxpayers would foot their own bill, by now estimated at over £250,000.

*

Finally, in December 1995, after what had been by far the longest food contamination case in British legal history, Sheriff Allen pronounced a devastating verdict. Showing remarkable grasp of the technicalities, he agreed that the council's scientific tests were not credible. He found there was no evidence that the strain of *Listeria monocytogenes* in the Lanark Blue posed any risk to human health. Therefore there was no case for Mr Errington's cheese to be condemned. Furthermore the sheriff described Dr McLauchlin as an 'evasive' and 'less than helpful' witness, who had failed to show the objectivity expected of a scientific expert. He spoke witheringly of the attempt to discredit Dr North, and directed criticism at the Clydesdale officials for the entire way they had conducted the case.

Of course the sting in the tail for Mr Errington was that he could not claim costs. Thanks to the officials' relentless war against him, he was now faced with a bill so enormous that even the appeal could not hope to raise more than a fraction. But even here, the terms in which the sheriff had condemned Clydesdale's tactics opened an unexpected door. Errington's QC Michael Jones realised that, under an obscure piece of law, if he could show the council as having been 'pugnacious litigants' it might be possible to claim costs after all. Sheriff Allan accepted this argument and awarded Mr Errington recompense for every penny. Although the laborious process of trying to get the money out of the council was to continue for many months, it had been a historic victory. In the end, the only real losers were the taxpayers, left to foot a bill amounting to more than £370,000.

The play safe culture

Inevitably, however, there was a further twist in the tail. Even though the case had not been brought directly under EC legislation, Brussels cast its long shadow over the whole affair. If it had not been for that directive on dairy hygiene, imposing a complete ban on cheese containing *Listeria monocytogenes* of any kind, the Clydesdale officials might not have been quite so confident in maintaining that all forms of this organism posed an equal threat to human health.

If there was one lesson everyone might have learned from the scientific expertise brought to bear on the case, it was that all forms of Listeria monocytogenes are not equally pathogenic. Most are harmless, and it was vital to the rational protection of public health that in future legislation this distinction should be made clear. Like so much else produced by that peculiar form of bureaucratised science which holds sway in Brussels, the EC directive was based on such crude over-simplification as to amount to dangerous nonsense. In the name of bogus science, the insane possibility had been created that many of Europe's finest cheeses might one day be declared illegal.

Yet only six months after the officials' resounding defeat a letter went out from MAFF minister Tony Baldry. This coolly stated 'the Government's view remains that all strains (of listeria) are potentially harmful to human health'. The officials were carrying on as if they learned nothing from the case at all. Echoing the Brussels line, and the argument which had been put for Clydesdale in the courtroom, their view was that, wherever it could be imagined there was the slightest possibility of risk, however improbable, the vital thing was to follow what is known in official circles as the 'precautionary principle'. It is always best to 'play safe', whatever the cost.

In recent years no principle has come to exercise a more subtly damaging influence on regulatory legislation, not least that emerging from Brussels. Wherever the shibboleths of hygiene, safety or environmental protection are invoked, we see the 'play safe culture' persuasively, insidiously, at work. The real significance of the Lanark Blue case was the way it showed how far officialdom was prepared to go in elevating the doctrine of 'play safe' above all else – even if it was based on abysmal scientific ignorance, and even if this might have meant putting an end to a successful business and a much-acclaimed make of cheese for no reason at all.

Part II

The Double Disaster

The more closely one looks at how this new System of government centred on Europe operates in practice, the more one sees how consistently it is governed by two principles.

The first is that the methods the System uses to achieve its declared intentions are such that, in themselves, they cannot work. They try to impose on the world an abstract bureaucratic framework which does not correspond to reality, which is why they so often end up producing results precisely the opposite of those intended. The whole System is thus fatally flawed.

The second is that Britain has made a unique mess of operating this System. Partly this is because her traditions are in so many respects different from those of continental countries, and invariably it is Britain which, in the name of 'harmonisation', must be squeezed into the continental mould, rather than the other way round. But also, as we have seen, it is because of the peculiarly damaging way in which Britain's own officials have chosen to operate the System.

In this second part of the book we illustrate these principles by looking at a series of particular examples. We begin with perhaps the most glaring example of all of this double-disaster, the Common Fisheries Policy. We then look at the curious story of how, by agreement with Brussels, Britain metricated her system of weights and measures, an obvious instance of how Britain was forced into a continental mould, with the active collaboration of her own officials. We go on to the bizarre fiascos of the Common Agricultural Policy and the Single Market. We end with a more general look at how Britain suffers doubly from this process, as ever-increasing areas of her national life become subject to a bureaucratic framework which is both alien and unworkable; and with a chapter on one of the finest achievements of the System, the form of taxation known as VAT.

7. Worse than a Blunder, a Crime – The Great Fish Disaster

In the North Sea discards of haddock may exceed what is retained from a single trawl; the global estimate for 1985 was 460 million discarded individuals, whereas landings amounted to 500 million. In the Bay of Biscay/Celtic Sea discards of hake were estimated at 130 million individuals, for a landing figuure of 110 million.

European Commission, *Mid-Term Review of Common Fisheries Policy*, 1991

In June 1993 the front page of *Fishing News*, Britain's leading fishing paper, carried a horrifying picture. Taken by Scottish skipper Jim Vanko from the deck of his trawler *Auriga III*, it showed a large trawl brimming with tens of thousands of silvery fish. The sea seemed to be boiling with these saithe, or coley as they are known in England. But the fish were not being taken back to the *Auriga*'s home port of Eyemouth, to provide a living for the crew and their families. The fishermen were having to throw all those fish back into the sea, dead. In just one day's trawling, the *Auriga* had caught 2,000 boxes, worth £100,000. Yet to bring them to shore would have been a criminal offence, for which Vanko and his men could have faced confiscation of their catch and fines of up to £50,000.

The only unusual thing about this picture was that it recorded a scene very rarely photographed. But to the fishermen it was only too familiar. Every year, as even the European Commission admits, billions of individual fish of every conceivable species must be 'discarded' or thrown overboard dead in the seas around the western coasts of Europe. And, astonishingly, this is made inevitable by nothing less than the bizarre system that the officials of the European Community have devised to 'conserve Europe's fish stocks'. Those billions of fish are being destroyed each year in the name of 'conservation'.

A year after Jim Vanko's picture was taken, in August 1994, the fishermen of Aldeburgh in Suffolk were staring in shock at a piece of paper they had been sent by officials of the Ministry of Agriculture, Fisheries and Food. The little wooden fishing boats which for centuries have been pulled up on the shingle at Aldeburgh are as symbolic of the town as the music of Benjamin Britten. But the Aldeburgh fishermen were being told that, on orders from Brussels, until the end of that year they would not be permitted to catch a single sole, the fish on which they relied for their living. For several months they would have no income at all. Yet out to sea the fishermen could see two large modern Norwegian trawlers, by permission of Brussels and British ministers, catching more sole in a day than their little boats could catch in a season.

Later that season, as we described in our first chapter, MAFF officials swooped on the little Essex port of West Mersea down the coast and caught a dozen small sole fishermen breaking those rules. They were charged with criminal offences and subjected to large fines by the local magistrates. And what enraged the fishermen most of all was that, under international law, those same areas of the North Sea from which they were being excluded, still full of large Norwegian and Dutch trawlers catching sole, were British waters. This was the sea they and their ancestors had freely fished for centuries, until the coming of the European Union's Common Fisheries Policy.

If one wanted just one example to illustrate both the crazy unworkability of the Brussels system and the way the British come out of it worse than anyone, the Common Fisheries Policy would have to be top of the list. And not the least significant feature of the CFP is that it is the EU's only example so far of a fully operational federal policy, the first real foretaste of what a federal Europe would look like in practice.

How Heath was tricked

The story of the CFP begins with what can only be described as a stitch-up. Back in June 1970, when four new countries were about to apply for membership of the Common Market – Britain, Ireland, Denmark and Norway – there was already much talk about a forthcoming international extension of national fisheries limits from the existing twelve miles out to 200 miles. South American countries had been trying to operate such a system, to protect fish stocks off their coasts, since the early 1950s. The original six Common Market members realised that, when this happened, the four new members would control the richest fishing grounds in the world. Just as Britain and Norway owned the rights to the oil just then being discovered in the North Sea, out to 200 miles or the median line between their coasts, so Britain's waters in particular would contain up to four-fifths of all the fish off western Europe, according to one estimate up to 85 per cent.

The Six therefore devised a trap. Although they had absolutely no authorisation to do this under the Treaty of Rome (see the end of this chapter), they drew up a Council Regulation, 2141/70, giving all Member States the right of 'equal access' to each other's fishing waters. The vital thing was to get this established as Community law before the applications for membership arrived, because the newcomers would then have to accept it as what is known as '*acquis communautaire*', the established body of Community law. As the late Mike Holden, a senior Commission fisheries official, described in his book, *The Common Fisheries Policy*, the regulation was cobbled together with such unseemly haste that it was only adopted on the morning of 30 June 1970, just hours before the applications for membership arrived. But the trap had been set.

At first the prospective new members, particularly Britain and Norway, simply refused to accept the new rule. Ministers of Edward Heath's Government promised the House of Commons that in no way would they agree to give away Britain's waters. The rule would have to be changed before Britain would sign the Treaty of Accession. But as the negotiations proceeded, the fisheries issue seemed curiously difficult to resolve. In June 1971, when the Heath Government sent out a shortened version of its White Paper on Europe to every household in the country, it claimed the negotiations had been successful, and that fishing was now the only issue left to be settled. But it also reassuringly stated that 'the Community has recognised the need to change its fisheries policy ... in regard to access to fishing grounds'. This was wholly untrue.

In October that year Britain's chief negotiator, Geoffrey Rippon, was still telling the Tory Party conference 'one thing is certain ... we should not sign a Treaty of Accession which would commit us to the present fisheries policy'. On 23 October he was still assuring the House of Commons that 'there is a clear understanding that either we must have an agreement on a new regulation ... or the Community will have to accept that we must maintain the status quo'.

But in November 1971 it became clear to Heath and his colleagues that the Six were not going to budge. This, after all, has been the whole point of setting the trap in the first place, and time was now running out. If negotiations were not wrapped up by the end of the year, the whole elaborate timetable for Britain to join the Common Market on 1 January 1973, on which Heath had set his heart, would fall apart. On Heath's insistence, therefore, Rippon capitulated. All Britain's fishing rights would be surrendered, right up to the shoreline. The only face-saver would be a temporary derogation in the Treaty, allowing the UK and other countries to retain control over their waters out to twelve miles 'until 31 December 1982'.

Rippon had done precisely what he had promised both MPs and his party conference he would not do. Yet on 13 December he told the House of Commons 'we retain full jurisdiction over the whole of our coastal waters', adding, 'I must emphasise that these are not just transitional arrangements which automatically lapse at the end of a fixed period.' Rippon was challenged on this by Denis Healey and failed to withdraw it. As he well knew, sight of the Treaty would show that it wasn't true. He had misled the House of Commons. However, the wording of the relevant passage in the treaty was kept secret until after MPs debated and voted on Britain's accession in January the following year, and Heath had signed the treaty on 22 January 1972. The British Government had already embarked on a deliberate policy to disguise just what had been given away, in which successive governments have persisted until today.

The other country which had been just as adamant as the British that it would not surrender to the Six's demands was Norway. In November 1971, when he had taken his fateful decision, Heath wrote a remarkable secret letter to the Norwegian prime minister (which was leaked to an Oslo newspaper), begging him to follow Britain's lead. The longer they spun out the negotiations, he argued, the harder it would be to retain public support for their common goal. He therefore urged Norway to surrender permanent control of her waters, the principle on which the Six refused to budge, in return for a private assurance that the transitional arrangement would be renewed in ten years' time.

In the end the Norwegian Government gave way. But this so enraged the country's fishing minister that he resigned in protest, provoking a political uproar. In Norway's referendum on joining the EEC later in the year, this 'betrayal' was a key reason why the Norwegians voted to stay out. They knew that fishing was a vital national interest. But in London, as we learned from someone close to the negotiations, Heath's calculation in 1971 was that there were 'only 22,000 British fishermen' and they were not 'politically significant'. Not for more than twenty years would it become clear just what a miscalculation that was.

*

One reason why the 'selling out' of the fishermen did not have more impact in 1972 was that half Britain's fishing fleet at that time still earned its living in 'distant waters'. The big deep-sea trawlers from Grimsby, Hull and Fleetwood still had unrestricted access to rich fishing grounds off Greenland and particularly around Iceland. Their representatives therefore did not oppose Heath's deal, which was translated by ministers at the time into a claim that the deal had 'the support of the industry'. But only a year or two later the Icelandic 'cod wars' began, and in 1976 a United Nations conference confirmed that it was now international law that countries could extend their fisheries limits out to 200 miles, or, where the coastlines of two nations were closer together, to the median line between them.

This had a devastating effect on Britain's deep-water fleet. The British trawlers were excluded from their traditional fishing grounds. Grimsby, Hull and Fleetwood filled with rusting hulks and unemployed ex-fishermen, and the industry's attention now focussed on the rich waters round Britain itself.

In 1976, in accordance with the new international law, parliament passed the Fisheries Limits Act, extending Britain's limit to 200 miles, which by happy geographical accident contained up to four-fifths of all western Europe's fish. This provided a dramatic opportunity for the British fishing industry to re-build, and there were immediate calls from the fishermen for Britain to establish an exclusive fishing zone out at least to 100 miles. One Labour minister promised that his Government would negotiate for this, and the Conservative opposition agreed. As front-bench spokesman Francis Pym put it, there was 'a strong argument' for 100 miles. After all, the wording of the Fisheries Limits Act 1976 was quite clear: 'no foreign fishing vessel' would be permitted to fish in British waters out to 200 miles, except by express permission of a British minister. Nowhere in the Act was there any mention of the EEC or the Treaty. But for all their brave promises to the British fishermen, when ministers talked to their officials in MAFF and the Foreign Office they had a rude awakening. Parliament might have passed an Act extending Britain's limits to 200 miles, with the full blessing of international law. But under the relevant articles of the Treaty Britain was now bound to accept Article 2 of Council Regulation 2141/70, now reissued, to underline the point, as 101/76. This made it crystal clear that all Member States had the right of 'equal access' to all fishing waters under Britain's jurisdiction. That temporary 'derogation' out to twelve miles was just a sideshow. The EC had landed the prize it had really been after.

7. Worse than a Blunder, a Crime – The Great Fish Disaster

Brussels creates a conservation disaster

It had always been planned that by 1982, when the transitional phase came to an end, the EC would be ready to put into place the fully-fledged version of its Common Fisheries Policy. When the plans drawn up by the officials of DG XIV in Brussels, given responsibility for fisheries, were approved at the first Maastricht summit, it became clear how the CFP was to be run.

The basic principle was that fishing vessels of each country would have access to 'Community waters' and be permitted to catch tonnages of fish of different species according to a complex 'quota' system. The Brussels officials would allocate quotas to each country, representing a maximum tonnage for each species, which they would not be permitted to exceed. This was to ensure that 'European' fish stocks were 'conserved' and not over-exploited.

But in this system lay the seeds of an astonishing disaster. What it demonstrated was just how little those officials, many of whom might not have seen a fishing boat in their lives, knew about fish. On paper the system, worked out with the aid of scientific reports on the current state of fish stocks, might have looked fine; as fine as those five-year plans drawn up by officials in the old Soviet Union showing just how many tractors were going to be produced in the state factories, and how many millions of tons of grain were going to be harvested on the collective farms. Every time an EC fisherman went out, he would know just how many fish of which species he was legally permitted to catch and bring to land. What could be more rational?

In reality, of course, fishing simply does not work like that. If a fisherman puts down his net for, say, whiting, which the officials have allowed him to catch, it may well come up full of fish of other species which swim in the same parts of the sea, such as haddock. But if the officials have told him he is not permitted to catch haddock, and that it would be a criminal offence for him to bring any haddock ashore, there is, legally, only one thing he can do. He must chuck back all those haddock, now dead because the change in pressure has burst their swim bladders. There they settle to the ocean floor, polluting it for hundreds of yards or even for miles around.

Again in the name of 'conservation', those Brussels officials draw up similarly rigid rules laying down the minimum sizes of each species which can legally be caught. This predictably produces exactly the same result as the quota system. If a fisherman pulls in his net full of thousands of cod, he may well find that half his catch consists of young fish, below the minimum size. Again he has no legal alternative but to chuck them back dead into the sea. And because there are more small fish to the same weight of large ones, he may end up destroying many more individual fish than he keeps.

The scale of the conservation disaster directly created by the system Brussels has set up to 'conserve Europe's fish stocks' is unimaginable. Every fisherman has his own horror stories, like the skipper who told us in 1994 how he had just came back from part of the North Sea called 'the plaice box'. Inside the 'box', a breeding ground for plaice, fishing for conservation reasons is strictly limited. Around the outside, however, as the plaice and other species swam out, 60 trawlers of different EC nations were catching anything that moved. But because those boats were only interested in mature, top-value plaice, as their decks became submerged in fish that were not wanted, they were chucking back 25 out of every 30 boxes they caught. Our observer calculated that, every day of the three weeks he was there, some 670 tonnes of juveniles or mature fish of other species such as turbot and sole were being thrown back. Nearly three million individual fish a day.

A Scottish crewman on a large modern Dutch trawler told us how, on just one five-week trip off Ireland, they caught 30 million horse mackerel. But for every fish they took on board, another – mainly herring or mackerel – had to be discarded. Thirty million fish thrown away to pollute the seabed, by just one vessel on one trip. A Newlyn fishermen told us how, in the 1970s, after one fierce assault by a mass of trawlers on mackerel shoals around the Cornish coast, a wall of discarded 'over-quota' fish covered the floor of St Michael's Bay to a depth of six feet over an area of thousands of square yards.

Even the European Commission itself, in its Mid-Term Review of the CFP in 1991, frankly admitted that 'discards' by fishermen account for 'hundreds of thousands of tons and billions of individuals' each year, and that these can be greater than the quantities of fish actually landed. Yet astonishingly the Commission continues to justify the CFP on the grounds that it is the only way to 'conserve' stocks. Repeatedly the Brussels officials, dutifully echoed by British ministers, intone their favourite mantra that the only problem is that of 'too many fishermen catching too few fish' – when in fact the very system they themselves have devised for 'conserving' those fish is inevitably creating one of the greatest man-made conservation disasters in the world.

Enter Spain – cuckoo in the nest

The CFP, as set up in 1983, thus represents the clearest of all examples of how the Brussels system of bureaucracy so often produces results precisely the opposite of those it is intended to achieve. But we must now return to the particular situation in which that new system placed Britain.

Under the 1983 share-out between the member states, the country which had contributed up to 85 per cent of all the fish to the common pool was allocated back the right to catch 37 per cent. One reason why Britain's share was so low was that this percentage was loosely based on each country's catches in the new 'Community waters' during the 1970s. But because, during much of the relevant period, a large part of Britain's fishing effort had still been directed at distant waters, her share of her own fish was much lower than would have been justified by her current needs. However, when the British fishermen came to look at the small print of the deal, they had an even nastier shock. In terms of money value, the fishermen saw that Britain's share was strongly loaded towards the lower-value fish, with a much smaller percentage of high-value species. Thus in cash terms Britain's allocation, the fishermen claimed, was not 37 per cent but only 12 per cent.

Britain's fishermen might have been able to live with even this, had it not been for the final disaster which began to loom over the horizon in the mid-1980s, with the applications to join the EC by Spain and Portugal. Spain in particular had by far the largest fishing fleet in Europe. Her 20,000 vessels equated in tonnage and power to three-quarters of the rest of the EC fleet put together. Estimates varied, but at the very least Spain's fleet was more than three times the size of Britain's. Yet when Spain joined the EC in 1986, she brought in with her very little 'marine resource'. The waters round the Iberian peninsula had, for geographical reasons, never been as rich as those of the continental shelf to the north, and much of what fish there were had been fished out by a Spanish fleet which was notoriously predatory, and paid little heed to any conservation rules.

In other words, the entry of the vast Spanish fleet presented the EC with an acute problem. Under the principle of 'equal access', the Spanish boats would have to be allowed into the rest of the 'Community waters'. But since she brought very few additional fish with her, the total pool remained much the same. It would now have to be shared out under new arrangements, which meant other countries like Britain would have to receive very much less.

So serious was this problem, unforeseen by the original Six when they set their trap to snare Britain's, Ireland's and Norway's fish into that common pool in 1970, that the immediate answer Brussels came up with was to postpone it. In return for other favours, it was made a condition of Spanish entry that she would not be granted full access to EC waters until 2002, when the CFP was destined for a full revision anyway. This would give Brussels 15 years to prepare the ground for Spanish entry in other ways, not least by devising alternative strategies for reducing the sizes of some of those other fleets before the Spanish cuckoo arrived fully in the nest.

In fact a first stratagem for achieving this was devised by the Spanish themselves, with the added benefit that it gave them access to EC waters long before this was formally allowed by their Treaty. This was to put Spanish vessels onto the registers of other EC countries. The advantage of this was that it allowed them to spend large sums of money, an unknown proportion from public funds, on buying up licences in those countries, with fishing quotas attached. The Spanish particularly targeted Britain in this way, sailing their vessels under the Red Ensign (hence the term 'flag boats'). This enabled them to buy an ever-larger share of the quotas allocated by Brussels to Britain (hence the alternative term, 'quota hoppers'), although they were sailing from Spanish ports and landing their catches back in Spain.

By 1988, only two years after Spanish accession, the problem of the 'quota hoppers' had already become so serious that the British Government passed the Merchant Shipping Act in an attempt to make the practice illegal. In future, to qualify for a share in UK quotas, vessels would have to be owned and crewed in Britain. But immediately one of the Spanish companies affected, Factortame, brought a legal case to show that, under Article 7 of the Treaty of Rome, this was illegal, because it constituted discrimination on grounds of nationality. And in 1991, by a historic judgement of the European Court of Justice, it was ruled that, where there was a conflict, European law was superior to any mere Act of the British Parliament. The Merchant Shipping Act had to be set aside. Quota hopping was established as something Britain was powerless to stop. And the Spanish companies which had been forced to stop fishing during the 18 months the Act was in force, sued the British Government for a minimum of £80 million, to compensate them for income of which they had illegally been deprived.

The next move in the grand plan came from Brussels. In 1992 the officials of DG XIV pushed the Council into a scheme whereby, in the name of 'conserving fish stocks', all national fleets should reduce their 'fishing effort', in effect a euphemism for cutting back the number of their vessels. But the true hidden agenda of this 'Multi-Annual Guidance Programme' (MAGP) could be seen from the cut-backs imposed on each country. Britain's MAGP target was 19 per cent, equivalent to nearly a fifth of her entire fleet. But the huge Spanish fleet was required to cut back effort by only 4 per cent. In other words, the shibboleth of 'conservation' was again being invoked, this time to disguise the real purpose of the scheme, which was drastically to reduce other fleets, particularly Britain's, to make room for the Spaniards when they won full access to 'Community waters' in 2002. For Britain it was an unmitigated disaster. But by a technique which was to become only too familiar, the British Minister of Agriculture, Fisheries and Food, John Gummer, came out from the Council meeting where the plan had been approved to announce that it represented 'a good deal for Britain's fishermen'. Once again to admit the reality of what had happened would be so unpalatable to the British people that it was better to say the exact opposite and hope to keep the truth under wraps.

In fact the British Government had already tried to prepare the ground for the huge cuts it now had to implement by introducing an extraordinary piece of legislation, the Sea Fish (Conservation) Bill. This proposed to give MAFF officials unprecedented new powers simply to order fishermen not to go to sea. The idea was that, by cutting down the number of days in the year when fishermen were permitted to fish, the officials might be able to meet the Brussels targets for reducing 'fishing effort', without having to pay large sums in compensation to the fishermen for the politically embarrassing sight of thousands of boats having to be destroyed. Again the name of 'conservation' was being invoked to hide the real political agenda, which was why we nicknamed this the Sea Fish (How to Destroy Britain's Fishing Industry Without Having to Pay Compensation) Bill. Conservative MPs meekly passed this cynical measure through parliament, but its legality was then challenged in the courts, and the Government eventually dropped the scheme. However, this left the officials with only one way to meet the Brussels targets, to pay compensation to fishermen to 'decommission' their boats. The Government refused to allocate more than £25 million for this, which would be nothing like enough to meet the target. But this was why, from 1994 on, smoke rose from beaches all round Britain and Northern Ireland, as fishing boats were burned to meet the strict rules under which compensation could only be paid when boats were physically destroyed.

*

From now on, the weird disaster overtaking Britain's fishing industry became harder and harder to conceal. In 1994 Spain dramatically upped the ante. She gave an ultimatum that, unless her vessels were given access to what were now called 'European Union' waters in 1996, seven years earlier than she had agreed under her Treaty of Accession, she would veto the accession of Austria, Finland, Sweden and Norway. This blackmail succeeded, although ironically what really turned the key was the possibility of the rich Norwegian waters being added to the 'EU' pool, which would have taken off some of the pressure – and at the last minute, of course, the Norwegians voted by a narrow majority to stay out, not least because, for a second time, they could not agree to handing over their fish.

After difficult negotiations in Brussels, the British and Irish had to agree to allow Spanish boats access to the 'Irish Box', and much greater access to other 'Western waters' where the Spanish already had limited historical fishing rights. Despite attempts by British ministers to play down the impact of allowing 40 Spanish boats into the Irish Box, Britain's fishermen pointed out that these would be large modern trawlers, with a catching capacity larger than that of the entire Irish and Cornish fleets combined, and that on their track record elsewhere, the Spanish would pay little regard to conservation rules. Indeed, such a row did this latest massive concession to Spain provoke that Britain's fisheries minister William Waldegrave had to buy off rebellious Tory backbenchers by more than doubling the money available to compensate British fishermen for 'decommissioning' their boats, to £53 million. But what a measure this was of the impotence to which Britain had been reduced, that the only way to buy off political trouble was now to pay even more British fishermen to give up fishing altogether.

Through 1995 the fishing issue became an increasing embarrassment to the British Government. In March it again hit the front pages with the 'Canadian-Spanish fish war', when the Canadian Government arrested a Spanish vessel just outside Canadian waters for blatantly flouting conservation rules. After Spanish trawlers had devastated fish stocks in the area, an international agreement had been drawn up, involving the EU on behalf of Spain, and under which the Canadians themselves agreed to lay off 50,000 people in their own fishing industry. But when the Spaniards continued to flout the rules, and one of her boats, the *Estai*, was caught concealing her illegal catch in a secret hold, and with a fraudulent log book, the row turned into an international crisis. EU Commissioners such as Sir Leon Brittan and Fisheries Commissioner Emma Bonino rushed to side with the Spanish, describing the Canadians as 'liars' and 'pirates'. At first Britain supported this EU line against her Commonwealth partner, but this provoked such anger that the Government quickly backed off. From Newlyn, England's largest fishing port, a symbolic rash of Canadian maple leaf flags spread round Britain's coastline, and the episode did more than anything so far to arouse British anger and alarm at the curious disaster which was unfolding.

At last, in fact, Britain's fishermen themselves were organising in a last-ditch effort to save their industry from final disaster. The Save Britain's Fish campaign, masterminded by a Yorkshire engineer, John Ashworth, who had worked all his life in the fishing industry, with a senior Scottish ex-trawler skipper, Tom Hay, was now winning support from thousands of fishermen all over the country, for their blunt demand that Britain should withdraw from the CFP altogether. The core of their argument was that this was the only way to achieve a double aim: first, to save Britain's own industry from the Brussels master-plan, which seemed bent on destroying it; secondly, to save Europe's fish stocks threatened with destruction by an insane quota system, and by the fact that other countries, not just Spain, were making a complete mockery of the rules. Indeed the country which took by far the largest tonnage of fish from 'EU waters' was Denmark which, by yet another astonishing anomaly of the Brussels system, was quite legally entitled to land

1,600,000 tons a year, nearly three times the legal British catch, mainly by what was called 'industrial fishing', targeting small sand-eels and sprats to be processed into fishmeal and fertiliser. This meant the Danish trawlers were removing from the marine food chain vast quantities of tiny fish, including hundreds of thousand of tons of juvenile herring, mackerel, cod and other valuable species, which represented a significant proportion of the fish stocks of the future.

The only rational way to avert this gathering catastrophe, the SBF campaigners insisted, lay in the lesson so painfully learned in other parts of the world, where fish stocks had been saved from destruction after years of reckless pillaging. Canada, Norway and Namibia, another victim of the Spanish predators, had all demonstrated that an effective conservation policy can only be run by one country, controlling its own waters. By operating scientifically-based conservation measures, properly monitored, it is possible to target catches much more precisely and to reduce discards to less than 5 per cent. As the SBF 's John Ashworth put it, speaking with the authority of a conservation adviser to the Canadian Government, the only way to save the stocks in British waters from final destruction would be for Britain to take back their management from Brussels, and to put in place a genuine, science-based conservation policy, permitting other countries only to fish on properly policed conditions.

*

By 1996 the CFP was being finally exposed for the complete charade it was. In Brussels the officials now spoke quite openly of the 'European Union fleet' fishing 'Union waters', as if the aim was simply to eliminate all national identities in one federal fishing fleet. But behind this lay the real hidden agenda. The great 'conservation' shibboleth – 'too many fishermen chasing too few fish' – was being quite cynically used as a front, to justify drastic reductions in some national fleets, particularly Britain's, to create room for the full access of Spain.

What this would mean in practice was already becoming clear in the waters off Ireland and the west coast of Britain, where nearly 300 powerful Spanish vessels in the summer of 1996 were fishing for anything that moved, in complete disregard of conservation rules, and often using their superior size to force any smaller Irish and British boats off their own traditional fishing grounds.

Meanwhile in Brussels, the Fisheries Commissioner Mrs Bonino read the riot act to the British Government, threatening to take Britain to the ECJ for not having cut back the British fleet fast enough in accordance with the 1992 agreement. To justify this she quite shamelessly claimed the British fleet had 'more than doubled in size' since 1986, from 116,000 tonnes to 239,000 tonnes, when official figures which the Commission itself had accepted showed that her figures were completely fictitious. It was true the British fleet had increased in size during that period, but only very marginally, from 206,000 tonnes to 211,000. And the only reason it had increased at all was through the explosion in the number of foreign-owned 'flagboats' which had rushed to join the British register after the ECJ's Factortame judgement. In 1996 the

British Government was at last forced to admit the true scale of the 'quota hopper' invasion, when it revealed that 22 per cent of Britain's tonnage of larger vessels, or more than a fifth of British tonnage, was now foreign-owned. Of 159 flagboats on the British register, 110 were Spanish and 42 were Dutch, including no less than 48 per cent of the entire British beam-trawler fleet, catching valuable species like sole. For some species, like hake and plaice, nearly 50 per cent of British quotas were now in foreign hands.

As if this wasn't implementing Brussels' hidden agenda fast enough, Mrs Bonino now issued two more demands. The first was that all national fleets would have to be cut back by a further 40 per cent. In Britain's case, this meant that Brussels was now demanding a total reduction of nearer 60 per cent, since the new cuts would come on top of those which it was claimed Britain should already have made, and the reductions would not affect flagboats (only one of which had been decommissioned from the British register, although 436 British boats had already disappeared). As for Spain, the demand for a 40 per cent reduction was in part only a gesture to make the policy seem 'fair', since the EC was pouring £739 million into a huge modernisation programme for the Spanish fleet, of which British taxpayers alone were contributing £103 million. But some reduction in the over-sized Spanish fleet would be necessary because it also came to light that, to accommodate its ever more rapacious needs, the EC was also having to pay an even larger sum, £894 million, to Third World governments, such as those of Morocco and Angola, to allow Spanish and Portuguese vessels to fish in those countries' waters. To this alone British taxpayers were contributing a further £125 million.

What finally revealed Brussels' hidden agenda more than anything, however, was a remarkable set of new 'conservation' measures proposed by Mrs Bonino in the summer of 1996. As usual, on the face of it, these looked as if they were just as they were described, technical measures to reduce sharply the total number of fish caught. These greatly increased the minimum permissible mesh sizes of nets, which would allow all but the largest sizes of most species to escape. The effect of this would be drastically to reduce permissible catches, making it much harder for fishermen to earn a living, Indeed, as the officials of DG XIV frankly confirmed behind closed doors, this was precisely its purpose: to force off the seas a great many more fishermen from countries, like Britain, where the rules were strictly enforced. At a meeting of DG XIV's Scientific, Technical and Economic Committee in May 1996 it was minuted that 'measures to reduce activity and catchability will improve the willingness of fishermen to leave the industry'.

But what made these new 'conservation' measures really curious was that, by what appeared to be a bizarre contradiction, they at the same time drastically reduced many of the minimum sizes of fish it was permissible to land. Furthermore, under another proposed change in the rules, these did not now have to be inspected until they reached their home port. This meant that for fishermen who did not obey the rules, like those from Spain, and whose few fisheries inspectors were so notoriously relaxed that they spent most of their time in Madrid, the new measures would be a blank cheque. Despite the new large mesh sizes, by the familiar device of putting a second 'blinder' net inside the first, it could be ensured that smaller fish did not escape. And the new, much smaller minimum landing sizes meant that the Spanish fishermen, who for years had been flouting the rules by landing colossal quantities of the undersized fish popular in Spain, could now do so legally. Even if they did happen to catch still smaller fish, no one would now be entitled to stop them until they arrived at their home port, where inspectors would be nowhere to be seen.

Thus the apparently crazy contradiction between, on the one hand, prohibiting the catching of any but the largest fish and, on the other, legalising the landing of much smaller fish, had a very simple explanation. In the empty name of 'conservation' it was just yet another devious move to push that hidden agenda: to force the law-abiding fishermen of the northern nations like Britain off the seas, and to featherbed that Spanish cuckoo even more firmly into the nest.

Then, in the autumn of 1996, there finally came to light the ultimate objective of the whole Grand Plan. It emerged that, for several years, the officials of DG XIV had been secretly putting together their strategy to achieve the final stage of the 'European Union Fisheries Policy'. Although they were careful not to reveal what they were up to in any single public document, the plan was based on a regulation issued as long ago as 1992, the so-called 'Basic Regulation', 3760/92. Step by step they had added further regulations and proposals (the final giveaway of what they were up to was only unearthed from an obscure article buried away in the 1994 Finnish Treaty of Accession) until the plan was complete. This was that, at the end of 2002, the entire existing CFP system would be scrapped. There would no longer be national quotas, or the principle of 'relative stability', supposedly guaranteeing the share allocated to fishermen of each Member State. After 1 January 2003 an individual EU fisherman would only be permitted to go fishing at all if he possessed a 'Special Fishing Permit', issued by Brussels through the local administration (national or regional authorities). This would lay down precisely how many fish of each species he was permitted to catch, where he was allowed to catch them and how many days he was permitted to stay at sea. Brussels would now decide just who was legally permitted to fish in 'Union' waters and who was not. And when the allocations were made, particular consideration would be given to the extent to which each country had complied with the earlier instructions to cut back on 'fishing effort'. Those countries which had 'met their targets', such as Spain, would be rewarded with an extra share of individual permits. Those which had fallen way short of their targets, particularly Britain, would be punished by receiving a much smaller share. Although the figures would not be finalised until just before the new scheme came into operation, the share for Britain's fishermen might well amount to only 10 per cent or less of the entire catch.

If this scheme came about it would deal the final coup de grâce to Britain's fishing industry. It would also be the first complete model of the new 'federal Europe' in all its glory.

*

Thus did we see finally unravelling in 1996 the consequences of that fateful decision by Edward Heath 25 years before to surrender Britain's fishing waters to the wolves, as the price of his ultimate dream to be the prime minister who took Britain into Europe. No one could then have predicted quite what a catastrophe this would lead to; except that it illustrated that old truth in human affairs of how often, once an initial wrong turning is taken, this can lead, further down the road, to more and more wrong turnings, compounding the original error, in ways quite unforeseen when the first false step was taken.

But a further consequence of this exposure of what a complete disaster the CFP was turning into was that it put the British Government more than ever on the spot. Ever since 1971 it had been official policy to hide from the British people just how far Britain's fishing waters had been given away; and now the practitioners of this deliberate culture of concealment, in MAFF and the Foreign Office, were having to work overtime to cover up each new facet of the disaster as it came to light. We saw John Major's ministers, even Mr Major himself, pitifully trying to obscure, deny and blur over almost everything that had happened.They continued to deny the existence of the principle of 'equal access', to which Mr Heath had signed up in 1972. They almost laughably tried to conceal the very existence of the 1976 Fisheries Limits Act, showing that Britain's fisheries limits extended to 200 miles; in a whole succession of government documents any mention of this Act was tellingly omitted, which was why we termed it 'The Act the Government Pretends Doesn't Exist'. For a time MAFF officials desperately tried to underplay the number of flagboats on the British register, claiming they amounted to only '4 per cent', until we finally forced them to admit it was five times that number. When the final stage of the CFP Grand Plan was brought to light, the system whereby after 2002 every fisherman in the EU would have to be allocated an individual Brussels 'fishing permit', the embarrassment of the MAFF officials knew no bounds. Their initial reaction was simply to deny, verbally, that such a plan existed, even though they had secretly approved it in 1994.

Indeed the bringing to light of the full extent of the fisheries disaster was already arousing so much political embarrassment in every direction that, at the start of 1996, the Government had decided to try to buy it off. Ministers' chosen tactic was to divert as much attention as possible onto the 'flagboat' problem, which until only a short time previously they had been playing down as of no importance. In the March 1996 White Paper for the forthcoming IGC, or Inter-Governmental Conference, ministers promised that, if necessary, they would 'seek' changes to the Treaty itself, to ensure the flagboat scandal was brought to an end. But this was only window dressing, mere displacement activity. Not only was there no chance they would actually get those treaty changes they pitifully promised to 'seek'. The real problem was the multiple insanity of the Common Fisheries Policy itself. And on that hook, as they knew, they were only too firmly impaled. Nothing had more discomfitingly exposed just how impotent British ministers now were to restore any sanity to a system which had them completely in its grip; a system which had not just, as was in this case only too obvious, gone completely off the rails. It had been hi-jacked to perpetrate a major international crime.

Why the CFP was illegal

One of the more bizarre footnotes to the sinister story of the CFP was the way in which for its first 22 years of operation it was completely illegal. When the Six rushed through that crucial regulation in 1970 establishing the principle of 'equal access', they had no authorisation to do this in the Treaty of Rome. When many years later this came to light, Commission officials desperately combed the Treaty trying to find some Article which might have justified the setting up of a Common Fisheries Policy. With relief they lighted on Article 38, authorising the setting up of 'a Common Market in agricultural products', because this goes on to say that this should include 'trade' in the products of 'fisheries'. But in no way was this intended to set up a federal fishing policy based on the pooling of all rights to fish in the waters of Member States. It simply authorised free trade across frontiers of fish once they had been caught.

In fact the officials who came up with this explanation made an elementary blunder. They had not even bothered to consult the preamble of the regulation to ascertain which Article was in fact cited as authorisation. Every piece of EC legislation cites in its preamble the article or articles of the Treaty which supposedly authorise it. In their eagerness to unearth some justification for the CFP, they overlooked the glaring fact that the regulation setting it up, 2141/70, made no mention of Article 38. Thr regulation was supposedly authorised under four quite different articles. These were:

Article 7, which is concerned with non-discrimination on grounds of nationality;

Articles 42 and 43, which relate solely to agricultural policy; and

Article 235. This is the giveaway, because it is a 'catch-all' article, giving authority to legislate when no other article can be found strictly relevant to the subject. But this can hardly be taken as a blank cheque to do anything under the sun.

The fact is that none of these Articles made any mention of fisheries, nor in any sense could they be taken to authorise the creation of a Common Fisheries Policy in anything like the form in which it was set up in 1970 – any more than they would have justified forcing Britain to give up its oil rights in the same waters. The truth is that Regulation 2141/70 was hastily cobbled together for purposes no one had dreamed of when the Treaty of Rome was drafted. The Commission lawyers then simply rootled around for anything which might, however vaguely or inadequately, seem to provide justification.

When the CFP's legality was called into question 20 years later this glaring error was remedied by the simple device of retrospectively inserting authorisation for a Common Fisheries Policy into Article 3 of the Treaty of Maastricht. But the very fact there was need to do this only confirmed the critics' point – that, for 22 years, the Common Fisheries Policy had been operating illegally. When this point continued to be made in subsequent controversy, the Commission and its supporters persisted in parroting the spurious claim that the CFP had been set up under Article 38, even though the merest glance at the preamble to the regulation would have showed how untrue this was. One such was Edward Heath in an article headed 'J'Accuse Booker' (*Sunday Telegraph*, 18 February 1996). Not the least curious characteristic of many of the EU's more enthusiastic supporters is how ignorant they are about even the most basic principles of its law.

8. Metrication by Stealth

'And what in hell's name is a pint?' said the barman, leaning forward with the tips of his fingers on the counter.

"ark at 'im! Calls 'isself a barman and don't know what a pint is! Why, a pint's the 'alf of a quart, and there's four quarts to the gallon. 'Ave to teach you the A, B, C next.'

'Never heard of 'em,' said the barman shortly. 'Litre and half litre – that's all we serve.'

George Orwell, Nineteen Eighty-Four

I have received a report from Mr A. Hickson regarding his recent visits to your premises when he discovered certain intoxicating liquors namely gin, rum vodka and whisky exposed for sale in one sixth of a gill quantities which became illegal on 1 January 1995 ... After careful consideration of all the facts I have decided that no further action will be taken by our Department on this occasion. I must however advise you again that offering, exposing or selling gin, run, vodka and whisky in quantities other than those required, namely 25 ml or 35 ml, is now illegal.

P.R. Mason, Head of Metrology, Cambridgeshire County Council,
in letter to Luigi Pragliola, landlord of the Gladstone
Arms pub, Peterborough, 15 November 1995

One of the tricks George Orwell used in *Nineteen Eighty-Four* when he wanted to conjure up his vision of a totalitarian Britain of the future was to show Englishmen forced to live under the metric system. To his readers at the end of the 1940s this immediately conveyed a chilling sense of their familiar world turned alien and bleak. Not even Orwell could have foreseen, however, that just 50 years after his novel was published it would actually become a criminal offence for one Englishman to sell another a pound of apples.

It was in 1995 that the British woke up to the fact that, under a series of regulations issued to comply with two EC directives, they were suddenly about to move into a world much more completely metricated than ever before. Even now, the moment when the change would be felt most acutely was still five years away. Not until 1 January 2000 would it finally became a criminal offence to sell fruit and vegetables except in metric measures, when a stallholder in an English market might face the threat of a fine up to £5,000 for shouting out 'Lovely toms – 70p a lb.'

The real point of the story of how Britain was metricated is not concerned with the advantages of one system of weights and measures over another. Our real interest centres on the way in which this was done. This has been one of the more curious episodes in recent politics, revealing much about the system of government we now live under and not least about the true workings of the relationship between Britain and Europe. And its one consistent thread is how, at every stage, metrication was slipped in on the British people by stealth, without officials or ministers ever coming fully into the open as to what they were up to. It has been a story shrouded in half-truths, evasions and sleight of hand for more than 30 years.

Hatching the plot

In 1963, around the time when Britain was making its first bid to enter Europe, officials of the British Standards Institute decided the time had come to convert Britain to the metric system. They knew there would be tremendous resistance to such a move, because the British were more deeply wedded to their traditional imperial system of yards and miles, pounds and ounces, pints and gallons, than any other nation in the world. The officials therefore decided their first move must be to create the impression that there was support for such a step from British industry. They asked the Federation of British Industries (later the Confederation of British Industry, or CBI) to organise a meeting with various trade associations. A confidential FBI report records that the meeting in January 1964 generally favoured the idea of a switch to metric, although it was admitted that 'for some industries this would present formidable difficulties'. When wider enquiries were made, however, it became 'clear that the nearly unanimous feeelings expressed at the January meeting had become modified ... some industries showed themselves definitely opposed to any early change'. Nevertheless it was finally agreed that a statement should be put to Government, advising that British industry was 'showing interest in changing over to the metric system'. If there was to be a complete switch, this 'would have to be preceded by extensive education of the public', and the FBI suggested that 'Government could help to this end by a general declaration of intent'.

It was hardly a ringing declaration, but for the officials lobbying for metrication behind the scenes it was enough. In May 1965, in a written parliamentary answer buried away at the back of Hansard, Board of Trade officials announced that, following representations from the FBI, the Government was giving support to 'a gradual change' to the metric system until this 'can become in time the primary system of weights and measures for the country as whole'. This might have seemed a curious way to announce a change which would have the most profound effect on the life of everyone in the country. But the chosen strategy had one enormous advantage. It meant work could now begin on planning the change, without the need for a public debate in parliament which might only serve to arouse opposition to the move. The lobbying of the FBI had achieved its purpose, and for 30 years the officials would be able to continue citing that FBI statement in support of their claim that metrication had come about only because 'industry wanted it'. However, their tale developed certain embellishments along the way. When the Heath Government issued its 1973 Metrication White Paper, it categorically stated that the FBI had conducted 'two polls of its members' (there had been no such polls), showing a majority 'in favour of the adoption of the metric system as

... ultimately the only method of measurement to be used in the United Kingdom'. This was scarcely what the FBI had actually said. But this was not to be the last time the FBI/CBI was used as a convenient 'front organisation' to promote a pro-European cause.

The next move came in July 1968 when, mixed in with a babble of other Government statements on the last afternoon before the summer recess, Technology Minister Tony Benn told MPs it was now the Government's intention that Britain should be 'fully metric' by 1975. But this was to be achieved voluntarily. 'Compulsion', he twice stated, 'is not part of the process.' Again this meant that there would be no need for a tiresome parliamentary debate. Only eight months later, in March 1969, the officials first gave the lie to the claim that metrication was to be entirely voluntary when they issued a statutory order making it a criminal offence not to use metric units for dispensing drugs.

Metrication now proceeded apace. The Government set up the Metrication Board. More statutory instruments were issued. Various industries, with Government encouragement, began the switch to metric. Officials of the Department of Education ensured that, after 1975, children would no longer be permitted to take exams in anything but metric measures, and imperial measures would no longer be taught in schools. But just before the 1970 election, when for the first time we publicised what was going on, this led to the first-ever parliamentary debate on the subject. A number of Tory backbenchers became concerned at how metrication was being smuggled in without consulting parliament, and particularly after Edward Heath was succeeded as Tory leader by Margaret Thatcher in 1975, party opinion moved firmly against it. In 1978 front-bench spokesman Sally Oppenheim declared that 'the Conservative Party is opposed to statutory metrication', and when Mrs Thatcher came to power the next year, one of her first acts was to announce the closing down of the Metrication Board. It seemed the whole process of compulsory metrication had been stopped in its tracks. But the officials now found another way round the problem.

Enter Europe

Before the Metrication Board was abolished British officials were already attending meetings in Brussels to discuss a new directive on weights and measures, known as 80/181. The argument put forward in its preamble was that the effect of differences in 'the laws which regulate the use of units of measurement in the Member States' was to 'hinder trade'. Of course only two countries in the EC did not use the metric system, Britain and Ireland. The directive's only real purpose was to bring them into line. A short transitional period until 1985 would be allowed (in the case of certain imperial measures, such as the inch, foot, mile, yard, acre, fathom and pound until 1989). But after that the only units of measurement legal in the Community would be those specified and defined in the annexes to the directive, all of course based on the metric system.

A claim commonly made for the metric system is that it is so much more 'rational' and 'logical' than the imperial system, based on such outdated concepts as the length of the human foot. Since it is the only measuring system in the world devised by bureaucrats this is of course unarguable. The metre was first adopted in the French Revolution as a minute decimal fraction of an arc of the earth's circumference, as measured on a line between Dunkirk in northern France and Mount-Jouy, near Barcelona. But by the time directive 80/181 came to lay down the Euro-definition of a metre, science itself had made giant strides. In an Annex to the directive the metre is defined as 'the length equal to 1,650,763.3 wavelengths in vacuum of the radiation corresponding to the transition between the levels $2p_{10}$ and $5d_5$ of the krypton 86 atom'. It would be hard to get more rational than that. What people really mean by the logicality of the metric system is, of course, only that it divides by ten.

Despite the best intentions of directive 80/181, Britain somehow managed through the Thatcherite 1980s completely to ignore the strict schedule it laid down. The process of voluntary metrication continued. On the urging of the major oil companies, most larger petrol stations switched from gallons to litres. More and more mass-produced foods carried metric measures on their packaging. But voluntary metrication was not what the officials were after. So in the late 80s, when the Single European Act had given the process of European integration new momentum, the officials decided it was time to put the process of compulsory metrication back on track. In 1989 a second directive was issued, 89/617, dutifully signed for Britain by Douglas Hurd, Lynda Chalker and Francis Maude, laying down a new timetable. This time the officials decided, to minimise public resentment, that the British might for certain purposes be now allowed to keep a tiny handful of measurements particularly close to their hearts.These included the mile, yard, foot and inch (but only for road signs and speed limits); the selling of beer and cider by the pint (but only in draught); and milk in the traditional 'pinta' bottle (but not in cartons). If all these familiar symbols of British national identity were suddenly outlawed, this might give metrication a bad name. So it was decided they should for the time being be retained, although in due course they would come to seem so anomalous that they could be quietly phased out. For similar reasons use of imperial measures such as pounds and ounces might for a limited period be still permitted on price tickets, as 'supplementary indications', but only so long as the metric equivalent was in larger print or otherwise given pride of place. Also to avoid trouble, the selling of certain 'non-packaged' items, such as fruit and veg, meat and cheese, could continue to be sold in non-metric measures until the end of 1999, giving people time to adjust. But otherwise, by 1995, the imperial system was for the scrapheap, and by 2000 Britain would have been brought completely into line. Europe would rejoice in one single, efficient continental system, leaving only America, the most prosperous and scientifically advanced nation in the world, struggling along with a few dozen others in backward isolation.

The officials go over the top

Armed with the authority of the two directives, the officials of the Department of Trade and Industry now set about drafting the sheaves of statutory instruments or regulations which would enable them to complete the metrication of Britain simply by official fiat. As in the earlier period, there would be no need to consult parliament, except by the merest formality of having to 'lay' their regulations before both Houses before they passed automatically into law. A first regulation, metricating the measures in which alcohol could be sold, was issued in 1990 (even the minister who signed this into law later confessed to us that he hadn't read it properly). Six more came out in a rush in 1994, preparing for 'M-Day' on 1 October 1995. And each was passed through parliament on the nod, using powers delegated to ministers under Section (2) 2 of the European Communities Act 1972, devised by the Heath Government to enable European legislation to be transposed into UK law with the minimum of fuss.

The most striking principle of the new legislation, again borrowed from the experience of earlier years, was that it made the failure to use metric measures a criminal offence. In fact these regulations created a whole series of new criminal offences, punishable by fines of up to £5,000 and/or imprisonment. One curiosity of this was that it would make Britain the only country in Europe where it would be a criminal offence to sell goods in non-metric measures. All over the continent there were survivals of pre-metric measures which had been retained in use, simply because in real life the imperial system is often more practical than metric, as it corresponds more naturally to everyday human needs. In several countries like France and Holland goods such as cheese continued to be sold using terms like 'livres' which dated back to pre-revolutionary times. Computer discs were sold as '3.5 inch' because this was an international standard. All over the French-speaking world pipes and taps continued to be sold in 'pousses', or inches, simply because plumbers and engineers found these to be much more practical measures than millimetres and centimetres. Even in Brussels itself, DIY shops still sold screws in inches. Only in Britain would this be made a criminal offence.

But why had the British officials been able to make it a criminal offence? Here was another curiosity. Weights and measures laws had traditionally carried a criminal sanction for centuries, but for one basic reason. This was because a powerful deterrent was needed to prevent traders trying to cheat or give short measure. Almost since the dawn of civilisation, a particular odium has attached to misuse of weights and measures to shortchange the public. As the Bible has it, 'an unjust measure is an abomination unto the Lord'. But our latter-day officials had hi-jacked this criminal sanction built into the heart of weights and measures law to put it to a totally different purpose. They were using it simply to enforce their compulsory metrication policy, even where there was not the slightest intention to defraud. And in practice, as we shall see, this flagrant misuse of that ancient legal sanction was to end up being stood on its head.

*

As was now routine when Whitehall officials came to turn Brussels directives into British law, they in fact went significantly further than the directives actually authorised. So determined were they this time to ensure that the metrication of Britain was complete, every 'i' dotted and every 't' crossed, that in the months before 'M Day' the officials of the DTI's 'Consumer Affairs' unit, in charge of metrication, not only took every step to ensure that metrication would apply to the selling of goods and all aspects of trade and industry; they also worked overtime to ensure that Britain's entire 'public administration' was metricated as well. Memoranda poured out to other departments and every branch of Government, instructing, for instance, that any reference to measurements in planning applications must now be in metric, or the applications would be sent back as unacceptable. Court proceedings would now have to be heard in metric, so that if a witness said 'he came at me with a six-inch knife' this would have to be translated into 'a 15.24-centimetre knife'. As we saw earlier, there was even a memo on the need to metricate Government contracts which ruled that departments ordering '3.5 inch floppy discs' should refer to these as '8.89 cm discs'.

As for any reference to a weight or measure in hundreds of thousands of minor public documents, local by-laws and official notices such as speed limits on canals, the DTI officials now ruled, under the Units of Measurement Regulations 1995, that these would all now have to be translated into their metric equivalents. A schedule to the regulations solemnly explained how each imperial unit should be translated. Any reference to 'a mile' should read '1.609344 kilometres'. A square mile must now be '2.589988110336 square kilometres'. A hundredweight must now be '50.802345544 kilograms'. Engineers, faced with an official document referring to foot-pounds, would have to understand each of these as '1.3558179483314004 joules'. Stresses measured in pound-force now had to be translated into units of '4.4482216152605 kilonewtons', while any reference to 'horsepower' must now be measured at a rate per unit of '0.74569987158227022 kilowatts'. It was hard to believe that the officials responsible for this particular regulation were not trying to send the whole thing up.

But the really odd thing, as we have seen, was that all this unbelievably cumbersome conversion of Britain's public administration to the new metric nirvana was supposedly authorised by two Brussels directives. Yet, as their preambles indicated, these in turn were authorised under Article 100 of the Treaty of European Union, which refers quite specifically only to 'trade'. Under EC law, therefore, Britain's compulsory metrication programme should only have been limited to 'public administration' where this was concerned with 'trade'. In no way could this be construed as referring to court proceedings or the work of police crime analysts or speed limits on canals. Strictly speaking, therefore, when the DTI officials used the European Communities Act 1972 to rush through their Units of Measurement Regulations they were acting in breach of the law. But this was not the sort of nit-picking consideration which could any longer be expected to concern those Whitehall officials. Acting above the law was something they were getting used to.

From theory into practice

As 1 October 1995 approached, when the British public would have to live with this new metricated world in practice, certain things became clear. First was that, because of the peculiar bureaucratic rigidity of the highly complex system the officials were trying to impose, it would inevitably throw up all sorts of silly little anomalies. For instance, to protect the metric system from too much of a popular backlash, there was that famous 'derogation' allowing British pubs to continue selling beer and cider by the time-honoured pint. But when officials considered this, they realised that it could not apply to 'mixed drinks' like shandy, made of beer and lemonade, because the derogation only applied to beer. So trading standards officials solemnly advised pubs all over the country that, since it would be a criminal offence to sell shandy by the pint, customers who asked for 'a pint of shandy' would have to be told they were being given 'a large shandy'. A half-pint could be described as a 'small shandy'. Similarly the officials laid down that wine could only now be sold by the glass in two quantities, 250 or 125 millilitres. No one had told them that this was ridiculous when applied to dessert wines, yet they had solemnly made it a criminal offence for a restaurant to serve Chateau d'Yquem, worth £150 a bottle, in anything other than the quantities appropriate for pub plonk.

In fact nothing was to throw up more anomalies than the drive to metricate every aspect of 'public administration'. In our Prologue we described the time-wasting inconvenience forced on the police as they had to grapple with transcribing descriptions of suspects into such incomprehensible formulae as 'height 1.82 metres, weight 88.98 kilograms' (instead of 6 foot, 14 stone). Shortly after M-Day serious confusion was caused in an Oxford courtroom, when Judge Wilson-Mellor reprimanded barristers in a drugs case for referring to cannabis in ounces. 'It is now', he intoned, 'against the law to refer to amounts in pounds and ounces.' But as a detective in the case observed afterwards, 'I don't think the drug dealers are taking much notice of Brussels. They would be pretty confused if someone came up and asked them for 0.28 kilograms of cannabis.' Even more ludicrous confusion was caused when the officials noted that the Brussels 'derogation' for miles and speed limits applied only to 'road signs', and therefore ruled that all speed limits on waterways should be metricated. Because these limits were laid down in by-laws, this led to signs going up on rivers and canals all over Britain indicating that speed limits were now '6.437 kph' or '12.87 kph'; while, as we recorded in the Prologue, the consequences of this on the Norfolk Broads, the most intricate network of inland waterways in Britain, produced almost a self-parodying nightmare of complexity, the costs of which could run into millions of pounds.

*

The groups in the community most immediately affected by the approach of M Day were Britain's hundreds of thousands of shopkeepers and traders, and it was noticeable how these divided into two distinct groups.

On the one hand, for many small shops, metrication was something of a nightmare. For shops selling a wide range of food items, the replacement of weighing machines and price tickets could run into thousands of pounds, quite apart from the confusion the new system would bring for assistants and customers alike. More serious was the problem faced by many smaller filling stations, which now found themselves compelled to buy new metric pumps, at costs which could easily run above £10,000, often more than their business justified. There were reports from all over the country of small garages closing

97

down, like J.D. Hunt's of Colchester, putting four people out of work, including two men who had been with the firm 35 years.

On the other hand no one welcomed the arrival of metrication more than the big supermarket chains. This was not just because they hoped it might make life more difficult for their smaller independent competitors, but because they could exploit the public's general confusion over the new weights to smuggle in a vast range of hidden price rises. We were sent many examples by readers, like the 99p bags of sweets sold by one store which over only a few months moved from 1lb/454 grams to 425g to 400g to 375g, with the price still at 99p. Two supermarkets which sold 'four pints of milk for 99p' took the advantage of M-Day to translate this into 'two litres for 99p' which, as only $3\frac{1}{2}$ pints, was a 14 per cent rise. One sharp-eyed reader had noticed how in 1993 Sainsbury's sold packs of Christmas puddings at 4 x 4oz (113g), but a year later was selling them at 4 x 100g, under a notice reading 'All Christmas puddings at same price or cheaper than last year'. When he took this up with Sainsbury's a spokesman for their 'Customer Services Department' replied, 'I have spoken to the Buyer of the Four Individual Rich Puddings and he has informed me that the ingredients of the recipe have changed to a higher quality, which explains the corresponding rise in price.' But the ingredients given on the labels were in each case identical. So our reader took this up with his local trading standards officials, who took the view that to tangle with a major supermarket chain was more than their jobs were worth.

Nevertheless there was a point of principle at stake here. The sole reason, it will be recalled, why a criminal sanction had been attached to weights and measures legislation in the first place was to prevent customers being sold short measure. This was why 'trading standards officers' had originally been known as 'weights and measures inspectors', checking measures and prices to ensure that the public was not being defrauded. The officials had then hi-jacked that criminal sanction for the quite different purpose of enforcing metrication. And now Britain's supermarkets were exploiting the resulting confusion to do precisely what that criminal penalty had been originally designed to prevent. The public was in effect being sold short measure – yet those same trading standards officials stood paralysed. It was a perfect small illustration of how our modern regulatory system can so often bring about consequences precisely the opposite of those it claims to be trying to achieve.

The real consequences of the wholesale switch to metrication was not to bring about a more logical, rational world. For a long time to come it was going to leave a large part of the population stuck in a neither-one-thing-nor-the-other fog, where they could no longer relate mentally to weights and measures with anything like their old instinctive confidence. As an Edinburgh surveyor pointed out, when he was told to post a notice on the floor of an old building warning staff not to exceed a floor-loading of '4 KN/m^2', not even the younger ones could define 'a kilonewton', although all could understand what the meaning of '80 lbs per sq. ft'. For many people it would just mean an enormous extension of the way, when petrol stopped being sold in gallons, they hadn't converted to thinking in litres. They simply stopped trying to relate to quantity at all, but just bought 'cash' instead. Obviously for many older people it was a particular source of irritation and inconvenience, like the semi-professional cook who told us how, after trying to work out with conversion charts how long she should leave a joint marked '1.45 kg' in the oven, she found herself expostulating 'I will not be persecuted by Brussels in my own kitchen'. She then broke the imperial measuring jug she had used for years and found the shops no longer stocked anything but metric replacements. But it was by no means only the old who continued to use imperial measures without thinking. One of us was invited on a BBC Watchdog programme, which it turned out wanted to put across the message that far too much fuss was being made about the switch to metric. Most young people in Britain, suggested the young interviewer, now thought in metric quite naturally. 'So how tall are you?' we asked him. 'Five feet ten,' he unthinkingly replied. An instinctive grasp of weights and measures is more deeply embedded in the unconscious of a culture than those 'rational' officials could ever imagine.

Puppet politicians defend the system

Perhaps the most revealing role in the drama surrounding Britain's metric conversion was that played by the politicians. In the months before M-Day we invited our readers to write to their MPs asking two simple questions on the most sensitive issue – in essence, did they approve of the fact that it would soon become a criminal offence not to use metric measures? More than 130 replied, but only a tiny handful even attempted a personal response to the question. It was obvious that most were almost wholly unaware of the change that was on the way, even though in theory the regulations had received the assent of parliament. Some were so ignorant they even flatly denied that it would be a criminal offence. Most MPs fell back on the routine device of sending back a form letter written by officials in the DTI, giving a highly selective history of why Britain was going metric which conspicuously omitted any mention of Europe or the two Brussels directives at all. This despite the fact that all the regulations had gone through parliament under the European Communities Act.

Even more revealing of the Government's growing sensitivity to charges that it simply carried out orders from Brussels was the response of Deputy Prime Minister Michael Heseltine, who flatly denied in a speech that Britain was making the change 'at the behest of Europe', even though it was his own department that had implemented the directives.

The Government was equally evasive when it came to questions about the use of criminal penalties to enforce metrication. The favourite response, adopted by the junior minister in charge of metrication, Jonathan Evans, was to say that Britain had been making the switch to metric for more than 20 years and so far no one had been prosecuted (not actually true). His audience was left to understand that therefore no prosecutions would be likely this time, although Mr Evans was very careful not to say that.

Sure enough, within weeks of M-Day, a first case appeared, of a publican in Peterborough who had fallen foul of the Cambridgeshire trading standards officials for refusing to instal new metric optics behind his bar. As luck would have it, Luigi Pragliola was not only the landlord of a 'free house', named the Gladstone Arms after a famous champion of liberty; he was also an Italian citizen, who had lived in Britain most of his life, and who roundly declared,

'I'm sick and tired of some prat in Europe dictating what we should do when the rest of Europe doesn't use optics. I'm prepared to stand up for this country, even if no one else is. None of my punters gives a monkey's about Brussels.' Orwell had got it wrong, it was to be the publican, not his customers, who stood up for the imperial system. No doubt heeding the minister's solemn assurances that enforcement would not be 'over-zealous', the officials did not prosecute Mr Pragliola. They merely confiscated his optics, forcing the pub to close. They later came back with the letter quoted at the head of this chapter, confirming that no further action would be taken. That is, until they noticed he had now installed a new set of imperial optics, when they threatened that, if he did not remove them, they would take him to court.

A new twist to the official line came when Norman Clarke was forced to close down his long-established business selling diesel fuel to boat-owners on a canal at Weedon, Northants, because of the prohibitive cost of installing metric pumps. 'It would mean doubling my prices, which for the sake of my customers I am not prepared to do,' he explained. When this was put to the DTI, the officials replied that 'the principal reason' it had been necessary to make it a criminal offence for Mr Clarke to sell diesel in gallons was 'to protect the consumer'. How 'consumers' were protected by denying them any service at all was a mystery which Mr Evans, who signed the letter, did not bother to explain.

A final example came up in May 1996 when Evans's successor as 'Minister for Consumer Affairs', John Taylor, signed a letter drafted by the officials, reassuring a fellow-Tory MP that in metrication matters officials did not 'take a heavy-handed or confrontational approach' unless there was 'clear evidence of fraudulent intent'. Scarcely had this admirable sentiment been intoned than trading standards officials in Birmingham swooped on 30 local carpet stores and found no fewer than 27 still committing the criminal offence of not selling their wares in metres. The officials threatened them all with heavy fines. Of course there was not the slightest suggestion of 'fradulent intent'. The stores only continued to sell in yards because this was what their customers preferred. But this was not the point. The real point was simply that the British had to be forced to go metric, whether they wanted it or not.

A 1995 opinion poll showed not only that the majority of the British people were still opposed to metrication, as they had been in 1975, but that after two decades of living with it that majority had slightly risen. In view of the methods the officials and the politicians had employed to foist it on them, this was not entirely surprising.

9. The CAP that Doesn't Fit

The huge cost of the policy to taxpayers and consumers far outweighs any benefit to them ... such large transfers into agriculture represent a major misallocation of resources and thus damage the economy as a whole ... the policy is extremely complex in detail, hence difficult and costly to administer and giving scope for fraud.

'The Government's View of the CAP', Memorandum by MAFF
to House of Lords European Communities Committee, 1995

Every year in a valley near Thessaloniki in northern Greece, billions of peaches are bulldozed into the ground because no one wishes to buy them. In the year to May 1995, according to European Commission figures, EC taxpayers handed over £89 million to Greek peach growers to pay for the destruction of 657,000 tonnes of these unwanted peaches, which are only produced in the first place because the growers know they will receive a guaranteed price for every one (although it is perhaps fair to add that when a British fruit expert wandered round one or two villages named as centres of Greek peach-growing, he was surprised how few peach trees he could actually set eyes on).

In 1994 EC taxpayers paid £439,000,000, more than £1.2 million a day, to destroy millions of tons of unwanted fruit and vegetables in this way. 94 per cent of this was in just four countries, Greece, France, Italy and Spain. In the years between 1992 and 1994, according to Commission figures, this accounted for up to 84 per cent of all the peaches claimed to have been grown in Greece; 77 per cent of French apples; 73 per cent of Italian pears; and no less than 97 per cent of the entire Spanish lemon crop.

In 1992 it was reported that Italian farmers had claimed EC subsidies for 4.3 million acres of durum wheat, used for pasta. But satellite photography showed that only 1.9 million acres of durum wheat had been under cultivation. Tens of millions of pounds had thus been claimed for wheat which was never grown.

In 1993 EC cereal farmers were paid £1 billion not to grow any crops on 15 per cent of their land under the compulsory set-aside scheme, to reduce grain surpluses. One consequence of this in Britain was that vast numbers of birds were attracted to nest on the 1.5 million acres left uncultivated. But to qualify for the subsidies farmers were told they had to mow their set-aside fields at least once before 1 July, before the end of the nesting season. This resulted in a wildlife catastrophe, as hundreds of thousands of lapwings, corn buntings, yellow hammers, partridges and other ground-nesting birds lost eggs and newly hatched chicks. The loss of skylark chicks and eggs alone, according to a detailed study by the British Trust for Ornithology, amounted to 250,000, of only 2 million breeding pairs left in the country. In this respect at least the rules were changed. But by 1996, after nearly £4 billion of taxpayers' money had been spent on this scheme to reduce EC grain production, annual production had risen over the four years by more than 10 per cent.

Despite the EC's politically-correct hostility to the evils of smoking (e.g. the health warnings ordered to be printed on every cigarette packet under directive 89/622), the CAP in 1995 gave £802,400,000 in subsidies to farmers mainly in Greece, Italy and Spain to grow tobacco. The Greek tobacco farmers alone received £332,400,000, equivalent to more than a tenth of all the CAP subsidies returned to farmers in Britain. The coarse, black tobacco the system encouraged to be grown was so low-grade that much of it had to be dumped at knockdown prices in North Africa and the Middle East.

*

The European Community's Common Agricultural Policy is one of the most bizarre creations ever devised by the human mind. We are entering here that mysterious, semi-mythical realm of beef mountains and wine lakes, where not only cattle but even plants must be issued with 'passports', where the Sicilian Mafia makes a fortune out of 'paper olives' (olive groves which exist only on paper), yet where British dairy farmers must pay fortunes to each other for official permits to allow their cows to continue producing milk at all.

Simply in terms of the mountains of taxpayers' money it disposes of, the CAP puts all the EC's other activities into the shade. In 1973 when Britain joined the Common Market, the CAP accounted for no less than 91 per cent of all Brussels' annual spending, at a cost of just over £3,000,000,000. Admittedly by 1995 the CAP's share of the EC budget had dropped to only 55 per cent, but this was only because other areas of spending had risen much faster. In money terms spending on the CAP had soared to £29,300,000,000, a rise of 976 per cent.

In *The Mad Officials* we quoted the calculation of a Blackburn carpet firm that it would cost less than this sum to cover every square inch of the EC's land area with top-quality carpet. But these direct payments are of course only part of the benefits the CAP bestows on EC farmers. Thanks to tariff barriers designed to keep out cheaper food from the rest of the world, EC citizens must subsidise the farmers twice over, firstly through their taxes, then by having to pay more for food in the shops. In 1993 this gave rise to probably the best-known single statistic about the EC, when the OECD estimated that, in one way or another, the CAP was adding £1,000 a year, or £20 a week, to the food bill of the average UK family. Even though this figure was disputed, and anyway has now fallen considerably as a result of reforms and changing patterns of world prices, the CAP still nevertheless maintains agriculture in a position of quite extraordinary privilege. It soaks up more public subsidies than all other sectors of the EC economy put together. And inevitably, with the dishing out of such astronomic sums of taxpayers' money, by far the greater part serves no useful or productive purpose at all. Billions of pounds go to rich farmers who do not need the financial help anyway.

Billions more are siphoned off in wholesale cheating and fraud. Billions more go to paying for produce which is not needed and has to be destroyed or dumped in the poorer countries of the third world. And yet further billions are swallowed up in paying the armies of officials required just to administer such an unbelievably complex system.

How on earth did such an extraordinary phenomenon come about?

Big is beautiful

As is not unusual with the EC's utopian schemes, the story of the CAP began with apparently high-minded intentions. The idea of a common agricultural policy originated in the years after the Second World War when Europe was determined never again to go through the desperate food shortages of the 1940s and the agricultural slump which preceded them. Written into Article 39 of the 1957 Treaty of Rome were the CAP's five central aims: that agricultural productivity in the Common Market should be increased by promoting 'the rational development of agricultural production'; that the earnings of those engaged in agriculture should be increased; that markets should be stabilised; that food supplies should be guaranteed; and that these should be made available to 'consumers at reasonable prices'.

The attempt to realise these aims has centred on three main pillars: first, by paying farmers direct cash subsidies to increase their food production; secondly, by the 'intervention' system, guaranteeing farmers that the EC will buy their products at a minimum price, even if the food is not wanted; and thirdly, by erecting a tariff wall to protect farmers against imports of food produced more cheaply elsewhere, thus enabling food prices in the Community to be kept higher than in the outside world (what the CAP calls making food available to 'consumers at reasonable prices').

As it happened, of course, this massive injection of state support for agriculture has directly coincided with the immense revolution brought about in farming over the past 50 years by advances in technology, centred on the use of ever more sophisticated and powerful machinery, the huge increase in the use of chemicals and the development of intensive methods of rearing livestock. And one of the more obvious characteristics of the CAP system has been the way it has been geared to reinforcing this process. One of its most striking features has been just how one-sidedly its largesse has been funnelled towards those sectors of the farming industry most identified with this technological revolution and the trend towards agri-business. In Britain, for instance, far and away the most conspicuous beneficiaries of the subsidy system have been the big grain growers, running the largest, most technologically-intense farms. For them the CAP has provided an almost unimaginable bonanza. In 1994 13 companies and landowners each received subsidy cheques from the taxpayers of more than £500,000; 5,000 farmers received more than £50,000; and the total given to farmers in just the county of Lincolnshire alone amounted to £107,101,476.

Certainly, by encouraging the most intensive use of land and resources, this system has led to a enormous increase in the quantity of food produced. But the net effect of the CAP has been to encourage those farmers who operate on the largest scale, while the majority of the EC's smaller and poorer farmers have been progressively squeezed out by a system dedicated to making the rich richer and the poor poorer. This has contributed not only to a drastic decline in the number of people involved in farming (e.g. the thousands of half-deserted villages in rural France), but also to the wholesale environmental devastation of the countryside, reflected in the disappearance of hedges and trees, the use on an enormous scale of poisonous and soil-destroying chemicals and all the other practices associated with the maximisation of production through modern factory farming. No one has supported the CAP more fervently than the manufacturers of machinery and the giant chemical combines, unless it be the National Farmers Union, representing the interests of those larger farmers for whom the CAP has been like Christmas coming every day of the year.

But for millions of smaller farmers the story has been very different. Nothing better demonstrates just how lop-sided the CAP's benefits are than the fact that 80 per cent of the £3 billion subsidies flowing back into Britain each year go to just 20 per cent of farmers. While the 'barley barons' on the hedgeless prairies of eastern England regularly pocket annual subsidy cheques of £500,000 or more, and 5,000 farmers claim subsidies of more than £50,000, the hard-pressed hill farmers of Wales or the Yorkshire Dales struggle along on average yearly incomes which more than once in the 1990s have dropped well below £10,000. In 1993/4 a quarter of British farms had living incomes of less than £5,000 and 53 per cent of farmers managed on less than £20,000.

Significant sectors of the farming community, like the breeders of pigs and poultry, draw no subsidies at all. Indeed this in itself highlights a further anomaly of this strangely distorted system, because the unsubsidised sectors must often then pay artificially-inflated prices for raw materials produced by the subsidised sector. More than half poultry breeders' costs come from grain produced by heavily subsidised and protected cereal growers, for which they may have had to pay 50 per cent more than the price on the world market. Big sugar users, such as the manufacturers of soft drinks, sweets and jam have had to pay £750 a tonne for sugar produced by subsidised and protected sugar beet growers, at times when the world sugar price outside the EC was only £350 a tonne or less.

All this in itself might recall the declared aim of the CAP, that 'the earnings of those engaged in agriculture should be increased'. What this means in practice is that for a minority of big farmers the CAP has assisted in increasing their earnings beyond all reason. But the 10 million people who have left the land altogether in the 40 years since the CAP began might see it rather differently.

The problems of excess

A second, even more predictable consequence of the CAP's blank-cheque system of support to farmers has been that, in terms of increasing food production, it has been only too successful. Many of the more glaring absurdities which have afflicted EC agriculture in recent years have resulted from the fact that farmers have been paid to produce more food than the EC can possibly consume. This has led the officials of DG VI in Brussels to introduce a whole series of immensely complex bureaucratic reforms intended to cut down the unnecessary surpluses, each creating further nonsenses of its own.

Few features of the EC Wonderland became more familiar in the late 1970s and 1980s than those supreme symbols of crazy over-production, the beef, grain and butter 'mountains'. These were held in vast warehouses, refrigerated stores or even container ships moored offshore, rented at a cost of tens of millions of pounds a year to house unwanted surpluses which only existed because farmers were subsidised to create them in the first place. These were set off by vast 'lakes' of unwanted wine and skimmed milk stored as powder. As for the surplus produce which could not be stored, such as fruit and vegetables, this was solved by bulldozing millions of tonnes a year into the ground. Such were the inevitable results of suspending the laws of the market by paying farmers to produce food even when there was no demand for it.

The first attempt by Brussels to cut down these surpluses was its imposition in 1984 of 'milk quotas'. The intention of this system was to reduce the 'milk lake' and the 'butter mountain' created by some countries' runaway overproduction. Each country was allocated a fixed ceiling on the amount of milk its farmers were allowed to produce, and we have already glimpsed some of the crazy consequences to which this almost Soviet example of state planning inevitably gave rise. But no country fared worse from this system than Britain, already forced to reduce her dairy herd in the 1970s as one of the conditions of joining the Common Market. It was on production figures after that time that quotas were fixed, with the result that Britain was permitted to produce only 85 per cent of its needs.

Britain had traditionally imported dairy products, particularly from New Zealand. But now she was in the EC, these imports had to surmount tariff barriers which could more than double the price of half a pound of New Zealand butter, from 29p to over 60p. This meant that much of the hundreds of millions of tonnes of the products Britain needed to import now came from her EC competitors. Meanwhile at home the new quota system created a horrendously distorted and bureaucratised system for Britain's own dairy producers. Inevitably a market grew up in buying and selling 'quota' to permit them to produce milk at all, encouraging the concentration of quota in fewer and fewer hands, Many smaller dairy farmers could not compete. Farmers faced drastic penalties if their cows 'over-produced', even if this was through circumstances completely beyond their control, like a warm, wet spring encouraging lush growth of grass. Eventually when, in 1994, the Milk Marketing Board was abolished and milk prices rose in the artificially restricted market, many butter and cheesemakers found it so hard to buy supplies at an economical price that some were forced out of business altogether.

Meanwhile they were forced to watch on the continent the unfolding farce of the Italian and Spanish Governments wilfully ignoring the quota rules for nearly ten years. Eventually in 1994 they were fined for non-compliance, but at the same time they were 'bought off' by Brussels with hugly increased quota allocations, which meant their producers scarcely suffered at all. In the same year, under the CAP dairy regime, the average subsidy for each cow in Britain was £81.50, less than half the EC average of £168.30, while dairy farmers in the Netherlands received £434 per cow, those in Denmark £407 and in Belgium £347.60.

Further reforms were introduced in the late 1980s and early 1990s in a bid to eliminate the 'grain mountain'. The best-known of these was the system of set-aside by which farmers were paid huge sums, amounting to more than a thirtieth of the CAP's entire expenditure, to leave a proportion of their fields uncultivated. Like so many schemes emerging from Brussels this ended up, as we have seen, producing results the very opposite of those intended, as farmers simply concentrated their efforts and use of chemicals on the acreages remaining, to produce more grain than ever before.

A further scandal was the 'intervention' system, whereby farmers who produced the fruit and vegetables which could not be stored were paid a guaranteed price for their produce. Year after year the tonnages of peaches, oranges, tomatoes and apples for which EC taxpayers had to pay to be destroyed rose inexorably. Almost the only measure introduced by Brussels to tackle a small part of this problem was its scheme to pay apple growers to grub up their orchards, mainly because of the wholesale over-production of inferior apples in southern Europe and France, where taxpayers had been paying for the destruction of more than seven out of every ten apples grown. As usual it was Britain which conspicuously came out worst, as a disproportionate number of her apple-growers applied for grants to destroy orchards of Cox's Orange Pippins and some of the best-quality apples grown anywhere.

Another answer to the problem of these huge unwanted surpluses was to dispose of them by exporting them to the outside world. Here the problem was that, thanks to the artificially-inflated prices created in the EC by subsidies and protection, such products could not compete with much lower world prices. As usual Brussels came up with a wonderfully bureaucratic solution in its immensely complicated system of 'export refunds', whereby exporters could receive a further subsidy to bring the price of their food down to or often way below the world market price. At one point it was calculated that the thickets of regulations issued to administer this system contained 170,000 paragraphs. This may have provided yet another bonanza for the EC producers, like those Greek and Italian tobacco farmers able to dump on the Third World much of the low-grade tobacco EC taxpayers paid them to grow in the first place. But this system of subsidised dumping also had a seriously damaging effect on the economies of scores of other countries, including those of the old Commonwealth such as Australia and New Zealand, and on some of the poorest countries the effect was devastating. One often-cited example is Upper Volta, where the influx of thousands of tonnes of frozen EC beef at knockdown prices so undercut the local subsistence cattle-farmers that many could no longer sell their animals and were driven out of business.

Another instance which in 1995 provided an illustration of the CAP system in all its glory was a deal whereby French and German farmers negotiated to sell 800,000 tonnes of surplus wheat to China. The world price of wheat at that time was £88 a tonne, whereas the EC price, thanks to subsidies and protection, was £131, or 50 per cent higher. But Brussels officials arranged a special 'export refund' scheme which would bring down the price to the Chinese even lower than the world level, to a mere £70 a tonne, the difference of £48,800,000 to be made up by British and other EC taxpayers. A sizeable quantity of this cheap grain would then be available to Chinese poultry producers keen to expand their export markets. Under strict Brussels health requirements, the Chinese would not normally be permitted to sell their chickens into the EC. But it turned out that Germany and France had also negotiated 'bilateral deals' to import cheap Chinese poultry, which under EC rules was quite legal. Furthermore, under Single Market rules, there was nothing to stop those imports being sold on to anywhere in the EC. So the net result of the arrangement was that EC taxpayers could pay first to subsidise the production of the wheat, which meant the EC's own unsubsidised poultry producers having to pay 50 per cent above the world price to feed their chickens; then they would have to pay more subsidies to allow the French and Germans to sell their wheat at knockdown prices to Chinese poultry producers; and finally the EC producers would have to see cheap Chinese poultry imported freely into Europe to compete with their own produce.

The primary declared aim of the CAP, it may be recalled, was that the agriculture of the EC should be developed in a 'rational' manner.

The fraud mountain

A third, entirely predictable consequence of the CAP system, with its astronomic sums of public money swilling around, is that it has led to fraud and corruption on a scale without historical precedent. No one can know precisely just how much of the hundreds of billions of pounds spent on the CAP since its inception have been improperly claimed or diverted. Undoubtedly the true figure is far higher than those given each year in the laughably inadequate annual report on EC spending by the Court of Auditors, which in a strangely opaque fashion, usually without quoting names, lists particular instances of fraud which have come to its attention. Estimates suggested by various official or semi-official sources over the years have put the annual cost of EC fraud at £2 billion, £4 billion, £5 billion, even £6 billion, much of it centred on the CAP. We shall never know the true figure, partly because so much fraud by its nature inevitably remains undetected, and partly because the system itself has absolutely no effective machinery for tracking it down.

Three points, however, can be made with certainty. The first is that fraud is so widespread that it has become endemic through almost the entire CAP system. One common form of fraud is the claiming of subsidies for crops which have not been grown at all, like the famous 'paper' olive groves of Greece and southern Italy, or those millions of acres of pasta wheat which satellite photographs showed never existed. A variation was the celebrated Greek case in 1989, involving the country's finance minister, other politicians, officials and prominent businessmen, who drew subsidies for growing huge quantities of maize. In this instance the crop had actually been grown, not in Greece but in Yugoslavia, from where it was smuggled over the border and given false documents of origin to claim the subsidy. After this case had come to light, the Greek Government was fined £5 million and some of those responsible were sent to prison. But after the Socialist election victory of 1993, they were all pardoned by the Greek parliament, at the request of the new Papandreou

Government, and some were promptly reinstated in high positions, including one appointed to run a state bank.

Another widespread form of cheating has involved making false claims for export refunds, as in the oft-quoted case of the ship in a north German port where meat was officially inspected as it was taken aboard at one end of the ship, to claim the refunds, only for it to be taken out of the other end and brought back to the loading point, so the subsidies could be claimed again. And CAP fraud is by no means just something practised at lower levels of the system. One of the most notorious cases concerned wholesale corruption in the administration of the vast subsidies, including export refunds, to tobacco growers. Eventually in 1993 the finger of suspicion pointed directly at Signor Antonio Quatraro, the Italian former head of the European Commission's Tobacco Division, who promptly committed suicide by jumping from the roof of his Brussels office building.

A second point to be made, however, is that it is a misconception for the British to imagine that fraud involves only the nationals of other countries, particularly those of southern Europe. So powerful are the incentives for cheating created by this labyrinthine system that countless rackets take place in Britain itself, as we have more than once discovered during our investigations. A worker in the packing shed of a large Lincolnshire horticulture concern described to us how an inspector from the Intervention Board would come in each day to check off 300 boxes of cauliflowers on which the grower received thousands of pounds worth of subsidy payments. Each day he would actually examine the fresh cauliflowers in only the same six boxes, taking the rest for granted. But these six were the only ones in which the cauliflowers were replaced. The grower also received payments on the other 294, even though day after day these contained only the same old cauliflowers.

Similarly we have seen boxes of British beef marked for export to Botswana, thus claiming export refunds. But Botswana just happens to be one of the few countries in Africa which is a net exporter of beef, under a special arrangement with the EC known as the Beef Protocol. It is therefore possible to re-import the same beef back to Europe at preferential rates, thus making a profit twice over.

We reported on a major racket operated at several major poultry processing plants in East Anglia, involving at least one supermarket chain, whereby millions of second-grade chickens were given fraudulent 'EC' stamps. These enabled the birds to be sold as prime quality, raising the value of each by 40p. What this example shows is that CAP fraud does not necessarily involve the misappropriation of EC funds. It may simply exploit the intricacies of CAP bureaucracy to work a scam directly against the public.

In none of these cases was any official action taken (in at least two, indeed, public officials were directly implicated). And ultimately the most chilling point about the massive scale of CAP fraud is how little can be done to stop it. When, as Chancellor of the Exchequer, that keen Euro-enthusiast Kenneth Clarke was interrogated on the fraud problem by a House of Lords committee, he recalled the Yugoslav maize scandal, recounting how those found guilty had been officially pardoned and reinstated. 'I think we should deplore what the Greeks have done,' he conceded, 'but there is nothing whatever that anybody can do about it.' In 1992 his rather less Euro-enthusiastic predecessor as Chancellor, Norman Lamont, took advantage of the British Presidency to put fraud at the top of the agenda of a meeting with his fellow EC finance ministers. As he recited some of the choicer horror stories from that year's report of the Court of Auditors, his fellow ministers ostentatiously read newspapers and talked among themselves. When he had finished Jacques Delors, then President of the Commission, condescendingly explained that fraud was nothing to do with the Council of Ministers or the Commission. What happened to EC funds, said M. Delors, was entirely a matter for individual governments. They then moved on to the next item.

Bureaucracy's ultimate empire

The final inevitable consequence of the CAP, as the most ambitious experiment in the centralised state planning and control of agriculture since Stalin's Five-Year Plans of the 1930s, was that it gave rise to one of the most labyrinthine systems of bureaucracy the world has ever seen. And as usual the zealous officials in Britain took this to lengths no other EC country could hope to rival.

An outsider reading through Britain's farming press in the 1990s might be astonished at the extent to which its pages are no longer dominated by traditional farming concerns but by bureaucracy and the tidal wave of red tape engulfing Britain's farmers. Poll after poll has shown how worries over paperwork, form-filling and new regulations have become the biggest cause of stress in farmers' lives. There have been new forms, licences, regulations and inspections to cover every conceivable aspect of farming activity. In *The Mad Officials* we described some of the more bizarre of these bureaucratic impositions, such as the 'plant passports' now required to sell any consignment of plants, complete with regular visits from officials of MAFF 's Plant Health and Seeds Inspectorate charging £70 an hour. 'Cattle passports' or Cattle Identification Documents had to be acquired to accompany every beast throughout its life, complete with ear tags and its own individual 18-digit number. In 1993 there was the incredible administrative shambles which surrounded MAFF 's implementation of the EC's new 'Integrated Administration and Control Scheme' (IACS), whereby British farmers were given six weeks with the 'aid' of a 79-page document to fill in a complex form giving the precise size in hectares of the cultivable area of each of their fields, down to two decimal places – when the equivalent documentation for Irish and Portuguese farmers covered only two pages.

At least many of these farmers were ultimately rewarded for their hours of form-filling by receiving subsidies – 'arable area payments' under the IACS scheme, 'beef premiums' payable on male cattle at 11 months and 23 months, 'ewe premiums' on female sheep. But for others there was no tangible benefit at all for the bureaucracy which now overshadowed their working lives: like the goat owners who had to fill in a form every time they moved a single animal off their holding; or those farmers who in 1996 suddenly found themselves having to operate under all the bizarre restrictions associated with the designation of their farms as 'Nitrate Vulnerable Zones'; or the cheesemakers suddenly instructed by the Intervention Board to weigh and record every drop of milk produced by their cows but not used for cheesemaking; or those abattoir owners who faced the utter devastation of much of their industry by the bizarre way in which the MAFF officials implemented the CAP's 'hygiene' directive 91/497. And everywhere as new regulations poured out from MAFF in an endless stream, new criminal offences were being created, to ensure that every last diktat from Brussels was obeyed to the letter.

For a more specific glimpse of what this ever-proliferating red tape means in practice let us consider just one relatively small example.

*

Near Bristol in the summer of 1995 Keith Pulman, secretary of an association representing Britain's smaller egg producers, is looking at the latest letter he has received from MAFF. This is a familiar experience for Mr Pulman. Scarcely a week goes by without a letter from MAFF advising him about some new set of regulations which his members will be expected to obey, even though they receive not a penny in subsidies. This particular missive, from Barbara McFadyen of the ministry's 'Pigs, Eggs and Poultry Division', gives Mr Pulman's members three weeks to comment on the new Eggs (Marketing Standards) Regulations 1995 due to come into force two months later. These, Ms McFadyen explains, provide for 'the enforcement of directly applicable EC legislation setting out quality, grading and labelling standards for the marketing of eggs'.

This has been established, the letter goes on, 'by Council Regulation 1907/90 (EEC) as amended by Council Regulations 2617/93 (EEC) and 3117/94 (EEC). The detailed rules are set out in Commission Regulation 1274/91 (EEC) as amended by Commission Regulations 3540/91 (EEC), 2221/92 (EEC), 3300/93 (EEC) and 1259/94 (EEC). There is also a Council Decision of 20 June 1994, 94/371/EC.' The new regulations, Ms McFadyen continues, also 'relate to the production and marketing of eggs for hatching and of farmyard poultry chicks'. Here the relevant Brussels legislation includes 'Council Regulation 2782/75 as amended by Council Regulations 3485/80, 3791/85, 3494/86 and Commission Regulations 3987/87 and 1057/91. Detailed rules are set out in Commission Regulation 1868/77 as amended by Commission Regulations 3759/85, 1351/87 and 2773/90.'

This is the kind of information which, as secretary of the United Kingdom Egg Producers Association, Mr Pulman is expected, month in and month out, to pass on to his members for 'consultation'. In one period of just a few weeks in 1992 he received no fewer than seven such new sets of regulations, running to well over 500 pages. Often he is given no more than a week or two to reply to the ministry with his members' views, of which the ministry takes not the slightest notice, since most of the legislation consists of Regulations issued in Brussels which are already automatically law throughout the EC anyway. This charade of 'consultation' is a device used by the officials of many ministries which enables them, first, to hand down their intentions to the industry concerned; then, subsequently, to claim that, since members of that industry have been 'consulted', no one is entitled to complain. The result in Mr Pulman's case is yet another set of regulations with which his association's members must comply, on anything from new wording to be inserted on egg-box labels to new rulings on the temperature at which eggs can be stored. To meet even one of these requirements may cost them hundreds of thousands of pounds.

In most other EC countries, as Mr Pulman learns from his network of continental contacts, many of these diktats are simply ignored. But if his own members ignore them, an army of zealous inspectors will ensure they are taken to court on criminal charges. However, Britain's food producers are not entirely alone in being beset by the armies of officialdom spawned by the CAP. In 1993 the Brussels office of the Danish agriculture ministry estimated that to administer the CAP in Denmark now required the services of 29,000 officials. As it happened there were just 29,000 farmers in the country. Denmark had thus become the first country in the EU to achieve the perfect bureaucratic equation of one official for every farmer.

*

In the summer of 1995 there appeared as devastating a critique of the Common Agricultural Policy system as has ever been published. This document stated that the CAP's 'huge cost' to Britain's 'taxpayers and consumers far outweighs any benefit'. The massive transfers of money into agriculture 'represent a major misallocation of resources and thus damage the economy as a whole'. The 'production of large surpluses which can only be sold at subsidised prices, besides being economically irrational, can result in unnecessary trade disputes with third countries'. The 'financing of the CAP from the EU budget gives rise to big financial flows between Member States, based on no objective justification, with the UK as a major contributor'. 'Quotas and similar devices' employed to 'limit production' inhibited 'competition and relative efficiency'. The CAP had 'increased the scope for modern agriculture to cause environmental damage'. The CAP was 'extremely complex' in its operations, hence 'difficult and costly to administer and giving scope for fraud'. And to the extent that the CAP was 'aimed at social ends', such as providing an adequate income for smaller farmers, it was 'a very inefficient mechanism'.

There followed a devastating analysis of how several of the CAP's central pillars were not authorised by the Treaty of Rome. These included the centralised payment of subsidies through Brussels; the intervention system giving producers guaranteed payments; and the erection of tariff barriers against food imported from the outside world. All three main pillars of the CAP system were thus, strictly speaking illegal. And the document then concluded with an equally devastating analysis of how the CAP had failed to honour or be guided by any of its original five central objectives laid down in Treaty Article 39.

No one reading this comprehensive demolition of the CAP could have imagined that its authors could contemplate remaining party to such a catastrophic fiasco for a moment. Yet what was particularly remarkable about this document, submitted as a memorandum to the House of Lords European Communities Committee, was that it represented the official view of the British Government. It was written by officials of MAFF, the very ministry which made the workings of the CAP in Britain more complex and burdensome than anywhere else in the Community. And most chilling of all was the report's admission that, although Britain would 'take every opportunity to shift the CAP in the right direction', 'most other EU Governments appear strongly attached to the CAP in its present form' and would be unlikely to support any significant reform. In other words, even though the British Government recognised the CAP as a complete and utter disaster, there was no hope whatever that anything could be done about it.

10. The Single Market – The Great Illusion

The Single Market has not developed as we had hoped at the macro-economic level.

> Mario Monti, European Commissioner in charge of the Internal Market, quoted in *The European*, 13 June 1996

If [Economic and Monetary Union did not come about] in what trap would we then find ourselves .... There would be a great danger of seeing Europe drift progressively towards a free trade zone – precisely what we have been trying to avoid for the past 25 years.

> Commissioner Yves-Thibault de Silguy, in charge of preparations for EMU, *Le Syndrome de Diplodocus*, 1996

At the time it was conceived, the creation of the Single Market was supposed to be the crowning glory of the whole European experiment.

There was always something odd about this claim. When Britain joined the Common Market in 1973, we were told we were entering a customs union which would enable businesses to sell freely to '255 million potential customers in the biggest home market in the world'. It would provide the greatest boost to trade and prosperity in history. But we then discovered things were not quite so simple. Maybe those tariff barriers were down. But it seemed trade within this Common Market was not yet free at all, because all sorts of other obstacles to selling between one EC country and another remained. As Margaret Thatcher put it in her memoirs, *The Downing Street Years*:

> These came in a great variety of more or less subtle forms. Different national standards on matters ranging from safety to health regulations discriminating against foreign products, public procurement policies, delays and over-elaborate procedures at customs posts – all these and many others served to frustrate the the existence of a real Common Market.

So in the 1980s moves were made, with Britain enthusiastically to the fore, to create a true 'common market', or 'single market' as it was now known. However, it was also decided that this was so radical a step that it required a whole new treaty to be drawn up, revising the Treaty of Rome. Just why it should need a new treaty to achieve something which had already been declared to be the chief aim of the original version was never clearly explained. In fact the truth was that, in return for other Member States' commitment to this new Single Market, Britain had to accept a number of other changes which had nothing to do with liberating trade at all, but were intended to further the cause of greater political unity, such as a large increase in the areas of legislation over which individual countries could not exercise a veto. There was to be much greater use of 'qualified majority voting'. Such was the real hidden agenda behind the Single European Act, signed in 1986. Although it was sold to the British people as simply an act promoting a 'single market', its real purpose, as its title clearly indicated, was to further the cause of a 'Single Europe'.

The target date for the new market was to be '1992', or rather 1 January 1993. Officials from all the Member States converged on the Commission in Brussels to plan the biggest concentration of new legislation since the Common Market began. 218 'harmonising' directives and hundreds of regulations would be required to bring the new Single Market into being, creating a 'level playing field' on which all Member States would share the same rules and standards. There were to be directives imposing new 'harmonised' standards on health and safety, covering everything from fire risks to the proper use of VDUs and the correct height of office desks and chairs. There were to be 'harmonised' standards on food 'hygiene' and standards covering the manufacture of every conceivable type of product, from machinery to buses, from computers to toys, from small boats to gas heaters, from lifts to cricket pads. There were to be directives to ensure that all public contracts were thrown open to tenders from every part of the Community. Customs controls at frontiers were to be abolished, so that '70 million customs forms will be swept away'.

All this frenzy of legislation was going to open up the biggest market in the world – now grown to '370 million customers' – on a scale never seen before. Everything, but everything was to be 'harmonised' to create that 'level playing field'. Britain's trade and industry minister Lord Young waxed almost mystical about how it would soon be possible 'to buy a television in Oxford Street, go to Paris, plug it into the wall and get a picture' (no one told him he only needed to pay nine francs for an adaptor). Millions of pounds were spent by the DTI asking British businesses whether they were 'ready for 1992'. It was to be the biggest moment of economic liberation in history. But when the great day came, and at midnight on 31 December 1992 John Major and Edward Heath lit a puny little beacon in London to launch the new Market on its way, it wasn't much like that at all.

There were three chief ways in which the Single Market turned out to be very different from what everyone had been led to expect. The first was that, for many people, trading across frontiers inside the EC did not now mean less red tape but more. The second was that the deluge of new 'harmonising' legislation itself, far from making business easier, imposed on many industries bizarre new burdens which made trading much more laborious, even when they had no intention of exporting abroad. Thirdly, as many firms discovered, the dream of the 'level playing field' often turned out in practice to be a chimera. Many countries simply ignored it, continuing to protect their own industries by every means the Single Market had been meant to abolish.

10. The Single Market – The Great Illusion

The red tape explosion

One of the first businessmen to discover what the coming of the Single Market meant in practice was Noel Ayliffe-Jones, whose company Eurocourt made body armour in Salisbury, Wiltshire. The firm had been steadily building up its export sales, but a major problem was that every time it sent any of its products overseas, even a sample, it had to get an export licence from officials of the Department of Trade and Industry. This might take as long as three weeks, by which time customers had more than once decided to shop elsewhere. At least, thought Mr Ayliffe-Jones, the coming of the Single Market would remove all this bureaucracy when he was exporting to the EC. But when January 1993 arrived, he was told he would not only have to continue obtaining licences from the DTI. He would also now have to supply an additional mass of information to HM Customs and Excise as well. And they would then have to come to inspect each consignment before he was allowed to send it off. The coming of the Single Market thus made it harder for him to export to the EC than anywhere else in the world.

A year later the officials discovered a further way to hamper Eurocourt's export drive. He had a call from the Foreign and Commonwealth Office to say that, because each of his applications for an export licence now had to be looked at by five separate committees in the FCO, as well as those in the DTI, the processing of his export licences would no longer take three weeks. They would now take six.

Noel Ayliffe-Jones was far from being the only British businessman who found the coming of the Single Market suddenly made it harder to export to the rest of the EC. And one of the largest of these new obstacles was the peculiar way in which the EC had chosen to dismantle 'customs barriers'. One of Brussels' proudest boasts about the creation of the Single Market was that '70 million customs documents had been abolished'. No longer would exporters and importers have to go through all that time-consuming and costly paperwork every time they moved goods across a frontier. But of course the officials were not going to lose such a valuable record of just what goods were being traded across frontiers. How could they measure the Single Market's success without the statistics to prove it? The solution was simple. If customs officials no longer recorded the information, the responsibility for collecting it must be imposed on the traders themselves. Enshrined in EC Regulation 3330/91, this launched the Alice in Wonderland system known as 'Intrastats', short for 'Intra-Community trade statistics'.

Typical of thousands of firms horrified to see what this involved was Mountune Racing in Maldon, Essex, which supplied engines and parts for racing cars which had won over 100 rallies and championships all over the world. 40 per cent of its £2.2 million a year business was with other EC countries.

Before the Single Market, when firms like Mountune needed to prove that an order had been exported they merely required a simple note from a shipping agent. After 1 January 1993 this system still applied to exports outside the EU. But under the Intrastats system, firms exporting to countries inside the EU were not only now expected to compile a quarterly 'EC Sales Listing', recording each separate order, complete with such details as its value and the VAT number of each customer. Where the new system, as Mountune director John Mountain put it, became 'madness of the highest order' lay in the fact that firms like his also had to provide a monthly 'Supplementary Statistical Declaration'. This required sheaves of forms listing every single item supplied, under ten separate headings. These include not just the exact value and weight of each item, but a special eight-figure Commodity Reference number which had to be looked up in a 750-page book supplied by HM Customs and Excise.

For companies selling only a limited number of models, or for very large firms with their own built-in corporate bureaucracy, this procedure might not necessarily be too onerous. But for Mountune, supplying tens of thousands of specialised engine parts, the Intrastats system threatened a complete nightmare. A typical invoice, for an order to Germany, might include 170 separate items. Each had to be weighed and given its own commodity number, looked up in the 750-page catalogue, along with all the other information required. The cost of this system would be so prohibitive that it would scarcely be worth exporting within the EU at all.

When John Mountain took up the matter with MPs and ministers, he was astonished to find that 'no one seemed to know anything about Intrastats'. After a battle lasting many months, HM Customs and Excise grudgingly granted a 'temporary concession'. The firm would only have to provide full details on orders above £600 in value, which in the three years up to 1996 saved Mountune £100,000 in hiring extra staff. But in March that year a series of meetings were due to begin in Luxembourg at which EU officials planned to thrash out a 'definitive Intrastats system', which might well bring that 'temporary concession' to an end.

Before the Intrastats system was introduced in 1993, the officials of HM Customs and Excise had claimed it would not cost British firms more than £100 million a year. One big accountancy firm, Coopers and Lybrand, then predicted that its clients alone were expecting to have to pay an extra £30-40 million, while other trade sources estimated that the true overall cost to industry would be 'over £1 billion'.

Among tens of thousands of firms which could not escape the full impact of Intrastats was Vee Kay Industries, run by Kim Shimwell and her husband in Stockport, Cheshire, selling £1 million-worth of packaging machinery a year worldwide. 'This system', she told us in 1996, 'is driving me crazy.' It 'takes at least a day a month to complete the forms, even if all the necessary information is available. There is no logic to the codes we have to use. Looking them all up is like being in the secret service – and if we are late with the information, we are committing a criminal offence.' Mrs Shimwell then had to spend another day each month filling in her separate EC Sales List, requiring much the same information, but arranged in different categories. 'Much the same data also then has to go on our VAT form, so we are providing Customs with the same information three times.' Mrs Shimwell explained she had become so bogged down in 'all the paperwork required by the Single Market' that she was now encouraging her fellow-directors to sell the company's goods 'anywhere in the world apart from Europe. When we recently sold a machine to Norway it was such a relief not to have to fill in all those complicated forms.'

Mrs Shimwell's greatest dread was a planned new system whereby firms like hers would have to register separately for VAT in every country in the EU to which they sell. This would mean having to complete 14 additional VAT returns every three months, one for each Member State, even if during that time they had not sold a single item to that country.

It was perhaps hardly surprising that in 1996 even the EC's own monitoring unit on 'Small and Medium-size Enterprises' estimated that the total annual costs of 'administrative burdens for businesses in Europe', including Intrastats and all the rest, were now 'between 180 and 230 billion ecus', a total of some £170,000,000,000.

One-way harmonisation

An even greater burden laid on many industries by the Single Market was the need to comply with the vast range of new directives intended to harmonise laws and standards across the Community. There were two ways in which this hit British businesses particularly hard. First, as we have seen, this was because of the peculiar way in which Britain's civil servants chose to implement and enforce the Brussels legislation, so that for British firms the new regulations became much more onerous than elsewhere in the Community. This was particularly absurd when firms had to comply with Single Market legislation even though they had no intention of exporting their products, as in the case of those abattoirs forced to pay huge sums to comply with 'EC export standards' even though their trade often only covered a small local area in Britain itself. A crucial fact which was generally overlooked, in all the initial excitement over the Single Market, was that most of Britain's trade was not with overseas countries at all, but at home. Yet businesses were forced to comply with all the deluge of Single Market legislation, even when their products never left Britain. Only a fifth of Britain's business involved other countries, and only 9 per cent of all trade was with other countries in the EC. Yet for the sake of less than a tenth of all Britain's economic activity, hundreds of thousands of businesses now had to conform with a mass of rules which in theory had only been introduced to make trade easier across frontiers. This helped to explain why, in 1995, a survey on the Single Market carried out amongst its members by the Federation of Small Businesses showed only 5 per cent saying that the Single Market had helped them to increase their business, while no fewer than 60 per cent said that it had led to 'increased administrative burdens'. In a survey carried out by the Institute of Chartered Accountants in 1996, firms were asked to place in order the 20 factors which they regarded as posing the greatest obstacle to the expansion of their business. Easily topping the list, among 'medium-sized firms', was 'European Union legislation'.

The second way in which Britain was peculiarly affected by Euro-legislation derived from the fact that her industrial and business practices were often so different from those on the Continent. Yet, when it came to the drafting of directives, this almost invariably meant British businesses having to conform to the Continental mould, rather than the other way round.

A classic instance was the long-running saga over two proposed directives which first hit the headlines in 1994 because they would have had the effect of outlawing the production of double-decker buses. This threatened to strike a devastating blow at Britain not only because the double-decker was such a distinctively British institution, but because her bus manufacturers had recently been building up a fast-growing export trade to Singapore, Hong Kong and other countries in the Far East.

The threat from the first directive on 'the size and dimensions of vehicles', proposing to limit the maximum height of buses below normal double-decker level, was eventually dropped. Much more serious, however, was the likely impact of the Bus and Coach Harmonisation directive. The problem here was that the relevant committee in Brussels was proposing to standardise all bus making in the EC round what was basically a continental model, openly described by the Commission as 'the Euro-bus', and entirely alien to the forms of bus design developed to suit British needs.

On the continent the commonest city bus type is one with several doors, fewer seats and most passengers standing, often with two vehicles articulated together, rather like the familiar airport bus. Such was the model which Brussels, keenly supported by continental manufacturers, planned to impose as standard throughout the EC, and it was a prospect which filled Britain's industry with horror. For a start the directive would impose huge costs on British manufacturers as most of their existing bus and coach models were prohibited. Requirements for wider gangways, fewer seats and lower floor heights to accommodate the disabled would render some types of British bus, such as midi and mini-buses, too uneconomical to operate. As for double-deckers, even though these were no longer to be banned outright, new EC requirements, such as that any bus holding more than 90 passengers must have six doors and three escape windows, would make them unrecognisable. It was even at one time proposed that every double-decker should have two staircases, although eventually, by a typical Brussels compromise, this was reduced to a requirement for one-and-a-half staircases, to provide an emergency exit in case of accident.

Not only did the proposed directive threaten to impose costs on Britain's manufacturers amounting to billions of pounds, and to halt in its tracks Britain's export drive to the Far East, worth hundreds of millions of pounds a year; even in Britain itself operators feared the consequent reductions in passenger loads would add further billions of pounds onto their operating costs. The justification claimed for all this was safety, though British firms vainly argued that forcing more passengers to stand would have the reverse effect, increasing the risk of injury. But the directive's real purpose, the British manufacturers feared, was to promote the commercial interests of their continental competitors who lobbied so hard for it in Brussels, knowing that under the system of 'qualified majority voting' (QMV) they would almost certainly get their way.

This was by no means the only instance of continental interests trying to use Single Market legislation to undermine their British competitors. Another example which came to light in 1996 affected the fine art market, in which London firms like Sotheby's and Christie's led the world. One reason why Britain had become the world centre of modern art dealing was that London dealers did not have to pay royalties to living artists or their heirs every time a work was sold, the so-called *droit de suite* system in force on the continent. But, thanks to fierce lobbying by the continental dealers, a new directive was now proposed to 'eliminate distortions of trade' by enforcing the *droit de suite* system throughout the EC, the impact of which would be all the greater because of another new directive already in force extending copyright from 50 to 70 years after an artist's death. The sellers of almost any work by a major 20th-century artist would now have to hand over up to 4 per cent of the sale price. As everyone in the art world agreed, this simply meant that the centre of modern art-selling would move overnight from London to New York and Geneva, losing Britain much of a trade worth £200 million a year. British officials insisted they would oppose the directive to the end. But as usual, thanks to the fact that they were outnumbered under QMV, this looked like no more than whistling in the wind.

A third proposed new directive which would deal an even more devastating blow to Britain was that being drafted in Brussels in 1996 to regulate 'Company Law concerning Takeover Bids'. Such alarm did this proposal, 5147/96, arouse in the City of London and Britain's business community that it was even, for once, rejected out of hand in a report by the pro-Brussels members of the House of Lords committee set up to review EC legislation. The most damaging innovation, which would undermine the whole basis of that system of company takeovers which had provided such a powerful (if not always desirable) dynamic to Britain's economy, was the new rights it would give shareholders. If they could in any way demonstrate that they would have been better off if a takeover had not taken place, they could now go to law to demand compensation. Many feared that this would so complicate the process of takeover bids, with the possibility of complex and expensive litigation lasting for years, that it would deter many companies from launching them at all. In fact the Commission's proposals aroused criticism from many countries in the EC. But it seemed that the officials of DG II were determined to push them through. And no country would be more damaged than Britain, simply because it was another pecularity of UK practice that Britain had more industrial takeovers than all other EC countries put together.

The unlevel playing field

A third way in which the high-sounding theory of the Single Market fell apart was the mockery many countries made of its much-vaunted intention to eliminate the 'hidden protectionism' which enabled them to exclude goods from outside by imposing national standards cunningly devised so that only their own firms could meet them. The theory was that so long as products complied with the new EC standards laid down under Single Market legislation, goods could be freely exported anywhere in the EC. But a striking example of how many British firms found this system worked in practice was the bizarre tale of how Whale Tankers of Solihull managed to sell a solitary hazardous-waste tanker into France.

In 1989, when Whale was already selling road tankers to 70 countries round the world, managing director Mike Fisher determined to use the arrival of the forthcoming Single Market to crack the hardest nut of all, the notoriously restricted French market for hazardous waste-tankers. He sent his employees to learn French and embarked on a sales drive which, in the autumn of 1992, was finally rewarded with promise of success. He landed the first order for such a tanker ever given to a non-French company. Despite the coming of the Single Market, Mr Fisher knew how fiercely the French protected their own manufacturers and was therefore not entirely surprised to learn that the only person in France who could explain the necessary regulations was a Madame Berkman, who was 'on maternity leave'. Undeterred, Fisher went back to the relevant ministry, and was then shunted from one ministry to another. In the end, having slogged his way through a whole succession of further bureaucratic obstacles, he even managed to contact Mme Berkman herself, and was finally allocated another official, M. Darmian, who would personally take charge of his 'case'.

By March 1993 the tanker was ready, seemingly complying with every last French requirement. It only required to be driven to Dijon for its final inspection by M. Darmian. But on 23 March, with just three days to go, came a hitch. M. Darmian suddenly demanded a certificate from Thyssen's, the giant German steel firm, to show the exact batch number of some of the steel which had been used in the tanker. Since this had been bought through a UK stockholder it was quite a challenge. Nevertheless, by superhuman efforts, a surprised M. Darmian was supplied with the paperwork he required the following day.

On 25 March, with less than 24 hours to go, Darmian played what he must have thought his masterstroke. At 5.30 in the afternooon, when the tanker had already left the UK for its inspection in Dijon, Whale received a fax to say that one tiny piece of equipment had to be certified by a French insurance company to say it was 'unique'. This would have to be done by the following morning or the inspection would be cancelled – and all offices were now closed.

By dint of telephoning around France through the night, Whale obtained the piece of paper in the nick of time. On the morning of 26 March it was handed to an even more startled M. Darmian, who grudgingly gave the tanker his official stamp. But then, with not even a hint of a smile, he solemnly explained that the tanker could not be given its 'formal papers' without yet another certificate from Thyssen's, and if this was not handed over within days, the whole deal was off. After further volleys of faxes and phone calls, which even involved ringing Thyssen's managing director on his car phone as he sped down an autobahn, the final miracle was achieved. It seemed M. Darmian had no further shots in his locker. Whale Tankers had become the first foreign firm ever to sell a hazardous-waste tanker in France, and now they had cracked the riddle, they hoped to sell many more.

But their triumph was shortlived. Days later Whale was told that the French regulations were to be changed, and 'no documents are available' to say what new specifications would be required. What annoyed Mr Fisher even more was that Michael Heseltine, President of the Board of Trade, should have chosen that very week to exhort his local Birmingham Chamber of Industry and Commerce to 'get out there and start selling' in the new 'Europe without barriers to trade'.

The great 'CE mark' fiasco

A glaring illustration of these three central failings in the Single Market system all in operation at once – the explosion in unnecessary paperwork, ludicrously cumbersome 'harmonisation' round some new supposed 'EC standard', then deliberate sabotage of the system by countries which still excluded goods from outside by continuing to apply their own rules – was the so-called 'CE mark' system.

This was introduced as a cornerstone of the Single Market in a series of so-called 'New Approach' directives, making it illegal to sell a vast range of goods unless they carried a 'CE mark', for Communauté Européene (as was pointed out, this seemed to have replaced the old common law principle of 'Caveat Emptor'). By supposedly guaranteeing that they had been tested to meet some new Community-wide safety standard, the idea was that this would enable the goods to be exported freely anywhere in the Community, although it equally applied to goods produced only for sale in the home market.

In our Prologue we glimpsed several examples of this CE mark system in action, such as the story of how the Liquid Gas Appliances directive 90/396 affected the only six tiny firms in Europe making specialised gas heaters for use in greenhouses. All six happened to be British. As the regulations prescribed, Hotbox Heaters of Lymington paid £20,000 to a Dutch-owned test house to qualify for a CE mark, fondly imagining this would now entitle the firm to sell its heaters throughout the EC – only to be told that, since EC countries used no fewer than 37 separate varieties of liquid gas, it would now have to pay out hundreds of thousands of pounds more for its heaters to be individually tested for each gas. Hotbox Heaters abandoned all attempts to sell its products in Europe and concentrated on its increasingly successful export trade to the USA, Africa and Asia where no such regulations applied.

The Toy Safety directive, 88/378, which made it illegal to sell new toys without the CE mark also threw up a host of absurdities. But these in the main resulted, as we have seen, from cockeyed enforcement of the measure in Britain itself, as in the 'Pig's Eye and Pipecleaner' case or the ban on charity shops selling second-hand toys which resulted from the DTI misapplying the directive. Indeed the only example involving exports which we came across in our investigations was that of a Clwyd firm, Piggery Potteries, which made novelty china nightlights for children's bedrooms in the shape of animals. Trading standards officials in another part of Britain suspended sale of these lamps for failing to comply with the Toy Safety Regulations, forcing the firm to the brink of closure, but the company continued to export its products to the continent, where they were sensibly regarded not as toys but as perfectly safe bedside lamps.

An example of CE marking with more serious application was the Machinery Directive 89/392. This laid down that all machines sold in the EC, from tiny car-jacks to huge processing plants, should carry the CE mark to show they had been tested for safety purposes. In the case of 'dangerous machinery' listed in Annex IV this testing had to be carried out by an independent test house, and under the UK regulations each machine also had to be accompanied by a detailed 'technical manual' up to 60 pages long.

These requirements might have been acceptable for a large firm mass-producing, say, tens of thousands of lawn mowers, which would need only pay to test each of its models once. But for smaller, more specialised firms with much shorter production runs, possibly assembling each machine separately to fit an individual customer's needs, the new regulations were a nightmare. For instance, Shemach Engineering of Castle Bromwich, near Birmingham, employing only 15 people, was the only British-owned firm producing custom-built press brakes, machines for bending metal. Under the new rules, which came into force on 1 January 1995, not only would each model have to be sent away for testing at a certified 'test house', at a cost of up to £20,000 a time, but each time a design was modified, to suit the needs of a particular customer, it would have to go through the elaborate testing procedures again. Managing director Victor Odell estimated that this might have cost his company £600,000 a year, more than its entire annual turnover.

Mr Odell's real problem, however, was that, six months after the new regulations came into force, he had still been unable to find a test house which could even quote him a figure for testing his machines. Six years after the directive had been issued there were still no agreed 'European safety standards' for the machines to be tested to. The only ones available were the highly-reliable British standards already in existence long before Europe began to interfere, to which Mr Odell's machines all conformed anyway. Despite repeated approaches to officials of the Department of Trade and Industry and the Health and Safety Executive, Mr Odell was unable to get any guidance as to what standards the testing houses should work to. Meanwhile Spanish and Italian machines, proudly carrying the CE mark, were now quite legally being sold in Britain, even though many would not meet the British safety standards.

Eventually Mr Odell challenged the Health and Safety Executive by telling them the new system was so unworkable that he would have to continue to sell his products without the CE mark. 'If necessary,' he said, 'I would even be prepared to go to prison.' Although the HSE's chief executive Mr John Rimington formally reminded Mr Odell that, if he wished to continue selling his machines, he was required to 'secure examination by a notified body', there was little he could do, since the 'EC standards' were simply not available. Fortunately Mr Odell had no need to get a CE mark to sell to any other EC countries, since all his exports were to the United States, which took no notice of the EC legislation.

The situation was one of complete confusion, and Mr Odell was far from alone. Tony Curry, technical director of Matcon Engineering, making discharge valves in Moreton-on-the-Marsh, told us the cost of collating technical files to compy with the CE system had 'increased by half the amount of time, effort and cost' spent by his firm's design team. 'We are worn down with sheer frustration tinged with anger,' he said, not least at the vagueness of DTI officials as to what technical data the new legislation required. 'I was amazed by their ignorance. No one knew what I was talking about.'

On the other hand, when the DTI was asked why other countries in Europe seemed to be getting away with putting CE marks on machines without any proper testing, a spokeswoman merely commented 'we cannot go on the basis that because Germany or Italy has not implemented a directive, nor should we. It doesn't work like that.' In fact another firm, experiencing similar difficulties in discovering what standards its woodworking machinery should be tested to, told us that when it exported machines to Germany, the CE mark would be irrelevant anyway. 'They still insist on all machines being tested to their own safety standards, which are much more severe even than ours here in Britain. They go completely over the top, adding around £1,000 to the price of each machine.'

Remarkably similar confusion, if not worse, surrounded the implementation of the Electromagnetic Compatibility (EMC) directive, 89/336, which came into force in Britain on 1 January 1996. Again this centred on the DTI's inability to provide any clear standard for testing electronic equipment to ensure that it did not cause interference (in fact the devices most likely to cause dangerous interference, mobile phones and radio transmitters, were excluded from the directive). Again the worst problems were faced not by large firms, with long production runs for items like videos, but by the thousands of smaller firms which produced specialised assemblies, often custom-made for a single customer, each of which to qualify for its CE mark would have to be sent off for testing by an 'approved test house' at up to £1,000 a day.

In the months before the regulations were due to come into force we were contacted by many such firms (this type of specialised small-scale electronics is a field in which Britain is a world leader), each recounting hair-raising stories of the chaos and expense the regulations were already inflicting on them. In June 1995 a letter from the ex-managing director of a successful firm specialising in electronic controls for wheelchairs described the situation as 'a bizarre shambles which (like the ERM) will cause untold havoc, destroying thousands of products and businesses and tens of thousands of jobs, before collapsing ignominiously in two or three years' time under the weight of its own anomalies. It is impossible to understand how grown men can (apparently seriously) contemplate and legislate for anything so manifestly unrealistic (indeed puerile), threatening criminal charges over requirements which in most cases are simply incapable of definition or evaluation.' Even a civil servant who worked on the drafting of the regulations privately confessed they were 'incomprehensible even to insiders, very hurriedly drafted in order to meet a political deadline and had caused great confusion in the industry'.

Almost the only virtue of the EMC regulations was that they were so clumsy and indefensible that, as 1996 went on, there were signs that the Government itself was not eager to see them enforced too zealously. But by this time huge damage had already been done, and not just by the expense and untold man-hours already wasted by firms trying to work out how to comply with such impossible requirements. Some of the worst damage resulted from contracts lost because larger companies refused to accept electronic equipment without a CE mark which was virtually unobtainable anyway. The few 'approved test houses' in operation had done such roaring trade they had waiting lists of up to two years. We heard of several small firms closing down or moving abroad. One company told us how one of its largest customers, which had been switching over to electronic controls for its fleet of cranes and earth-moving equipment had decided to phase these out and return to less sophisticated and less safe hydraulic controls, simply because of the expense and confusion of the CE system. The havoc inflicted on British industry by this episode was incalculable. And it was scarcely consolation to know that many other EC countries, most of whose electronics industries were much less advanced, had not bothered to enforce the EMC directive at all because it was too complicated.

Another directive which threw up innumerable anomalies was that on Personal Protective Equipment, 89/686, not least because this covered such a vast range of products. Some of these were just silly nonsenses, like the CE-marked wellington boots bought by a reader which came with a 24-page 'User's Manual' instructing purchasers how to use wellies in all the languages of the Community (the Finnish for 'user's manual' is Kayttajalle). This included such invaluable information as that the 'heel energy absorption' of the boots equated to '20 joules', while their 'penetration resistance is up to 1100 Newton'.

Some were more aggravating, like the variety of clips and other safety equipment no longer available to rock-climbers, because of the prohibitive cost of compliance with CE marking in a market which hardly achieves mass-sales.

A London dentist Brian Karet discovered the Brussels officials had specifically included mouthguards on the list of products which required testing by an approved test house at a cost of up to £1,000. Since the average mouthguard is individually made and costs only around £35, this would put up their price by 2,850 per cent. After more than a year of trying to get this nonsense sorted out, he was finally assured by Brussels that mouthguards could be taken off the list, and could now be approved very much more cheaply under a different directive by the Medical Devices Agency. But since the MDA officials would make very little income from approving mouthguards, they refused to take the job on. It thus remained a criminal offence for Mr Karet to supply his patients with mouthguards unless each had been given an individual CE mark at a cost of up to £1,000.

Some anomalies thrown up by the new PPE regulations were still more serious. We discovered, for instance, that manufacturers of 'coveralls' were advertising some of their 'CE marked' products as suitable for use when sheep-dipping with organo-phosphorous (OP) chemicals. These OPs had caused irreparable damage to the health of thousands of farmers and others, and the directive specifically laid down that protective equipment for use with dangerous chemicals could only be given a CE mark when it had been specifically tested for each chemical by an independent test house. The tests had not met these requirements, and when we contacted the manufacturers they confirmed that they had only tested the coveralls themselves 'in house'. When this apparent breach of the law was put to the Health and Safety Executive, normally only too zealous in enforcing safety law but with a conspicuously poor record on anything to do with OPs, a spokesman commented that 'the CE mark is merely a marketing issue'. Yet that same week a row was raging in the cricketing world over the revelation that, under the same PPE legislation, almost all makes of cricket helmet on the market were illegal, leaving manufacturers 'open to legal action from players injured while using them'. This was because only one make of helmet had been tested by 'an independent inspection body', and the European standards body CEN had ruled that, although it was all right to test pads and batting gloves 'in house', for helmets 'third-party verification' was definitely necessary. So for sports equipment, the officials were adamant that independent testing was required. But when it came to protection against chemicals which had destroyed the health of thousands of victims, they were happy to regard the same law as 'merely a marketing issue'.

As usual, however, what particularly frustrated many British firms about this Single Market legislation was the way it was being disregarded elsewhere in the EC. In Aspatria, Cumbria, Graham Travell ran a small firm, Alpine Marketing, making a special energy-absorbent padding used in protective clothing for motorcyclists. When the PPE regulations came into force, the firm spent over £20,000 to have its padding tested to the required CE safety standard. Although this increased its price substantially, the firm decided to use its CE mark to launch a major sales drive in Germany. But Alpine's German distributors were informed by their trade association that 'Germany does not accept this directive'. Therefore the British product could no longer be marketed in Germany at all. Mr Travell then learned that a German firm had geared up to make almost identical padding for a well-known German manufacturer of motorcycle clothing whose products could then be freely imported into Britain because they carried the CE mark which the UK officials would accept without question, because those were the rules of the Single Market.

A last example of the CE mark system, the full impact of which has not yet hit Britain, is the Recreational Craft directive, 94/25. This lays down that it will be illegal to sell any small boat for recreational use unless it carries a CE mark to show that it complies with 50 separate safety standards. These cover every conceivable aspect of boat design, and are of such bewildering complexity that most practical boat builders, however experienced, can scarcely make head or tail of them. Experts who have examined them in detail, however, are convinced of two things: first, that whoever drew up these standards knew so little about boat design they might never have been in one; and, secondly, that several requirements will help to make certain small craft less safe. The British team responsible for negotiating this highly technical directive in Brussels included officials from the DTI, the Department of the Environment, the British Waterways Board, the National Rivers Authority and a 'big ships man' from the Department of Transport, but not one with direct experience of small boats. In 1990, when the directive emerged from technical committee discussions to be considered by the Economic and Social Committee, Robin Sjoberg, a senior officer both of the Royal Yachting Association and the European Boating Association, representing ten million owners of small boats, travelled to Brussels in the hope of introducing some realism into their deliberations. He found a room full of 'officials and lawyers'. Although not a single genuine expert on small boat design was present, he was peremptorily informed he had no status at the meeting and ordered to leave the room.

Such is how the system which produced those 218 directives considered necessary to set up the Single Market works in practice.

The 'procurement' fiasco

As a final example we turn to what was promised in advance to be one of the Single Market's greatest triumphs, one of the central pillars on which the whole institution would rest. This was the principle that public contracts for goods and services would have to be open to tenders from all over the Community. The intention was that this would 'open up trade' and 'promote competition' like almost nothing else. If a public body of any kind wished to buy ambulances or dustcarts or large consignments of filing cabinets, it would have to advertise in a special daily edition of the Commission's Official Journal, inviting tenders from throughout the EC. Bidders would have to provide details to prove they were bona fide, but the contract must then go to the lowest bidder.

In due course three 'procurement directives' emerged, relating to contracts for public utilities (90/531), public services (92/50) and public works (93/36), and it did not take long for the usual discrepancies to emerge between the theory of any Euro-legislation and how it works out in practice.

A first anomaly came to light when we heard from the angry managing director of a Birmingham firm, Latch and Bachelor, which for years had been supplying Yorkshire Electricity with modest amounts of steel cable worth around £1,500 a year. The firm was now told that, under the Public Utilities Directive, it must now fill in a detailed 13-page questionnaire and supply large quantities of paperwork, such as a copy of its 'Environment Policy' and five copies of the annual report and accounts for each of the previous three years. If all this was not received by 1 January 1993, the firm would receive no further no contract. What was odd about this was that, as the EC directive clearly stated, it did not apply to contracts below the value of 400,000 ecus (£330,000). But it soon became clear that Yorkshire was far from alone in not reading the rules correctly. All over Britain firms were being bombarded with similar requests on contracts way below the threshold. A Kent consultant who did work worth £5,000 a year for London Underground was asked to complete a questionnaire of no fewer than 56 pages. An Isle of Wight firm Davall Relays was asked to supply yards of paperwork for a Ministry of Defence contract worth a mere £51. This was so patently ridiculous that managing director Tony Gower replied by imposing his own barrage of conditions on the ministry, in a superb parody of official prose.

As usual with Single Market legislation, anomaly number two arose when the dutiful way it was obeyed by the British was contrasted with the attitude of other Member States. In 1995 British engineers were surprised to observe that nearly half the engineering design contracts advertised in the EC's Official Journal came from Britain. In other words Britain was far more compliant than anyone else. But when the £1.2 million contract for the organ in a new Manchester concert hall went to a Danish company, British organ builders were outraged. They said they could have built the organ for much less, but had never been given a chance to tender. It was then revealed that, because the organ was part-subsidised by the EC, the Central Manchester Development Corporation had accepted as a condition that the contract should only be advertised in the Official Journal, a periodical few British organ builders normally read.

A third anomaly was the way the British Government appeared happily to ignore the very requirements it was so keen to enforce on everyone else. In 1994 it was revealed that the Government was routinely sidestepping the Public Services Directive in awarding computer consultancy contracts worth millions to a favoured few firms without going through the required procedure. A particular row arose over a substantial contract given by officials of the Department of Social Security to the Government's favourite consultants, Andersen's. A spokesman explained the DSS did not need to advertise because it had a 'framework agreement' with 34 'preferred suppliers'. This seemed an odd way to demonstrate ministers' insistence that the British should be the 'good boys of Europe' when it came to obeying directives. The British people must obey, but not it seemed their Government.

But the point which more than anything exposed what a charade the procurement system was in practice might best be illustrated by an episode in the summer of 1996, when holidaymakers travelling to South Wales were caught up in long delays on link road between the M5 motorway and the newly opened Second Severn Bridge. This was because millions of pounds of repair work were having to be carried out on steel plating supplied by a Spanish steel company, Ensidesa of Madrid. Quality assessors had found this to be seriously defective, even dangerous. Wrongly constructed steel plates had been loosely welded over to conceal the fact they did not fit together properly. When the new bridge was put out to tender this had been advertised in the Official Journal and several big contracts had been awarded to Italian and Spanish companies, because they put in offers much lower than their British competitors. Under the rules these had to be accepted. But the highly-efficient British steel industry pointed out that the Italians and Spanish were only able to offer such low prices because they benefited from vast hidden state subsidies. In 1995 Ensidesa, the company which supplied steelwork for the M5 link road, made an £800 million loss which was simply written off by Spanish taxpayers.

This was not the first time similar errors had come to light. A bridge on the M25 was long out of service because of faulty steelwork supplied by a subsidised Italian company. British steel firms complained they had lost hundreds of millions of pounds through such unfair competition from subsidised continental competitors – and this in turn raises what had become one of the most glaring of all anomalies in the Single Market.

The great subsidies racket

One of the key principles laid down in the Treaty of Rome had been an agreement to declare illegal any practices which would bring about the 'restriction or distortion of competition within the common market'. Article 92 had in particular made it clear that this applied to any Member State giving subsidies to its own industries in such a way as to promote unfair competition with those of other countries.

With the coming of the Single Market and the 'level playing field', it might have been supposed that these solemnly agreed rules would be enforced more rigorously than ever. Yet one of the greatest scandals of the years after 1987 was not just the extent to which certain countries continued illegally to pour huge subsidies into their own ailing industries, enabling them to undercut competitors from countries which abided by the rules, but also the way the Commission took so little effective action to intervene. The inefficient, over-manned and heavily subsidised steel industries of Spain, Italy and Germany provided one instance, to the particular rage of the British steel industry which, after being painfully weaned off subsidies and over-manning in the 1980s, had been transformed into the most efficient and competitive in the world. In 1994 British Steel was so frustrated by the rampant distortions Brussels was allowing to persist in the European steel market that it announced it could not afford to build its major new £100 million rolling plant, providing hundreds of jobs, in Britain. To 'reduce its exposure to Europe', the new plant would be re-sited in Alabama, USA, where a genuine free market still existed.*

Another grotesque distortion of competition was that created in air travel, by the shameless way in which certain governments continued to pour subsidies into their inefficient and over-manned airlines. Between 1991 and 1994 Sabena, Iberia, Aer Lingus, Portugal's TAP, Greece's Olympic and Air France between them received nearly £6 billion in subsidies, which alone enabled them to offer fares competitive with those of unsubsidised and incomparably more efficient carriers such as British Airways and KLM. Yet in 1994, only months after a so-called 'Committee of Wise Men' appointed by Brussels had condemned such persistent flouting of the Treaty of Rome, the Commission meekly approved the biggest subsidy of all, a £2.4 billion pay-ment by the French Government to Air France. In 1995 BA and six other private airlines, with the backing of their governments, took the issue to the ECJ in a bid to get Air France to pay back the money.

The French Government seemed particularly adept in persuading the Brussels officials to approve huge subsidies which flouted the law in this way, to recipients ranging from their lame-duck computer company Bull to their leading bank Credit Lyonnais which in 1996, with Commission approval, was given subsidies of £500 million. In the same year it actually came to light that the leading German shipbuilding group Bremer Vulkan had 'misappropri-

---

* It was noticeable how British ministers carefully avoided any mention of this damning decision by British Steel. As minister for trade and industry, Michael Heseltine was only too keen to publicise any examples of major foreign companies investing in Britain, which he invariably ascribed to the attractions of winning 'access to the Single Market' (although this usually featured well down the list of reasons given by the companies themselves). In October 1994 Heseltine and other ministers made enormous play with the decision by Samsung, the 14th largest company in the world, to build a large new plant on Teesside, providing 3,000 jobs. Although a major factor in Samsung's decision was the offer of £58 million of British taxpayers' money, all the official emphasis was placed on how this was another benefit derived from Britain 'being in Europe'. But there was complete silence from Mr Heseltine at the same time about the decision to close down ICI's huge nylon fibre plant at Wilton, also on Teeside, turning over £140 million a year and providing 760 jobs. This was a direct result of EC legislation, because the plant was responsible for most of Britain's emissions of the 'greenhouse gas' nitrous oxide, and Britain was now exceeding the quota of such emissions it was allowed under directive 84/360. The plant's new owners Dupont were therefore moving it to Alsace, because France, with a much smaller chemical industry, still had plenty of N_2O 'quota' to spare. The global quantity of 'greenhouse gas' emissions would thus not be affected. But thanks to the System, Britain lost 760 jobs and a significant chunk of exports, while her keenly Europhile trade and industry minister looked the other way, hoping no one would notice the glaring absurdity.

ated' DM850 million of 'guarantees' given by the German Government to prop up its shipyards in the former East Germany, by diverting them instead to save its main West German operation from bankruptcy. The Commission had approved the original 'extension of credit', but when it was discovered that this had been put to a different and quite illegal purpose, Brussels took no action, merely agreeing to 'consider conditions' on which the deal might retrospectively be approved.

Yet only a few years earlier, in Britain in 1988, two companies had been eagerly vying to buy North-East Shipbuilders, one of the most efficiently modernised shipyards in Europe. At the last minute the company was told to its astonishment that the sale could not be 'permitted' by Brussels. It seemed that when, the previous year, the British Government had sold off the Govan shipyard on the Clyde to a Norwegian company for £6 million, Britain's trade minister Kenneth Clarke had been allowed by the Commission to provide £12 million of taxpayers' money as an additional 'sweetener'. But Brussels only permitted this on conditions so secret that even Clarke's ministerial successor Tony Newton had not been told about them. These conditions, intended to ensure that shipbuilding facilities were 'fairly distributed' round the Community, meant that if the sale of the Sunderland shipyard went ahead, the Govan deal would have to be 'called in'. Newton only learned of this during an interview in Brussels with Trade Commissioner Sir Leon Brittan. He was shocked. The highly efficient Sunderland yard was thus forced to close altogether, though it did not need a penny in subsidies. Hundreds of skilled men were put on the dole. And, as an extraordinary denouement, millions of pounds worth of expensive modern machinery then had to be sold off at knockdown prices, because it was another of the conditions imposed by Sir Leon's officials in Brussels that none of the equipment could be sold for the purpose for which it was designed – building ships.

*

Two final points must be made about the sad mess so much of the Single Market was turning out to be in practice.

The first is that, although every point made in this chapter was public knowledge, not one was ever acknowledged by British ministers. Because Britain 'supported' the Single Market, it had come to occupy a position of unique sanctity. However often it could be shown that its operations were riddled with anomalies, that British businesses were suffering immense damage, both from the failure of other EC countries to obey the rules and from the ludicrously over-zealous fashion in which these were applied by Britain's own officialdom, the Single Market was the one aspect of the EC regarded as above all criticism. Belief in it had been elevated into an article of almost religious faith.

An example of this refusal to accept even a whisper of criticism came in the House of Lords on 7 June 1995, when Lord Pearson of Rannoch tried to pin down foreign minister Baroness Chalker into conceding that not every single British industry had enjoyed unalloyed benefit from Britain's membership of the EC. He named three groups, all conspicuously under severe threat: bus manufacturers, glasshouse lettuce growers and fishermen. Lady Chalker brushed this aside and immediately went into the Government's familiar incantation of how British 'action at Community level has created the Single Market which is of huge benefit to both British businesses and consumers'. Pressed further, she again carefully avoided mentioning the specific examples, but suggested that, if British businesses did not like legislation from Brussels intended 'to encourage free trade' they had 'nobody to blame but themselves'. They should put their point 'directly to government' (all three industries had in fact repeatedly made their case to government, with no effect whatever). For much of the rest of the debate, Lady Chalker centred her case on the way the Single Market had 'so greatly expanded the opportunities for British firms', repeatedly citing 'a recent CBI survey' which 'showed that 71 per cent of firms were enjoying greater trading opportunities with Europe due to the Single Market'. What she did not mention was that the survey in question was answered by only 7 per cent of the CBI's members; that an even larger percentage of firms said they were actively seeking greater trading opportunities outside the EC; and that in general the answers were a great deal less favourable to the Single Market than Lady Chalker implied (we shall take a closer look at the peculiar way in which the CBI was used to play a leading role in promoting the EC cause in a later chapter).

Nevertheless here was the real point. In 1973 the British people had been assured that joining the Common Market would greatly increase Britain's trade with Europe. They had been told this again with the coming of the Single Market. And so it turned out. Britain's exports to the EC did increase substantially. But the EC's exports to Britain increased even more. Just before joining in 1973, Britain still enjoyed a trading surplus with the Common Market countries. But from then on her trade with the EC ran progressively into the red, to the point where by 1995 she had run up an accumulated deficit over 22 years of £100,000,000,000. Yet so well was the UK doing in the rest of the world market that she now enjoyed a trading surplus with every continent, except Europe. That Common or Single Market had turned out to be a very good bargain indeed – for our continental competitors. But this was not something any British minister would admit to, because it contradicted the central article of their faith.

11. Earthquakes for Everyone

England is insular and maritime ... her nature, her structure, her economic position differ profoundly from those of the continentals.
President de Gaulle, explaining why he could not accept Britain's application to join the Common Market, 14 January 1963

In 1995 Britain's engineers stared in amazement at something called 'Eurocode 8' which proposed that all new structures in the European Community larger than a private house should be designed to withstand a major earthquake. As NCE, the journal of the Institution of Civil Engineers, pointed out, the problem was not so much the cost of making the buildings earthquake proof. It would be the tens of millions of pounds a year added to design costs by having to run the drawings for every structure through the complex computerised tests required to show that it complied with the new Euro-specifications.

Of course it was accepted that not every part of Europe was quite so much at risk from major earthquakes as Italy and Greece. But in the name of 'harmonisation' and the 'level playing field', the officials argued, it would be unfair if all countries were not made subject to the same rules.

A year or two earlier owners of grouse moors and deer forests had stared in similar amazement at a draft of something called the Wild Game Meat directive. This proposed that anyone slaughtering game birds or animals intended for sale to the public would have to ensure that a vet was present to inspect each animal at point of kill, and that its meat was immediately refrigerated. These were provisions which had simply been transferred by DG VI officials from the standard form of other meat hygiene directives. At least on this occasion the absurdity of shooting parties having to hump a refrigerator 3,000 feet up a Scottish mountain, accompanied by a vet who was meant to carry out an ante-mortem inspection of every wild stag before the stalker pressed the trigger, became so self-evident that the proposals were dropped.

What is remarkable about the Euro-system in action is that, wherever one touches it, the same sorts of absurdities present themselves. The overall theme of this part of the book has been twofold. First, in each chapter, we have been looking at a specific example of a system which is constantly trying to impose on the world some tortuous bureaucratic framework, dreamed up by officials in their concrete equivalents of ivory towers, which does not begin to correspond with the complexities of the real world. Secondly, it is a system which, with quite baffling ingenuity and determination, the British then contrive to operate uniquely to their disadvantage. Again and again it is as if we are looking at a jigsaw puzzle which not only does not fit properly together on its own account; but which then makes Britain appear like a piece belonging to some different puzzle altogether. In this chapter we look at other instances of how the only lesson to be learned from trying to squeeze the world into a uniform, homogenised mould is that it can never work.

The banning of the English oak

One celebrated instance of how Britain was made to fit into a peculiarly inappropriate continental set of rules was the strange story of the English oak trees and the directive on Forestry Reproductive Materials, 66/404. This was a particularly odd piece of legislation because it was based on a German forestry law of 1963, which in turn was copied from a so-called Forestry Race Law introduced by the Nazis in 1934 to preserve the genetic purity of forests in the Third Reich. The intention of the Brussels directive was exactly the same, to preserve the genetic purity of trees. And of course when Britain joined, it was translated into regulations by the UK authorities and applied more rigorously than anywhere else in Europe.

The problem was that the British oak tree, that symbol of gnarled and sturdy national character down the ages, has a natural tendency to hybridise. This meant that only comparatively few stands of oaks in British woods and forests met the exacting purity standards laid down by the directive Brussels had borrowed from Hitler. And it was now a criminal offence to sell acorns from any trees which did not meet those standards. The result was that British commercial growers, who traditionally used only British acorns, were forced to import them. By 1995, according to MAFF, more than three-quarters of all new oaks in Britain's forests came from acorns imported from abroad, mainly from eastern Europe. Experts like Dr Andrew Gordon of Forestart warned that, because these were not so well adapted to British conditions as native oaks, this was already leading to problems. In years to come, it was not impossible that Britain's oak forests would be prey to a disaster comparable to the one which in the 1970s devastated her elm trees.

Euro-seeds only

The curious fate of the English oak was only a tiny part of one of the most grandiosely ambitious of all the utopian schemes dreamed up by those officials in Brussels. This was the attempt to impose the most rigorous controls on the varieties of plant seeds permitted to be sold in the Community. As so often, the idea behind this seemed well-meaning enough, to prevent the spread of plant diseases and to protect consumers against 'inferior' varieties. But in practice, as so often, this bureaucratic Grand Design threatened to produce results exactly the opposite of those intended.

Under this unbelievably complex scheme, which required nearly 600 directives, regulations and other pieces of legislation to set up, for any variety of seed to win official acceptance required extensive testing, with the payment of an initial fee as high as £3,000 plus a further annual fee up to £700 to keep it on the list. This inevitably meant that it was no longer economical to keep most varieties of crop plants, vegetables, fruits or flowers on the market. Tens of thousands of traditional varieties disappeared, as it became a criminal offence to sell them. For instance, between 95 and 98 per cent of all the 2,500 naturally occurring varieties of tomato were banned, because it would not have paid any seed firm to keep them on the list.

Inevitably this system threw up countless individual anomalies. In 1978 an old lady named Miss Cutbush living in Kent gave Jeremy Cherfas of the Henry Doubleday Research Association four broad beans of a carefully-preserved variety which had probably been grown in English cottage gardens since Elizabethan times. When Mr Cherfas grew them, they turned out to be particularly delicious. However, under the new EC rules, it was now a criminal offence for anyone to sell these beans. But this only applied if they were sold for eating. They could still legally be sold for ornamental purposes, for anyone who merely wished to admire their beautiful crimson flowers. However, as soon as the beans themselves appeared, the gardener was in theory obliged to throw them away.

In Oxted, Surrey, Colin Simpson ordered an old variety of tomato seeds from an American catalogue. When he grew them on his allotment, he was amazed by their superb flavour. Everyone who tried them agreed they had never eaten tomatoes with such taste. So Mr Simpson advertised some of his seeds for sale. This brought down on him the wrath of the MAFF's Seeds and Plant Health Inspectorate because they were not on the EC-approved list. After a long battle with the officials, Mr Simpson was eventually allowed a compromise. He was allowed to germinate the seeds himself and then sell them to the public as tiny plants, because this was not considered to break the law.

The most serious consequence of the EC's seed control scheme, however, was that by making it so expensive to keep any particular variety on the list, seed merchants inevitably concentrated only on those varieties which suited the homogenised needs of commercial growers. These might well lack many of the qualities, like taste, which made them popular with amateur gardeners, for whom seedsmen could no longer afford to cater. The result was that, as those thousands of crop, vegetable and fruit varieties disappeared from the market, the surviving gene pool shrank dramatically. As growers became dependent on only a comparatively tiny reservoir of varieties, what many experts feared was that, if these were attacked by diseases, no genetic alternatives would be left to fall back on. In other words, the EC's farmers and growers might ultimately be left much more vulnerable to precisely those genetic deficiencies which the scheme was designed to eliminate.

Copyright über alles

In January 1996 many publishers, theatres, orchestras, and owners of photographic archives were landed with all sorts of complicated and sometimes costly problems by the new Duration of Copyright and Rights in Performance Regulations 1996. Traditionally in Britain, and by international agreement in most other countries, copyright had lasted for 50 years after the artist's death. But suddenly this had been extended to 70 years, which meant that huge quantities of books, music, films, pictures and photographs which had gone out of copyright were now brought back into it again. This affected all the writers and artists who had died between 1926 and 1946, including such famous names as Elgar, Holst, Delius, Thomas Hardy, James Joyce, Virginia Woolf and H.G. Wells. The reason for the change was to comply with an EC directive, 93/98. But particularly odd was the reason for this directive. The only country in Europe which had a 70-year copyright rule was Germany, and this had come about for a very particular historical reason. So many German artists and writers had died young or prematurely in World War Two that it was thought only fair that copyright on their works should be extended from 50 years to 70, so their heirs might enjoy the same benefits they might have expected if the artists had lived to a more normal span. But 50 years after the war, just as the reasons for this were fading into history, all other countries in the EC were compelled by Brussels to fall in behind Germany.

Offshore islands

Someone who unwittingly stumbled over one of the EC's stranger anomalies was John Buckland of Fishbourne, Sussex, who for some years placed regular orders with a Channel Islands firm for Guernsey sweaters to sell in his museum shop. But in 1996 he was surprised to be told that his latest order had been sent to the HM Customs and Excise Parcel Concentration Office in Southampton and could not be released until he had filled in 'European Community Form C88A'.

When Mr Buckland obtained this form he discovered that he needed to fill in no fewer than 56 boxes, with the aid of a twelve-page explanatory booklet. But one thing this didn't explain was the meaning of five different codes, such as 'Community Code' and 'Country of Origin Code', without which it was impossible to complete the form. He rang HM Customs to ask whether they knew what these codes were? 'Oh yes,' they replied. 'But under regulations we are not allowed to tell you. You will have to look them up at a public library.' The nearest library which held the codes, Mr Buckland was told, was Fareham, so he had to spend several hours on a 50-mile round trip to obtain the information.

Mr Buckland was staggered that the EC could have been allowed to impose such crazy red tape on trade between Britain and Guernsey. As he pointed out in a letter to his MP, 'The Channel Islands have been virtually part of the United Kingdom for nearly 1,000 years. No bunch of unelected foreigners have ever been allowed to interfere with our trade before.'

What Mr Buckland had come up against was a consequence of the curious fact that, when Britain joined 'Europe' in 1973, the Channel Islands and the Isle of Man insisted that they did not wish to become members. Although they are British soil, Brussels therefore insists that for Customs purposes we must treat them as a foreign country. In Mr Buckland's case, he had little sympathy from Customs minister David Heathcoat-Amory, who merely replied via his MP that, if he had problems over filling in his customs form he should retain 'the services of a professional customs agent'.

But a further irony about the peculiar relationship of these British offshore islands to the EC is that, although not part of the EC, they are in some respects compelled to obey its laws. This gave rise to a particularly disastrous saga in the Isle of Man when, after talks between the island's government vets and officials of MAFF in Britain, the Manx Government decided it would have to rebuild the island's only abattoir to conform with the EC's meat hygiene directive, 91/497. Although independent consultants advised that the existing abattoir, which already complied with an earlier EC directive, could be 'upgraded' at a cost of £1 million, the Manx vets decreed that an entirely new building should be constructed, at a cost eventually exceeding £6.5 million. Its capacity far exceeded anything the island was ever likely to need. The workforce was doubled to handle the same throughput of animals. And the result was a white elephant so expensive that Manx farmers received significantly less for their stock, butchers had to pay more for their meat and every taxpayer on the island had to contribute to a hefty annual subsidy, all to achieve no improvement in hygiene whatever.

Even this paled, however, beside the tale of the only abattoir on the Falkland Islands, 8,000 miles from Europe, which for years had provided meat for everyone on the islands without a single incident of food poisoning. In 1992 Ministry of Defence officials in London ruled that, since the abattoir did not comply with 'EC standards', the 2,500 strong British garrison should no longer be allowed to eat its meat. Beef was therefore bought in Uruguay, shipped to Britain and back to the islands. Lamb was imported from New Zealand, while 60,000 Falklands sheep must be destroyed each year, some by being pushed over cliffs into the sea, because there are not enough people to eat them.

Mr Huxley and the meaningless form

Another perfect little illustration of the way the officials were constantly contriving to create bureaucratic structures which did not correspond to the real world was highlighted by the curious problem confronting Paul Huxley, whose company employs 30 people in Arlesford, Hampshire, making special-ised machines to cut the grass on the greens of golf courses. In January 1994 Mr Huxley had a letter from the Central Statistical Office concerning a new scheme with the Soviet-style title of PRODCOM (Products of the European Community). Devised by the Statistical Office of the European Communities (EUROSTAT), this was designed to collect statistics relating to the new Single Market. Mr Huxley was asked to fill in a 15-page form with the details of his products and sales. He read carefully through the boxes listing 70 categories of machine, such as 'self-propelled powered mowers with the cutting device rotating in a horizontal plane for lawns, parks or sports grounds, excluding those with a seat'. Not one corresponded to the type of machines made by his company, so he returned the form, politely explaining that he could not fill in the form because 'our products do not fit any of the categories shown'.

Thus began an extraordinary saga which was to last over a year, involving no fewer than four ministers of the Crown, three MPs, four MEPs and numerous officials. The point at issue was very simple. All Mr Huxley was trying to convey was that it was impossible for him to complete the form because it had no entry describing his products. But not one of his correspon-dents, as the file of letters grew several inches thick, seemed able to grasp his point. The CSO threatened him with criminal prosecution. His MP Gerry

Malone told him to comply with the officials' 'important and reasonable request'. Even 10 Downing Street replied that 'the Prime Minister thinks it would be best if you were to provide them with data they have asked for'. Yet all Mr Huxley was trying to point out was the simple fact that he could not do this. The form was so drafted that it was impossible for him to give a meaningful or honest answer.

A point many of his official correspondents emphasised was just how 'important', even 'vital', was the information collected under the PRODCOM scheme. In January 1995, with the dispute still unresolved, Mr Huxley received a further form from the officials, together with an illustration of the 'vital' data garnered by earlier surveys on the products of 'your industry'. This quoted a category including 'Parts for seed dusting machines, fertiliser crushing or mixing mills, machines for cutting slips, hedge cutting machines, tree-felling machines, tree stump removers, machines for chipping branches and twigs, honey presses, machines for forming wax into comb foundations'. It was obviously extraordinarily useful to know that total sales for all these items lumped together had in 1993 amounted to £11,134,00. Mr Huxley then read through the new 15-page questionnaire. There was still no entry corresponding to his machines, so he went through all 70 boxes, in each case writing 'nil'. He did not hear from the officials again.

Mr Huxley was not alone. In Penrith, Cumbria, David Kennedy and his sister ran a tiny, two-person business making top-quality hand-made chocolates. The PRODCOM form arrived at their busiest time of the year, just before St Valentine's Day, Mothering Sunday and Easter. Mr Kennedy had to take off three days from chocolate making to trawl back through months of invoices, laboriously working out how much of each item they had produced by weight and value. The only product they could think of which remotely corresponded to one entry was their 'novelty chocolate mice'. So they solemnly filled this in as 'weight 17 kilograms, value (to nearest thousands of pounds) nil'. John Broughton, who ran a company making false teeth, told us how he had looked through a similar form from the CSO and, finding no entry for 'dentures', concluded the nearest thing to a box relevant to his products was that for 'food processing machinery'. 'Given the number of units we produce,' he wrote, 'I understand that ever since we have been classified as the country's largest manufacturer of food processing machinery.'

Will travel, won't have job

Another feature of the post-Maastricht Europe on which we received regular letters was the claim that there were no longer obstacles to 'citizens of the European Community' seeking work anywhere in the EC. As Britain's Foreign Secretary Douglas Hurd boasted in an open letter to the Conservative Party in January 1995, one benefit of Britain's membership was that 'professionals find it easier to live and work anywhere in the EU'.

Only that week we heard from Dr Mark Kidger, a professional astronomer who, since 1983, had been working in Tenerife. The island's clear skies meant that opportunities for star-gazing were 'far superior' to those in the UK, and he had been employed on a series of short-term contracts by the local Institute of Astrophysics, part of the local university. But under the university's rules he now had to apply for a permanent post and one at his institute was vacant. Under the EC's new rules, Dr Kidger assumed there would be no problem. All Member States were now bound to recognise each other's academic qualifications, and professional posts should be open to any EC national.

Dr Kidger's first problem was to win acceptance of his UK academic credentials. Even though he had been working for the University of the Canaries for nearly ten years, this ended up costing him £800. He then applied for the job he was after. Even though the advertisement said applicants 'must be Spanish', he knew that under a Spanish royal decree of 1993 such scientific posts were open to all EC citizens, in accordance with EC law. Nevertheless he was rejected, because he had not proved his 'Spanish nationality'. He appealed and was told that, although his application was acceptable under Spanish national law, the final authority in this case rested with the 'regional government', and under local rules he was turned down. Although he was told he could appeal and would almost certainly win, this would take several years, by which time the vacancy would be filled. At the age of 35 Dr Kidger was thus completely stuck, no longer allowed to earn a living in the place he had come to think of as home. Throughout this episode he had received friendly advice from the British consul in Tenerife. But Mr Hurd's Consulate General in Madrid now instructed the Tenerife consulate 'not to intervene' on his behalf.

Worms, winkles and chicks

Yet another example of the officials dreaming up legislation which failed to allow for the complexities of the real world was directive 91/628, intended to safeguard the welfare of animals when they were being transported. The animals should be regularly fed, watered and rested; a 'journey plan' should be produced showing exactly how they were to be cared for; and journeys must not last twelve hours without a break. All this might have seemed fine as applied to larger animals such as horses, cattle, sheep, goats and pigs (or as the directive insisted on calling them, 'domestic solipeds and domestic animals of the bovine, ovine, caprine and porcine species'). But by a slight oversight in drafting, the directive's requirements, faithfully echoed in the UK regulations, also applied to all other creatures, including 'cold-blooded animals' and 'birds', and here in due course some bizarre anomalies emerged.

Philip and Heather Gorringe ran the Wiggly Wormers Worm Farm in Herefordshire, breeding earthworms for use in compost heaps. In 1994 they were surprised to be told by a trading standards official that, under the new regulations, it would now be a criminal offence for them to send out worms which were 'pregnant' (not easy to discern since earthworms are hermaphrodites). The worms must also be provided with suitable food and drink on their journey, and accompanied by a journey plan showing arrangements for the animals to be 'rested'. The solution eventually solemnly found to this problem was that the worms might be sent by first-class post. In September 1995 there was further publicity when the RSPCA halted a consignment of winkles, again on the grounds that these were not accompanied by a journey plan and that no proper arrangements had been made to provide them with rest on their journey.

Behind these lighter examples, however, lay the real disaster which hit many specialist breeders of poultry and ducks. They often had to supply customers with small numbers of day-old chicks or ducklings, and an efficient system had been evolved to load these up after they had fed in the afternoon, transport them during the night while they were asleep and deliver them the next day. Long experience had shown that this was the best way to reduce stress on the birds. But under the new regulations this was no longer possible, because the time between loading and unloading lasted more than twelve hours, and did not provide for regular feeding and watering during transit. So complex did the system now become that the firm which specialised in moving such small consignments of birds round Britain decided it could no longer provide the service. The result for dozens of specialist breeders like David Bland of Chichester, Sussex, one of the country's best-known experts on rare poultry breeds, was disastrous. In June 1994 Mr Bland announced to the trade that he could no longer operate his business, and that he was having to sell up his farm. All because, before drafting their regulations, the officials had never bothered to ascertain that the welfare needs of day-old chicks are not the same as those of horses, cows and elephants.

At least in 1995 the officials in Brussels rectified some of the crazier anomalies of this directive by producing a new version, 95/29. No longer was it necessary to ensure that oysters and mussels were rested and fed on their way to restaurants. But, inevitably, the new directive then created new problems of its own. One of these was a ruling that, if animals were transported for eight hours, they must now be rested for a full 24 hours before they could be moved again. Hardly was the ink dry on this edict than we were contacted by a farmer in the Scottish Highlands pointing out what devastating effect it would have on the economy of far-flung regions like his own. For the largest sheep fair in Europe, held every August at Lairgs, farmers bring animals from all over northern Scotland. Some must be brought by ferry from outlying islands, on journeys inevitably taking more than eight hours. Yet under the new rules, accommodation would now have to be found for all those 35,000 sheep to be rested, fed and watered for a full 24 hours before they could be sold and moved on. In practice this was so impracticable that it would mean an end to the centuries-old Lairgs sheep fair. Once again, something which might have made perfect sense in a Brussels committee room, to officials happy to legislate for the real world without ever setting foot in it, threatened to inflict maximum havoc on those affected, to achieve no benefit whatever.

*

Typical of the directives pouring out of Brussels in the early 1990s, preparing for the Single Market, was 92/29 on 'the minimum safety and health requirements for improved medical treatment on board vessels'. This laid down immensely detailed lists of medical equipment, ranging from splints to prescription-only drugs, which had to be carried on all sea-going vessels, at costs ranging from £1,600 for a fairly large craft down to £290 for a dinghy. Naturally these were implemented in Britain with the usual commendable zeal by officials of the Marine Safety Agency, with the result that, for instance, the ferry across the Tamar between Devon and Cornwall had to carry 120 seasickness pills for the benefit of passengers. The only snag was that these had to be taken 'half an hour before the journey begins'. Since most passengers for the ferry arrive only a minute or two before it begins its seven-minute journey across the river, this presented rather a problem.

*

In 1994, on instructions from Brussels, Britain introduced a new telephone emergency line, dialling 112, to bring her into conformity with the rest of the Community. In its first twelve months of operation, police and operators were inundated by two million calls. Police had to investigate 300,000 'silent calls' where operators were unable to make contact with a caller. Most calls resulted from dialling errors or children playing with telephones. Only 500 turned out to be genuine. A BT spokeswoman said, 'we checked with other European countries and they had the same problems'. BT planned to keep its existing 999 service, which works very efficiently. But Britain would still have to retain the 112 line, even though it wasted millions of man-hours a year.

*

In 1995 the oyster farmers of Argyll received a rude shock from officials of the 'environmental services department' of Argyll and Bute district council. Their long-standing practice was simply to pull their oysters out of the water, sort them into string bags on the sea-shore and dispatch them as quickly as possible to customers all over the country. But no longer. Under the Food Safety (Live Bivalve Molluscs) Regulations 1992, implementing EC directive 91/493, they would now have to spend tens of thousands of pounds building a 'dispatch station', complete with stainless-steel 'sorting tables', changing rooms and showers for employees and walls that must be 'seamlessly cladded'. Because the cost of building such a pointless facility would drive them all out of business, the oystermen asked the officials whether their 'dispatch station' could not just be an open shed, since fresh air is the most hygienic environment known. This was out of the question. The regulations specifically stated that the 'walls' must be 'seamlessly cladded'. And if the 'station' did not have walls, how could it comply with the requirement for 'seamless cladding'?

*

Britain's safety experts were amazed in 1996 to see the Home Office's new Health and Safety (Safety Signs and Signals) Regulations 1996, implementing EC directive 92/58 on 'the minimun requirements for the provision of safety and/or health signs at work'. These laid down that all the millions of fire 'EXIT' signs in Britain should be converted to an EU approved sign showing a crude little pictogram of a running figure. Although the directive very clearly stated that this requirement only applied to new signs, the Whitehall officials with their customary zeal had laid down that, as from Christmas Eve 1998, it would be a criminal offence for any office, factory, shop, hotel, cinema theatre or village hall not to have replaced all their existing 'EXIT' signs with the running man. So unconcerned were the officials about the cost of their diktat that when their junior minister, Baroness Blatch, was asked in the House of Lords how much this might come to, all they could come up with was 'between £2 million and £12 million'. In other words, they hadn't a clue, although independent experts thought that the true figure would be far higher. But what really irritated those experts even more was that picture of a man running. It had long been established as almost the first rule of fire safety that, if fire breaks out in any workplace or public building, the one thing people must be instructed never to do, on any account, is run.

Whisky – square peg in a round bottle

No trade better exemplified the mismatch between the dreamworld of EC regulation and practical reality than the whisky industry, Britain's fifth largest export earner. There seemed to be something about Scotch whisky which repeatedly made it the square peg in a whole sequence of Brussels round holes.

We have seen earlier how two separate directives, on the transporting by road of 'flammable liquids' and on fire safety in chemical plants, imposed ludicrously inappropriate costs on the industry by equating whisky with the most dangerous chemicals. But these were not its only problems. Another came from a proposed new directive on animal feed. This might seem curiously unrelated to whisky, until one realises the vital part played in the Scottish rural economy by feeding cattle with 'draff', the wet barley mash left over from whisky distilling, which sustains more than half Scotland's dairy herds. The new directive laid down that the contents of animal feed should be weighed and analysed. This would mean each distiller having to pay up to £50,000 for a weighbridge, to give the exact weight of draff which, by the time it reached the farm and much of the moisture had evaporated, would weigh much less; also for costly laboratory analysis which in every case would simply show the contents of the feed as 'barley and water'.

The distillers were also informed by the Scottish River Purification Boards that, to comply with the Freshwater Fisheries directive, the water they discharged into streams after distilling must never raise the temperature of the water by more than 1.5 degrees Celsius. In fact they already took care not to discharge water that was too hot into the streams, and all the scientific evidence available showed that the slight warming of the water downstream from distilleries attracted abnormal numbers of salmon and trout. But to meet the ludicrously exact requirements of the directive, they were told they would now have to spend millions of pounds on cooling equipment, although technology sophisticated enough to monitor such temperature changes exactly did not yet exist.

But ultimately no anomaly affecting the whisky industry was more absurd than the fact that, despite the arrival of the Single Market, in 1995 a '70 centilitre' bottle of whisky cost twice as much in the Highland village where it was distilled, £11.05, as it did in Rome, where the same bottle cost only £5.10. This was because in Britain £7.41, or more than 70 per cent of the purchase price, went in tax. Herein lay one of the most glaring contradictions of all in the Single Market.

Single Market, double dealing

Although no country's politicians were more enthusiastic for the Single Market in theory than Britain's, in practice there was a supremely important respect in which they were quite determined to prevent that 'level playing field' coming about. Nothing made so blatant a mockery of the Single Market as the huge difference between British and continental prices for alcohol and tobacco because of the much higher taxes Britain charged on these products. But there was no way in which even a fervent Europhile like Chancellor Kenneth Clarke was going to give up the £14 billion a year those taxes gave him.

When the Single Market eliminated customs controls, this yawning tax gap of course immediately gave rise to a huge new import trade, as thousands of Britons crossed over to France each day for the specific purpose of buying alchohol at much cheaper prices (in Britain wine duty was £1.16 a bottle, in France only 2.5p). Although for 'personal consumption' this was now quite legal, many were doing so only to sell their purchases back in Britain, thus illegally undercutting the British drinks trade which had to pay full duty. In 1995 a detailed study by the Wine and Spirits Association indicated that 1.4 million barrels of beer alone were imported in this way, equivalent to 5 per cent of total British beer sales; 289 million bottles of wine; and 35.65 million bottles of spirits. Over a fifth of all the spirits drunk in Britain, it was estimated, did not pay UK taxes. Altogether this semi-licit smuggling, according to the WSA, cost the Exchequer £978 million in lost revenue. But in the view of politicians like Mr Clarke, this was a small price to avoid the greater loss which would result from lowering duties to a level which might bring the scandal to an end. The fact that this farce also cost Britain's own drinks industry more than £2 billion a year in lost sales, along with thousands of lost jobs in pubs, breweries and wine merchants, was not something over which ministers showed any concern.

A tiny example of how topsy-turvy this system had become was provided in a letter to *The Times* in 1994 from Devon hotelier Paul Henderson, describing how on a visit to France he had bought 15 cases of wine to sell in his restaurant. Being an honest man, on arrival in Dover he tried to declare them for duty. He was told that, thanks to the Single Market, Dover was no longer a 'customs port' and he should therefore contact his local excise officials in Devon. They told him he should have paid the duty on the wine before he left England for France. Because he had not done so, the wine could now be confiscated. Mr Henderson patiently explained that, before he left for France, he had no idea what wine he was likely to buy. He received the historic reply that what he should therefore have done, after making his purchases, was to return to England to pay the duty and then go back to France to pick up his wine.

It was later that year, however, that a tiny South London firm, the Enlightened Tobacco Company, decided to put ministers' belief in the Single Market to the ultimate test. The ETC advertised that it would act as agents for British smokers, to import cigarettes from Luxembourg costing only £1.60 a packet, £1.10 less than they cost in Britain. Before launching their scheme the firm's directors B.J. Cunningham and Stan Bertelsen consulted a leading tax lawyer, who advised that it should be entirely within the law for the firm to act as agent in importing cigarettes for customers' personal consumption, because under an ancient principle of British common law, an agent and the person for whom he acts are legally the same person. Thousands of customers signed up for the scheme. In February 1995 Customs and Excise began detaining the imports until full duty was paid. The company applied for an injunction to stop them, and in July the case came before Mr Justice Popplewell in the High Court. ETC was opposed not only by HM Government, terrified at the prospect of losing a large part of its £8.5 billion a year tobacco revenues, but also by the giant Imperial Tobacco Company, which saw a serious threat to its control of 35 per cent of the British market.

The legal argument centred on the wording of an EC directive, which stated that if people wished to avoid excise duty, the goods had to be 'transported by themselves'. Thanks to that ancient principle of British law that buyer and agent count as the same person, this was the heart of ETC's case. But at the last minute the QC for the Imperial Tobacco Company pulled a masterstroke. The version of the directive the court had been considering, it seemed, was 'a Dutch translation of the German translation of the original French version'. But now, the QC claimed, a new translation had turned up, direct from the French, and very conveniently this added a crucial word. Instead of just saying that the goods had to be transported 'by themselves' the directive's text now read 'by themselves personally', which made a mockery of the English law. ETC's lawyers were astonished when Judge Popplewell accepted this supposed new version without demur. Such a casual response would have been unthinkable if the High Court had been considering a point of British law. Nevertheless the judge did suggest that, if ETC's lawyers didn't like his ruling, they should appeal, and when they did, the Court of Appeal simply referred the case to the European Court of Justice. Such matters were much too arcane to be decided by any mere British court. But one thing at least the case confirmed beyond question. When all those fine words about the 'level playing field' were really put to the test, British ministers and officials would stop at nothing to keep at least part of that field as 'unlevel' as possible.

12. VAT – The Bureaucrats' Dream Tax

> I know it is too late to do anything about it, and that it is all part of making
> Britain more efficient and bringing us into line with the Continental way of life.
> But it is surely not too late simply to stand and marvel at how this extraordi-
> nary tax came to be – which, for human ingenuity, must rank with the Gothic
> cathedrals, the law of relativity and the utterances of Mr Wedgwood Benn as
> one of the great achievements of the European mind.
>
> Christopher Booker, *Daily Telegraph*, February 1973

Undoubtedly one of the EC's finest gifts to Britain was Value Added Tax. This
system of indirect taxation, adding a percentage for the Government on
transactions in goods and services, was devised in the 1960s by those masters
of Cartesian logic, the officials of the French Government. It was adopted by
the EEC in 1969, and of course Britain was forced to take it on when she
joined the Common Market in 1973. When first invented it was described as
'fiscal anaesthesia', because for the first time in history a means had been
devised to collect taxes from people without them being aware of it.

The cleverest trick about VAT was the way it forced millions of businesses
to become unpaid tax collectors for the Government. As the House of Commons Public Accounts Committee pointed out in August 1994, collecting VAT
now cost Britain's businesses in time and paperwork £1.6 billion a year, while
the cost to the Government itself was only £400 million. But a far greater cost
lay in the ultimate peculiarity of the system, which was the way businesses
were forced to hand over billions of pounds a year which then had to be
claimed back.

Dr Bernard Juby of the Federation of Small Businesses liked to illustrate
this with the example of the paper bag. A timber company fells a tree and
sells it to a wood-pulper, charging him VAT. The pulper then claims the VAT
back as an 'allowable input' and sells his product to a paper manufacturer,
again charging VAT. The paper company claims this back as an 'allowable
input', and sells its product, again charging VAT, to a paper-bag manufacturer, who then reclaims the VAT and sells his paper-bags onto a shopkeeper.
Again the VAT is reclaimed by the shopkeeper, who gives the bag to a
customer full of sweets. This time no VAT is payable because the customer
is given the bag free. So, at the end of the day, VAT has been collected, paid
and reclaimed four times, and it might seem the only money which stays with
the Government is that collected by the timber-company in the first place.
Except that the next time that company buys an expensive chain saw, it will
be able to subtract the VAT it paid on the saw from its next payment to the
Government, as another 'allowable input'.

Admittedly the end result of this system, as the PAC found in 1994, was that the Government ended up keeping £63 billion a year. But to collect this another £25 billion was shuffled uselessly to and fro, some of which the Government received as a temporary interest-free loan and much of which was meanwhile taken out of the productive economy.

One reason why the EC was so keen on VAT was that it provided one of the chief ways in which it raised funds for its own purposes. A proportion of the VAT paid in each Member State went to Brussels, as part of what were called the EC's 'own resources'. Another provider of 'own resources' was the customs duties levied on goods from the outside world, and this was a major reason why Britain's contribution to the EC budget was originally so absurdly disproportionate, because she imported more goods from outside the EC than other countries, particularly from her old Commonwealth partners. This disparity got so out of hand that, by the mid-1980s, Britain was contributing up to 25 per cent of the EC's entire budget, which was why Mrs Thatcher fought her long and bitter battle to win a reduction in Britain's share of payments.

The formula eventually devised to calculate this 'abatement' or 'Budget rebate' was based on Britain's VAT payments, and in itself represented one of the shining triumphs of the EC official mind. As Treasury minister Sir John Cope told MPs in 1992, to work out Britain's yearly rebate you must:

> (a) Calculate the difference between: (i) on the one hand, the UK's percentage share of member states' total VAT-based contributions to Community resources as if pre-1988 'uncapped VAT' arrangements were still in place, and (ii) on the other hand, the UK's percentage share of total 'allocated expenditure' – ie the total of intra-Community budget expenditure, excluding aid;
>
> (b) Apply the percentage difference obtained (the 'VAT expenditure share gap') to total allocated expenditure;
>
> (c) Multiply the result by 66 per cent;
>
> (d) Deduct the benefit for the UK arising from the new own-resources structure agreed in 1988 (calculated by multiplying (1) the percentage difference between the UK's share of uncapped VAT and its share of capped VAT and fourth resources payments by (2) member states' overall capped VAT and fourth resources payments)'.

*

In every way the VAT system was a bureaucrats' dream. In *The Mad Officials* we told the story of the international opera singer, David Wilson-Johnson, who with the coming of the Single Market in 1993 was told by his local VAT office in London that he must now register for VAT in every one of the other Member States. This meant he would now have to fill in twelve separate VAT returns every three months, even if he had not earned any money in any of those countries during the period in question, with a penalty for every day his returns were late. The local VAT officials were unable to advise him as to what rates applied to the services of an opera singer in other countries – in Italy, for instance, VAT percentage rates were 0, 4, 9, 12, 19 and 38. But when he dutifully wrote to all the other national VAT authorities for advice, he had only two highly unhelpful replies, including one in such dense bureaucratic German that, although he was a linguist, he had to send it off for translation.

Of course another glory of the VAT system, from the bureaucrats' point of view, was that it was so unbelievably complicated that it gave rise to endless opportunities for catching people out by picking them up on arcane points of procedure. The legal quibbles to which the VAT system gave rise made those mediaeval disputations over the number of angels which can dance on the head of a pin look like something out of nursery school. And no area of VAT law provided more fees for the legal profession than the interminable battles over whether some particular product or service was liable to pay VAT or not ('standard-rated', 'zero-rated' or 'exempt' in the jargon). Immensely technical cases wound their way laboriously through the courts for years, often involving sums of money so vast as to be wholly unreal, like the one under which Barclay's Bank and others claimed they had been wrongly forced to pay VAT on company cars. The total sum they were demanding the Government should repay amounted to no less than £15 billion, equivalent to half the entire annual cost of the National Health Service.

But it was at a much lower level that the real viciousness often created by these countless anomalies of the VAT system showed itself, as in the story in 1996 of the Cardiff charity, the Trust for Sick Children in Wales, which had raised £500,000 to build a new hotel unit at the University of Hospital in Wales. This was to provide parents with accommodation while their babies were receiving life-saving treatment in the hospital's Special Care Baby Unit. The charity assumed that because the unit was a new building, although connected to the hospital, VAT would not be chargeable. But it was told by Customs and Excise that £70,000 of the money raised by thousands of volunteers in coffee mornings and charity events must now be paid in VAT, because the new building did not have 'a separate entrance'. It was therefore 'an extension to an existing building' and 'zero rating' as an official smugly confirmed, 'only applies to new buildings'.

Another example we reported in 1996 was the bizarre story of Kathy's Kones, a successful small Manchester company threatened with bankruptcy simply because Customs and Excise officials could not grasp the difference between a biscuit and a sweet. John Oldfield had been making his novelty biscuits, from ice cream cones filled with marshmallow, for more than 20 years. In 1992 the firm was reorganised under his daughter Kathy, an England netball captain, and renamed Kathy's Kones. Their product caught on with supermarket chains, turnover rose to £670,000 a year and the firm was employing 30 people until, in September 1993, the blow fell. A new VAT inspector on a routine visit ruled, after only a few minutes in the factory, that Kathy's Kones were not biscuits after all. They were sweets. The significance of this was enormous, because biscuits are free of VAT, but sweets must pay at the full rate of 17.5 per cent. Furthermore the officials ruled that the firm must therefore pay back taxes of £250,000.

John and Kathy Oldfield couldn't believe what had happened. Over 20 years, John Oldfield had received no less than ten visits from VAT inspectors. All had accepted the cones were biscuits. In every supermarket Kathy's Kones were placed with other biscuits in the bakery department, not sold as confectionery. Worse still, the products they competed with were all officially

145

classed as biscuits and, if Kathy's Kones alone now had to pay VAT, adding 7p to the price of a 39p packet, this would price them right out of a highly price-sensitive market. Mr Oldfield was so confident common sense would prevail that, when he put his case to a VAT tribunal, he didn't even take a lawyer with him. Instead of the normal three assessors, however, he found only one. And when the assessor was shown three products, including one called an Oyster Delight, he was so confused that he assumed all three were made by Kathy's Kones. He promptly ruled that all three were 'sweets' and must pay VAT.

What apparently the assessor didn't grasp was that the only reason he had been shown the Oyster Delight, made by another firm, was that, like Kathy's Kones, it was made of wafer biscuit filled with marshmallow, but had already been officially ruled as not liable for VAT. In 1988 Customs and Excise had specifically ruled that 'wafer products' like the Oyster Delight were only subject to VAT 'if the covering on them is similar to chocolate in taste and appearance'. Other 'wafer products', wrote Customs, 'are eligible for relief'.

So horrified was Mr Oldfield by the assessor's confusion over the law that he applied for leave to have the case looked at by a High Court judge. But the VAT officials were determined that it should not be re-heard and the application was turned down, which for Kathy's Kones threatened final disaster. Although the officials had at one point offered to waive the £250,000 back tax claim if Oldfield dropped his court case, they now demanded payment in full. Already the case had dealt such a body-blow to sales that the firm had been forced to lay off more than two-thirds of its workforce. And if it was now forced to close, the taxmen would get virtually nothing, because the company had no assets to pay the back tax.

The final irony was that, if the officials withdrew their ruling, other taxes paid by the firm and its workers might once again contribute hundreds of thousands of pounds to the Government. But all this the officials were prepared to chuck away, just to defend another of those Alice in Wonderland issues of 'principle' which the VAT system seemed almost designed to create.

*

The real point of VAT, as the EC's very own tax, was that Brussels had long been working for the day when it was applied uniformly throughout the Community. This was the purpose of the so-called 'Sixth VAT Directive', issued as long ago as 1977 on 'the harmonisation of the laws of the member states relating to turnover taxes', proposing a 'common system of value added tax' and a 'uniform basis of assessment'. The aim of directive 77/388, with its long sequence of subsequent amendments, was to ensure that, by 1997, VAT was levied on exactly the same goods and services in every Member State. The idea of a uniform tax system, controlled by the Community and transcending the power of individual member states, has played an important role in the continuous momentum towards political unity, and Brussels has issued frequent reminders that certain countries, particularly Britain, were falling behind on their timetable for stepping into line.

Indeed it was ironic that, although Britain was normally so eager to comply with Brussels legislation, when it came to VAT the British Government remained strangely recalcitrant. A small instance was the curious story we told in *The Mad Officials* of how, when VAT was first introduced, Customs and Excise refused to accept a clear Brussels ruling that sports facilities run on a non-profit making basis were exempt from paying VAT. From 1973 onwards thousands of Britain's amateur sporting organisations, such as golf clubs, tennis clubs or village cricket clubs, were forced to pay VAT in a way which was actually illegal under EC law. When this meant having to find thousands of pounds extra on the cost of building new tennis courts or extending a club house, it represented a substantial penalty. As in so many contexts, the British Government seemed determined to use the EC system to inflict unnecessary damage on its own people, even when in 1990 this meant ignoring a reminder from the Commission that it was in flagrant breach of EC law. But a gallant hero then entered the fray. Ernest Virgo, Honorary Secretary of the Kent Playing Fields Association, was a retired civil servant who had served in Brussels and knew his way around the system. As a public servant of the old school he was so outraged by this arrogant disregard for the law that he launched a stubborn one-man campaign to get the injustice righted. He finally managed so to embarrass the Government that in 1994 it was forced to give way. But for Mr Virgo this was not enough. He demanded that clubs should be repaid all the taxes which had been illegally claimed, to such effect that sports clubs all over Britain found themselves sharing in an unexpected windfall amounting to more than £150 million.

*

However, the most serious effect of Britain's reluctance to accept moves towards the 'harmonisation' of VAT throughout the Community was that it led her politicians into deliberately concealing from the British people the extent to which they were being led up a cul de sac. The Sixth Vat Directive made it clear that all Member States, including Britain, were legally obliged to harmonise their VAT systems by 1997. This would mean the imposition of VAT on a whole range of goods and services which as yet remained exempt. These included domestic heating, books and newspapers, travel, including rail, bus and air tickets, new houses, above all food. On all these items most other countries had already fallen into line, and Britain became increasingly isolated.

The problem was that, particularly after Britain's standard rate of VAT was raised to 17.5 per cent, imposing VAT on all these items would mean a sudden huge jump in the cost of living. 17.5 per cent VAT on a £200,000 new house would put up its price by £35,000. VAT on food alone would add a staggering £7 billion a year to Britain's shopping bills. Just how politically embarrassing this could be was demonstrated in 1993 when the Government's first tentative step towards meeting its obligations, by putting VAT on domestic heating, caused a political storm lasting months. Even then, since 'Europe' was now an ever-more sensitive political issue, the Government was very careful not to admit openly the extent to which this was being done in obedience to Brussels, and in this deception it was abetted by the main opposition parties, even more committed to Europe than the Government.

But the inexorable logic of EC law was closing in. Britain could continue to defy the Sixth VAT Directive by asking Brussels for further 'derogations'. But these would have to be paid for by major concessions elsewhere. And the Maastricht Treaty laid down that by 2005 all Member States must accept a fully-harmonised VAT system without exceptions. Somewhere before then all those additional items, food, newspapers, travel and the rest would have to be brought into the VAT system. It was perhaps hardly surprising ministers kept as quiet about this as Brer Fox's tar baby, for nothing could bring home more forcibly to the British people how far tax-making powers had passed from Westminster to Brussels. It was yet another example of how 'Europe' was luring Britain's politicians ever further into a culture of deceit, where it had now become almost impossible for any of them to admit frankly just where the European adventure was leading, and just how far Britain had already travelled down the road.

It is that extraordinary state to which Britain's membership of the 'European Union' had reduced her politicians which is the theme of our next chapter.

Part III

The New Totalitarianism

13. The Strange Death of Democracy

The battles with Communism are yesterday's battles. Today's enemy is bureaucracy and the people are losing the struggle.
Vaclav Klaus, Prime Minister of the Czech Republic, 1995

When Britain's MPs returned to Westminster after their long summer recess in October 1994, they found their offices furnished with shiny new desks and filing cabinets. There had been nothing much wrong with their old desks and filing cabinets. Indeed many were comparatively new. But during the holidays thousands of them had been removed by a fleet of furniture vans down to an airfield in Devon, to be auctioned off at knockdown prices. Very few MPs knew why this had happened. The orders had been given by the officials who run the Palace of Westminster, and their reasoning was that the old furniture did not comply with new regulations implementing six EC directives on health and safety in the workplace.

What made this strangely symbolic was that, hitherto, it had been a jealously guarded privilege of parliament that, in all matters relating to health and safety, Westminster was sovereign over its own affairs. It was not bound by regulations applying to the rest of the population. As had been confirmed in a celebrated King's Bench judgement in 1935, MPs were literally masters in their own house. But with the arrival of the Single Market, the officials had decided that this privilege no longer applied. From now on the Palace of Westminister must be subject to the dictates of Brussels. And most significantly of all, MPs were not even consulted on the matter.

Rule by decree

During the late 1980s and early 1990s, a profound and almost entirely unnoticed revolution took place in the way Britain was governed. Outwardly it seemed the world's oldest parliamentary democracy was still functioning much as it had evolved over many centuries. Parliament was still the central political forum of the nation. MPs debated issues of the day and put questions to ministers. Television screens regularly showed the House of Commons packed for exchanges between the Prime Minister and the Leader of the Opposition. The media still projected politicians as if they were figures of power and importance. Above all, most people still fondly imagined that parliament was where their laws were made, and that laws only came into being when politicians had been given a chance to examine them, discuss them and vote on them. Only with their consent could such measures become the law of the land.

But, by the mid-1990s, to an astonishing degree this was no longer so. Almost all significant legislation was now carried out, not by Acts of Parliament, but by what were called 'statutory instruments', SIs, or sets of regulations. Drafted by anonymous Whitehall officials, these might never even be read by MPs, or even by the ministers who had to 'sign them into law'. In the ten years up to 1996 there was a huge jump in the number of statutory instruments being issued each year. In 1986 there were 2,336 SIs, not many more than 30 years earlier, and many of these were just concerned with routine matters involved in the administration of government. But in the late 1980s the yearly figure began a steep rise. By 1990 it had reached 2,667. The following year it was 2,953. In 1992 it soared for the first time past 3,000, to 3,359, and from then on it remained at this all-time record level. The 1993 total was 3,279, in 1994 3,334, in 1995 3,345. And the most obvious single reason for this increase was the need to translate into British law the avalanche of new legislation coming out of Brussels. In 1995 the Department of Trade and Industry estimated that the need to implement European legislation accounted for a third of all the new statutory instruments now pouring annually out of the Whitehall machine.

Almost equally revealing over the same years was what happened to the number of statutes initiated by the British parliament. In the mid-1980s these were running at around 70 a year, but in the late 1980s a general downward trend set in. In 1994 the total was only 41. Even this concealed the full picture, because some of the most important statutes of the period around 1990, the late-Thatcher era, were what are known as 'enabling Acts'. That is to say, their chief purpose was to give ministers – or more precisely the Whitehall machine – the power to pass regulations. In *The Mad Officials* we reported on the extraordinary regulatory explosion which had such devastating effect in so many areas of British life in the early 1990s, much of it stemming from those same enabling Acts, such as the Children Act 1989, the Food Safety Act 1990, the Environmental Protection Act 1990. All these empowered Whitehall to issue a stream of new regulations, while at the same time giving unprecedented new powers to petty enforcement officials, such as social workers, environmental health officers and pollution inspectors. But the biggest enabling Act of them all was one passed more than two decades earlier, the European Communities Act 1972.

It was this Act which gave ministers and their officials their chief instrument for turning Brussels directives directly into British law; as was the case with many of the regulations cited in this book, such as the spate of SIs implementing the Brussels metrication directives. It was Section 2 (2) of the European Communities Act which enabled the DTI officials to slip these regulations into law without most MPs even knowing about them. However a range of other enabling Acts could be used for the same purpose. It was under the Food Safety Act 1990 that MAFF was able to issue the Fresh Meat (Hygiene and Inspection) Regulations 1992 which inflicted such havoc on Britain's abattoirs. Most of the thousands of pages of environmental regulations derived from Brussels directives were issued by DoE officials under the Environmental Protection Act. And the significance of many of these edicts, in terms of their impact on the life of the nation, could scarcely be overestimated.

13. The Strange Death of Democracy

For a start they created literally hundreds of new criminal offences. They had the power to impose quite astronomic new costs on all those industries and businesses which were being regulated, whether these took the form of direct charges or just the costs of complying with the regulations. When officials of the Health and Safety Executive introduced the Construction (Design and Management) Regulations implementing Council Directive 92/57 'on the implementation of minimum health and safety requirements at temporary or mobile construction sites', they estimated these would cost the construction industry £550 million a year. When officials of the DoE put forward their Producer Responsibility (Packaging Waste) Regulations, implementing Council Directive 94/62, they estimated these would cost industries using packaging materials up to £573 million a year. The Home Office's proposed Workplace (Fire Precautions) Regulations 1992, implementing just 34 lines of the Workplace Directive 89/654 would have cost Britain's businesses an estimated £8,000 million, equivalent to nearly £150 for every man, woman and child in Britain. In 1996 the Water Services Association estimated that the total cost over the next nine years of meeting the quality standards set by just four new EC environmental directives would be a scarcely believable £24,000 million. This would have to be paid for by every water user in the country, through water bills set to rise even more drastically in the future than they already had done in the recent past. And all these costs were to be imposed, not after lengthy deliberation by elected MPs in parliament, but simply by way of regulations drawn up and issued by officials, in response to diktats passed down from Brussels.

Another thing this strange new system of lawmaking enabled the Whitehall machine to do was to set up whole new phalanxes of officialdom to enforce the regulations, without any need to consult parliament. The officials were now able off their own bat to create new bureaucratic 'organs', armed with draconian powers, and financed by the charges they imposed on those they were regulating. This truly remarkable constitutional innovation, almost wholly unnoticed by MPs or the media, was the emergence of the Sefra, or Self-Financing Regulatory Agency, and legislation from Brussels provided the chief cover for calling these new bodies into being. One instance was the Meat Hygiene Service, set up in 1995 with its 1,000 officials, headed by a Chief Executive on £78,000 a year, to enforce a string of EC 'hygiene' directives on the meat industry. Eventually it was planned that all the MHS's £50 million a year running costs, including lavish 'performance-related bonuses' for its top officials, would derive from the charges imposed on the industry. The Medicines Control Agency was hived off in 1992 from the Department of Health, to license drugs under the requirements of Brussels directives. Since charges for licensing a new drug amounted to £84,000 a time, with annual 'subsistence' and inspection fees to follow, this provided its officials with very lucrative employment. When the agency had still been part of the ministry, its top official, Dr Jones, had earned £49,000 as a Grade 3 civil servant. In its first year as an independent agency or Sefra, the MCA doubled its 'profits' from licensing and inspection fees from £9 million to £18 million. Dr Jones's salary as 'chief executive' now shot up with 'performance' bonuses to £78,000. The number of his officials earning £40,000-50,000 a year more than doubled, from 13 to 30.

But of the new Sefras spawned by this boom in Brussels legislation, all others paled beside the monster new Environment Agency launched on 1 April 1996, to enforce a whole array of EC environment directives on the pollution of water, air and land. The new agency was made up by merging a string of existing Sefras, the National Rivers Authority, Her Majesty's Inspectorate of Pollution and the scores of Waste Regulation Authorities which had previously been run by local councils. It derived 70 per cent of its £560 million a year income from charges. These ranged from 'authorisation' fees permitting chemical plants to discharge pollutants into the air, under directive 84/360, to the 'management' licences now required under the EC's waste directive 91/156 to run landfill sites. Almost no business could now escape these 'hidden taxes'. Even a corner shop or a plumber had to pay for a 'Waste Carrier's Licence' to handle 'Controlled Waste'. And the Sefra which benefited from all this bonanza of new money, with its 12,000 officials and a Chief Executive earning £88,000 a year, more than the Prime Minister, was now by far the largest public regulatory body in the land.

Yet very few outside the System would have realised that almost all the mass of regulations this monster 'organ' was set up to enforce derived from Brussels. So vast was the flood of new regulatory legislation now pouring out of System in all directions that few people in Britain had any idea how wide-ranging and influential in British life it had become. Indeed one of its most remarkable features was how much of it passed into law with scarcely anyone, including MPs, being aware that it had originated in Europe at all, although several ministries, particularly MAFF and large parts of the DTI and DoE, were now so completely driven by the task of imposing the never-ending flow of EC laws that they had become little more than branch offices of Brussels in London.

One of the more controversial steps taken by Government in the 1990s was the decision to split off Railtrack from the ownership of the trains running on Britain's railways. Most people assumed that this had been dreamed up just as a rather odd way to prepare for railway privatisation. Even a former member of the British Rail Board who, like several of his colleagues, regarded it as a pretty crazy way to proceed, told us he assumed it must have emanated from 'somewhere in the Treasury'. It was never debated in parliament. But the reason for this was that the move was put through by means of a statutory instrument, the Railways Regulations 1992; and the preamble to this revealed the startling fact that it had been introduced under Section 2 (2) of the European Communities Act 1972. The real reason why the Government had split off Railtrack's ownership in this way was simply that it had been ordered to do so by a Brussels directive, 91/440. This had originated from the fact that so many continental railways cross frontiers: the idea was to promote the Single Market by allowing trains to be operated by international companies while ensuring that each country could retain national ownership of its track. How typical, therefore, that the first country immediately to implement this to the letter was the only EC country whose railways do not cross land frontiers. As so often Britain had contrived to turn to her disadvantage a piece of Brussels legislation never really relevant to her in the first place.

Not the least interesting feature of this episode, however, was the way ministers were so careful not to explain to the British people why it had happened. By the mid-1990s it was becoming by no means uncommon for ministers to try to conceal just how much of what they were doing was only being done because they had been ordered to do it by Brussels. And inevitably as the new system took more and more of a hold over the Government machine, the question arose – precisely what power did democratically elected politicians now exercise in this system at all?

The swing doors of Brussels

In theory there were three main ways in which elected politicians still exercised democratic control over this new Brussels-centred system of government.

The first and most important was that all the most significant decisions in the European Community were made by the Council of Ministers. Week after week ministers representing every government in the EC converged on Brussels or some other Euro-capital to attend endless meetings of this nebulous 'Council', in all its different manifestations. One week it would be a 'Fisheries Council' or an 'Agriculture Council', attended by fisheries or farming ministers; another it would be a meeting of finance ministers, 'Ecofin'; another it might be a full 'Summit', usually staged in some picturesque old European city, involving prime ministers themselves, attended by their foreign ministers with swarms of lesser dignitaries and officials. The theory was that it was at these get-togethers of elected politicians that all the key policy decisions were arrived at. It was only at these working Council meetings that the main items of Community legislation, the Council Directives, were discussed and approved. Ministers were filmed disappearing through the glass doors with their briefcases to enter the large mysterious rooms where their discussions took place in secret. Eventually, sometimes only in the small hours of the morning, they would wearily emerge again to give statements to the cameras about how 'useful' the discussions had been, how 'progress' had been made on some contentious issue, how they had won 'a good deal' for some industry back home.

All this elaborate exercise this was meant to convey the reassuring impression that the whole machine of Euro-government was ultimately under democratic control. Those ministers, each the member of a democratically elected government, were there to represent the wishes and the interests of their own people. And in theory their deliberations were meant to constitute the highest expression of democracy in the Community system, so that no important item of legislation could emerge unless it had been 'considered by the Council' and if relevant put to a 'democratic', if secret, vote around the table.

A minister who attended some of those meetings once told us what a shock it had been to discover, at his first 'Council', just how the system really worked. The night before, when he arrived in Brussels, he had attended a dinner with all his fellow-ministers in a château outside the city. As the ministers plodded through a lavish banquet, protocol dictated that each should speak only in his or her own language. Behind glass screens above them, banks of interpreters kept up a running translation of every language combination required, from Greek into Portuguese, from Danish into Italian, from English into French (although the Frenchman sitting next to our own minister spoke very good English). Next morning, when they arrived for their formal discussions, our minister was astonished to see that the item heading the agenda was 'the communiqué' to be issued after the meeting. When he expressed surprise to his officials, saying that surely the communiqué should come last, after they had settled all the other matters on the agenda, he was condescendingly told, 'Oh no, minister, all the other items have already been agreed at last week's Coreper.' The only point of summoning those ministers from all over Europe was to rubber-stamp decisions already arrived at in endless committee meetings of officials further down the line, culminating in the meeting of Coreper (the Committee of Permanent Representatives made up of senior officials from each member state). The only real contribution asked from the elected politicians was to consider how best to present what had happened to the outside world, in the form of a statement for the media.

Of course there are occasions where an issue so contentious arises between governments that it is necessary, by elaborate procedures, to try to resolve their differences during a meeting of the Council itself. But by far the greater part of Community law- and decision-making is something already agreed by officials before the ministers arrive. The politicians are there only to create the illusion that the process still contains some semblance of democratic control and consultation. But the real business has been conducted behind the scenes by the officials. And in recent years this has become ever more obvious, as more and more legislation emerging from Brussels has taken the form not of Council Directives, which at least on paper require the assent of ministers in Council, but of Commission Regulations, requiring no political involvement at all. These are the EC's equivalent of those statutory instruments which now form by far the greater part of lawmaking in Britain. Between 1993 and 1994, according to figures from the Commission's CELEX Database, the number of Council Directives dropped from 65 to 17. But the number of Commission Regulations rose from 1,160 to 1,579, representing 88 per cent of all Community legislation. The largest and fastest-growing form of legislation in the EC thus comprised edicts issued by officials without any political control. It was the purest distillation of rule by bureaucracy.

The irrelevance of parliament

A second way in which democratic control was supposed to be exercised over EC legislation was the procedure whereby, before directives were finally approved in Brussels, they were submitted for scrutiny by parliaments of the member states. Just how effective this procedure turned out to be in practice was illustrated by a report issued in July 1995 by the House of Commons Select Committee on European Legislation. This began by reprinting a Resolution of the House of Commons in 1990 that 'No Minister of the Crown should give agreement in the Council of Ministers to any proposal for European Community legislation' until the MPs on the committee had completed their scrutiny of that proposal, or unless there were special circumstances for making an exception which ministers had to explain.

This could scarcely have been clearer – a solemn Resolution, approved by the British House of Commons, insisting that MPs should at least be given a chance to look at Community legislation before ministers, acting on their behalf, agreed to it. But five years later the report presented a startling picture of how this had worked. In general the MPs concluded that the Commission's decision-making process was 'chaotic', 'in deep crisis' and showed 'total disregard for the rights of national parliaments'. They cited dozens of instances where Commission officials in Brussels had made available the texts of directives and regulations only just in time for ministers meeting in Council to nod them through. 'Time and again an English text emerges only just before a Council.' Sometimes no English version was available at all; texts were only supplied in French. And this was how ministers themselves were treated. When it came to Britain's MPs almost no effort was made to supply documents in time at all. All too often the Commission relied on the Belgian post service 'which may take upwards of a week'; although, the MPs noted, documents were sent from Brussels to the French and German Governments by 'electronic transmission'.

All this confirmed just how insignificant the British parliament was considered to be by the Commission officials. And just as telling was the failure of British ministers themselves to take any steps to rectify the situation. As members of the British parliament, they should have been bound to respect that Resolution passed by their colleagues in 1990, by refusing to agree to any proposal at a Council meeting unless parliament had considered it. The only faint gesture in this direction was in 1994, when Agriculture and Fisheries Minister William Waldegrave appeared before the Committee to give his 'personal undertaking' that something would be done. A year later, the Committee observed, 'We are not yet able to report an improvement.'

The real point, however, was that even if this system worked perfectly, and MPs were given all the time in the world to scrutinise Brussels legislation, their views would not have made a shred of difference. From the lofty perspectives of Brussels, the opinions of the British parliament were wholly irrelevant. All the time and effort these MPs gave to discussing EC legislation became just another part of the charade. The only purpose of all those committee meetings and worthy reports was to help maintain the fiction that parliament still had some 'democratic' part to play in the EC's legislative process. In reality it had nothing of the kind.

Politicians as rubber stamps

The third way in which elected politicians were still supposed to retain some control over this mass of new legislation lay in the method whereby directives from Brussels were turned into British law. This was done, of course, by transposing them into statutory instruments, or regulations. And in theory these could not become law until first they had been read and signed by the appropriate minister, then presented to parliament for approval. In practice, however, when the officials had completed the task of drafting their own version of the EC legislation, often adding on every kind of embellishment, the signing of them into law by ministers was no more than a formality. Very few ministers ever dared question what the officials placed into front of them for signature. The contents were usually too technical for ministers to grasp their full implications unaided; and anyway the whole system relied on the assumption that the officials knew what they were doing, and would draw to their minister's attention anything it was relevant for him to know. We cited earlier the case of the ex-minister who, when we embarrassed him by publicising a particularly absurd consequence of a regulation bearing his signature, admitted he had not even read it.

The regulations then had to be laid before parliament, and again in theory this gave 40 days during which MPs or peers could object. But in practice this happened so rarely that the procedure was no more than a final rubber stamp before they became law. For a start, by the mid-1990s, so many regulations were being spewed out by the system, at a rate of up to 50 or more in a single week, some containing as many as 100 densely packed pages, that it would have been quite impossible for MPs to read them all. And even if in theory it might be possible to marshal enough opposition to a particular regulation for it to be 'prayed against', the system ensured that little would come of it. When in March 1995 the Ministry of Agriculture issued its Fresh Meat (Hygiene and Inspection) Regulations, these proposed using the excuse of an EC directive in effect to set up a major new Government agency, costing £50 million a year and employing 1,000 officials. Yet parliament had never been consulted on the matter. By determined lobbying, we managed to stir enough interest in the issues this raised for more than 100 MPs of all parties, including Tony Blair, several Labour front-benchers and a number of Tory 'Euro-rebels', to sign an Early Day Motion calling for a debate. The Government response was to refer the matter to a Committee, packed with a majority of ministers and loyal Tory backbenchers. These sat through the formality of a two-hour discussion, mostly looking bored or reading their correspondence, until they could obediently vote the regulations the officials wanted into law. Such was the first serious attempt to halt a regulation in nearly 20 years. And this, with more than 3,000 regulations being issued each year, was now the measure of parliament's 'democratic' control over the system.

Politicians as puppets

The truth was that, to a quite startling degree, elected politicians had by the 1990s lost control of Britain's system of government. More than ever before ministers and politicians were controlled by the civil servants. Indeed this phenomenon was not only obvious at national level. It was just as evident in local government, where councillors were more than ever run by their officials. There were several reasons for this shift of power, not least the hugely increased complexity of modern government, which favoured complicated bureaucratic responses to almost any problem, even if the problem was imaginary. This in itself ensured the proliferation of an ever more bureaucratic system of government, encouraging ever more use of technical jargon, paperwork, committee meetings, fancy titles and acronyms, arcane management structures, all of which in turn gave greater power and control to those most naturally at home in such a milieu, the officials themselves.

But nowhere did this evolution in the nature of Britain's government show more clearly than in the spell cast by Europe. If the power of politicians was already diminished by the new bureaucratic ethos of domestic politics, this was nothing compared with the state of subservience to which they were reduced by the all-pervasive influence of Brussels. Across vast areas of government they were no longer able to act independently, because they had constantly to take account of the demands of that shadowy new master, the Euro-system, with its 'centre' in Brussels. For many ministers, much of their working lives was now dominated by the need to consider what that system compelled them to do, proposals for EC legislation which had to be discussed, edicts handed down from Brussels which had to be implemented. And this above all placed them more than ever in the hands of the mediators of the mysteries of that system, the officials, who instructed ministers not just what was required of them but also how their own room for independent thought and action was in so many respects now circumscribed.

This was not to say there was no longer any role for the elected politicians in this System. On the contrary, they had a very significant role. Their function was to act as its front men; to represent it to the outside world; to be interviewed on television and radio explaining and defending its actions; to appear in parliament giving answers to questions or reading out statements which had been drafted for them by the officials; to put their signatures to the endless mass of letters the officials placed in front of them; in short to give the whole system the appearance of democratic legitimacy. Of course the bureaucracy has always been powerful in government. Politicians have always been prisoners of circumstances and the system of their time to a greater extent than they like to imagine. But by the 1990s this tendency was so pronounced that it had given rise to a wholly new form of government. And one of the chief functions of the politicians was to pretend that none of this was happening: to carry on outwardly as if nothing had changed; to protect the public from knowing just how far and how deep this revolution behind the scenes had gone.

Nevertheless anyone who had the chance to study ministers at close quarters in the 1990s might have been struck by a peculiar change which had come over their demeanour. As so many people who had dealings with them observed, particularly if those dealings concerned any of the sort of issues which are the subject of this book, they seemed in a quite new way to have become cut off from the everyday world. They were so cocooned in the System that they could no longer talk or think outside its terms of reference. They had withdrawn behind what we called the 'glass wall', so that although one could still see and talk to them, it was impossible to have proper dialogue with them. They could no longer hear what the outside world was trying to say to them, and could only reply in the strange, dead, endlessly self-justificatory language of the System.

The farce of 'deregulation'

Nothing better exemplified the strange effect this new System was having on Britain's politicians than their response to the growing dismay expressed by so many businesses at the avalanche of new regulations which was suddenly engulfing them. This first became a political issue just before the Conservative Party conference in 1992, and a trigger for this was an article we published in the *Daily Telegraph* on 14 September headed 'Who's That

Lurking Behind the Brussels Book of Rules?', showing how many of the disasters being blamed on 'EC regulations' were in fact due to the way Whitehall civil servants were adding on all sorts of damaging new elements when they translated directives into UK regulations. The article was discussed at some length in the Cabinet, as if the point it was making had come as a surprise to the ministers responsible for passing those regulations into law. The need to roll back the tide of bureaucracy was chosen as a theme of the conference a month later, and several ministers highlighted it in their speeches, culminating, as we have seen, in the invitation from the Prime Minister to Michael Heseltine to act as Tarzan in 'hacking back' the 'jungle' of red tape.

Thus Mr Major launched his 'deregulation' drive, which was to remain a flagship policy of his Government for the next four years.

One of its first steps was the setting up of a special 'Scrutiny Unit' in Mr Heseltine's ministry, the DTI, to produce an urgent report on 'the implementation and enforcement of EC law in the UK'. It should already have been a warning sign that, when ministers wanted to know what to do about the excesses of bureaucracy, they immediately turned for advice to the very people responsible for them, their own civil servants. In fact the Scrutiny Review, published in July 1993, was not altogether a bad document. In particular it examined two areas of legislation. The section on the Meat Hygiene directive 91/497 completely failed to understand the disaster that was falling on hundreds of craft slaughterhouses, and bore all the marks of a MAFF whitewash. But the other main section, on the EC's six Health and Safety directives, contained some penetrating analysis, and in particular levelled devastating criticism at the notorious Workplace (Fire Precautions) Regulations. These were the ones which in September 1992 had been at the last minute withdrawn, just before they lumbered industry, shops and all other businesses, including the self-employed, with costs of £8,000 million.

In December 1992, at the EC's Edinburgh summit, Britain as holder of the 'revolving' Presidency was able to push through a general declaration on the need for 'subsidiarity', the principle that, wherever possible, Member States should be left to legislate for themselves and the Commission should only demand EC-wide rules where they were absolutely essential. This was hailed as a triumph for 'deregulation' in curbing 'unnecessary interference' by Brussels. Meanwhile, under the auspices of the DTI's 'deregulation unit', seven 'task forces' of businessmen produced 650 recommendations for rolling back the regulatory juggernaut and a lengthy 'Deregulation Bill' began its progress through parliament, hailed as yet another epoch-making blow in the great counter-attack on red tape.

But then, in every direction, Mr Major's policy began to unravel. Businessmen read through the Deregulation Bill with astonishment. It became clear it would do nothing at all to tackle the wave of recent regulations which were inflicting such havoc on so many sectors of industry. The recommendations of those task forces of businessmen were quietly buried. Most of the targets chosen for deregulation turned out to be long-obsolete laws causing no problems to anyone, like the Gun Barrel Proving Order 1851 or the Metal Hollow-ware, Iron Drums and Harness Furniture Regulations 1922. It seemed the officials had quite unashamedly turned the whole deregulation exercise into a joke. On more than one occasion they even used 'deregulation' as an excuse to introduce what amounted to new and more onerous regulations. Only right at the end of the passage of the Deregulation Bill through parliament did a junior minister in the House of Lords at last openly admit that any legislation related to Europe had deliberately been excluded from the scope of deregulation. This was particularly revealing, since it was the damage caused by Whitehall's over-eager implementation of Single Market directives which more than anything gave rise to the policy in the first place. Furthermore, to underline the futility of all Mr Major's high-sounding claims for his policy, the EC's Essen 'Summit' in 1994 put out an amendment to the previous year's Edinburgh statement on 'subsidiarity'. This made clear that the subsidiarity principle would not apply to any legislation related to the Single Market: in other words, precisely the legislation which was causing most of the problems, and which subsidiarity had been specifically invoked to restrict.

Although in public Mr Major and Mr Heseltine continued to proclaim that deregulation was high on the Government's list of priorities, the spate of new regulations pouring out of the Whitehall machine continued unabated, at record levels. Between 1992, when the policy was launched, and 1995, the total of new regulations was more than 13,000, easily the largest number for any four-year period in history. And nothing more poignantly illustrated why this was happening than the bizarre battle which raged behind the scenes over one piece of legislation which had now become a test case for the success or failure of the entire policy.

After the DTI Scrutiny Report had savaged the original version of those fire safety regulations intended to implement just 34 lines of a 1989 health and safety directive, the officials were instructed to come up with a more sensible version which would not cost businesses billions of pounds. Again and again they came up with new versions, many scarcely differing from those which had been rejected. In their tenth draft in 1995 the officials were still proposing to implement those 34 lines from Brussels by way of 16 pages of regulations and 123 pages of guidance, totalling 3,698 lines. In vain did members of the deregulation unit, Britain's chief fire officers and other experts argue that there was no need to implement the directive at all, since it added nothing to the protection already given by Britain's own highly-effective legislation on fire safety in the workplace. In the summer of 1996 the officials came up with their final version of the Workplace (Fire Precautions) Regulations. They privately agreed these would add nothing to Britain's fire safety, but explained that they were forced to implement the directive, because they been told by Brussels that, if they didn't, Britain would be taken to the ECJ for breaking EC law. At least, the officials claimed, they had produced a version of the directive which they thought would not cost very much, although they had not yet consulted industry for estimates of what those costs might be. On this basis on 31 July 1996 the Prime Minister wrote reassuringly to Anthony Steen MP, a fierce Conservative backbench critic of his deregulation policy, 'We have reduced the cost of the new fire regulations … to almost nothing.' But the deadline for industry to provide its figures was still nine days off, by which time the British Retail Consortium came up with its estimate of what the new regulations would cost Britain's shops alone.

This was '£758 million'. It was only just short of what the BRC had estimated as the cost of those original regulations ditched in 1992. And this was what Mr Major described as 'almost nothing', because this was what the officials had told him.

The world of mirrors

The Danish philosopher Kierkegaard once wrote that the most dangerous revolutions are not those which tear everything down and cause the streets to run with blood, but the kind which 'leave everything standing, while cunningly emptying it of significance'.

Such was the nature of the change which had been at work in Britain's system of government since she joined the Common Market in 1973, but which only became glaringly obvious in the 1990s. Outwardly the British constitution, the parliamentary system, the processes of lawmaking, the role of the courts, all looked much as they had done 25 years before. But to a remarkable extent this was all now just a façade. Behind it, to a very marked degree, the real government of Britain had been taken over by this strange new System, run by anonymous armies of officials, ultimately looking to Brussels as its centre. It was in this system that the real power now lay. And not its least unnerving feature was the curious way in which politicians tried to disguise or even deny what was happening.

It became almost a matter of wonder how determined ministers were to conceal how far they were now just creatures of this System, and how far their actions were now dictated by Brussels. So keen was Michael Heseltine to imply that Britain was still sovereign in its own affairs that he was prepared quite categorically to deny that his officials were introducing their metrication regulations 'at the behest of Europe', even though these had been put into law under the European Communities Act. When transport minister Steven Norris came under fire for introducing new eyesight tests for lorry drivers exactly as specified in the EC's directive on driving licences, he wrote a letter to the *Sunday Telegraph* not mentioning Europe once, claiming 'the decision to introduce the new standards was mine' and trying to convey the impression that it was nothing to do with Brussels at all. Fisheries minister Tony Baldry repeatedly claimed in 1996 that Britain's jurisdiction over the fishing waters immediately round her coasts was 'not negotiable', implying that no power on earth could take it away. Yet our Treaty of Accession in 1972 clearly showed that we had handed it over lock stock and barrel, only qualified by a proviso that it would be lent back to Britain on the basis of a temporary 'derogation', which at any relevant time could be revoked.

An even more marked feature of the new system was the way, whatever it did, it was always right. We have referred before to the curious phenomenon of those letters which in the mid-1990s poured out of the ministerial word processors of Whitehall in every direction, to MPs writing on behalf of constituents, to trade associations and firms in the business community, to members of the public, defending some policy or action in terms which could not possibly allow that the System was ever wrong. We saw many hundreds of these letters. And what was uncanny about them was just how consistently they presented a version of what the System was up to which did not accord with the way it looked from the outside world. Scarcely one of these letters, often carrying a ministerial signature, did not cry out for an accompanying commentary, drawing attention to just which key points were being carefully skated around or omitted, the half-truths and weasel words which managed to convey a wholly false impression without actually telling a direct lie. The skill with which the civil servants had learned how to put across a misleading point without ever quite falling into a complete untruth was elevated almost to an art form. A classic instance was that phrase so often used in letters signed by MAFF ministers in 1992 and 1993 to explain why dozens of slaughterhouses were being forced to close by the crippling costs of the new meat hygiene regulations, that their owners had 'taken a commercial decision not to invest in the future of their business'.

Ultimately, in fact, the most revealing thing of all about this new System of government was precisely the extent to which it seemed so routinely to rely on bending and distorting the truth. Trying to understand what it was up to constantly took one into what we came to call 'the world of mirrors'. Nothing was ever quite what it seemed. There was something about the all-pervading influence of 'Europe' which had seemed to cast an extraordinary spell over the whole machine of government, so that it was invariably trying to put over to the outside world a version of events which turned out, in reality, wherever one put it to the test, to be subtly misleading, a colossal, carefully contrived fake. It is time to look at the crucially important part played in this new System by propaganda.

14. Lies, Damned Lies and Euromyths

The true object of propaganda is neither to convince nor to persuade, but to produce a uniform pattern of public utterance in which the first trace of unorthodox thought reveals itself as a jarring dissonance.

Leonard Schapiro, writing of Stalin, quoted by Bernard Connolly
in *The Rotten Heart of Europe*, 1995

You can fool all of the people some of the time, and some of the people all of the time, but you cannot fool all of the people all of the time.

Abraham Lincoln, 1858

In the summer of 1995 householders in Kent received a copies of a free colour newspaper called *L'Echo du Pas-de-Calais*. If they bothered to glance at it, they might have read on its front page that its intention was 'to draw closer together' the people of Kent with their French, Belgian and Walloon neighbours just across the Channel. The paper's purpose, it declared, was 'to modestly participate in the necessary and vast project of the construction of Europe'.

750,000 copies of this paper had been printed, using taxpayers' money from the European Commission, local authorities in France and Belgium and Kent County Council. On an inside page, next to a long statement by the 'European Commissioner for Information, Communication, Culture and Audio-Visual Techniques', Senhor Joao de Deus Pinheiro, was an interview with a Mr John Purchese, described as immediate past Chairman of Kent County Council.

The first question put to ex-Chairman Purchese was, 'What is the meaning of Europe Day?', 'Europe Day', came the reply, 'shows the ability of Kent County Council to celebrate with our people our deep attachment to Europe.' He was then asked, 'What are the main initiatives to strengthen the links between Kent and the Pas-de-Calais?' The answer was 'We have both worked on very factual programmes concerning the exchange of social workers, tourism, environment and culture.' 'Do you think', it was put to Mr Purchese, 'that the European idea is on the right track?' 'The Pro-Europeans', he replied, 'think as I do that European construction is a decisive step in the building of our common history.'

To anyone familiar with the Party literature put out in the old Soviet Union, there was something about the bland, leaden, dehumanised tone of these answers, with their talk of 'very factual programmes' and the 'vast project' of the 'European construction', which might have struck a startling chord. It was precisely the sort of Dalek-language one read in those Soviet propaganda booklets extolling the 'vast project' of 'the construction of Socialism'.

Mr Purchese then turned to the problem of those dissidents who had not yet learned to love Big Brother, the people he called 'the Euro skepticals'. These 'Euro skepticals', he said, 'cannot make up their minds about Europe, because they still fail to understand what it means in their daily life, not only for themselves but also for their family and their neighbourhood. In order to convince them I strongly feel that the European Union, the Parliament and the Commission in particular must find a way to communicate. We have to make people understand that without Europe nothing important can be achieved.'

The need to 'make people understand' was one which preoccupied a great many minds in the European Commission and elsewhere in the 1990s. In 1993 an unusual press conference was called in Brussels to hear the proposals of what was described as the 'Comité des Sages', a 'Committee of Wise Men', led by a Belgian MEP, M. Willy de Clerq, who had been given four months to deliberate on ways to 'strengthen the image of Europe' in the minds of its citizens. Among the report's recommendations were that the European Community should in future be 'systematically called the European Union'. Its flag with the ring of stars should be shown as widely as possible. Money should be given to pay for 'pan-European television broadcasts' by the then-President of the Commission, Jacques Delors, and in particular he should make a programme 'directed at the women of Europe'. 'This will probably be the first time', the report solemnly intoned, 'that a statesman makes a direct appeal to women.' Europe should be treated as 'a branded product', to be sold under slogans such as 'Together For Europe For The Benefit Of Us All'. and 'Mother Europe Must Protect Her Children'. There should be a European Order of Merit, for those who had played a leading part in building the new Europe. EC Governments should stop trying to explain the Maastricht Treaty. As M. de Clerq put it, 'It is unexplainable. Treaty decisions are far too technical and removed from daily life for people to understand.'

At least it was to the credit of the journalists present at this bizarre press conference that for once they began to get restive. When the Sages suggested that money should be provided to persuade the media to take 'a more positive line' about the EC, that broadcasters should be paid to introduce 'the European dimension' into television soap operas and game shows, and that history books should be rewritten 'to reflect the European dimension', some journalists even walked out in protest. The Greek president of the Brussels association of journalists, Costas Verros, accused the Commission of 'acting like a military junta'. But the Commissioner responsible for 'Information, Communication, Culture and Audio-Visual Techniques', Senhor de Pinheiro, gave an assurance that he would be acting on some of the report's suggestions. And so it was to be.

*

It would be impossible to understand the workings of the new System of government which has been developing in recent years without recognising the crucial role played in its operations by propaganda. To surround its activities with the correct aura, the Euro-system continually has to convey three messages about itself:

1. that it is in every respect working successfully, bringing the peoples of Europe ever closer together, to the benefit of all;
2. that it enjoys enthusiastic support for what it is doing, particularly from corporate groups, such as organisations representing industry and local government;
3. that it is rolling forward by an irresistible historical momentum, so that it is on the side of the future and not least the young.

The most obvious way it pursues these ends, of course, is simply by pouring out propaganda of the most straightforward kind. In this sense it spends hundreds of millions of pounds a year on publicity material, on staging conferences, seminars and exhibitions or on sending people on free or highly subsidised trips to Brussels or Strasbourg, or from one EC country to another. A good deal of this effort is deliberately targeted at schools and the 'young Europeans of tomorrow' because, as the report by the Committee of Wise Men put it in 1993, 'it is strategically judicious to act where resistance is weakest'. Under the SOCRATES programme, a 'European Education Project' designed to target the young of all ages, from nursery school up to university, aimed at building up 'awareness of our common European identity' with posters, videos, training courses for teachers and booklets designed to be used as teaching aids. Typical of these is a booklet issued free to schools by the Commission, 'A Portrait of Our Europe', describing 'the development of the European Union', with glossy pictures of its cultural achievements, such as the Parthenon, Notre Dame, Dutch windmills and the London red double-decker bus. Under headings such as 'The road to European Union' and 'Solving problems together', this presents children with a wonderful success story, of how 'Europe' has brought peace, prosperity and 'co-operation in the interest of all concerned'. There are still one or two little problems, like the fact that 'unfortunately payments still have to be made in a different currency in each Union country'. However 'even that should change', with monetary union and a European central bank to 'ensure the stability of the European currency'. Oh yes, and the 'organs and institutions of the EU are there to ensure that European rules are complied with'.

We must now, however, look at some of the subtler ways in which the System tries to win the battle for hearts and minds – beginning with the curious techniques employed to convey the impression that it has the full support of industry.

Front organisations and the CBI

Those familiar with the workings of the old Soviet Union will recall the significant role played in the Soviet system by what were known as 'front organisations'. These were bodies set up by the system itself, purportedly to represent every kind of key group in society, coal miners, steel workers, fishermen, artists, writers, composers, doctors, scientists, to declare slavish support for the policies of the Soviet Government. The purpose of these declarations was that they could then endlessly be quoted by Party spokesmen and reprinted in the media, to convey the impression that all miners, fishermen, composers or whatever were solidly behind the Party line.

Anyone following the news in Britain in 1994 and 1995 could scarcely have avoided coming across references to the views on Europe of the Confederation of British Industry. The fanatically pro-EU leadership of the CBI, under their director general Howard Davies and president Sir Bryan Nicholson, conducted two polls of members, on the Single Market and the Single Currency, the findings of which were then incessantly quoted as representing 'the view of British industry'. Both polls were presented as ringing endorsements of Britain's membership of the EC in general and these aspects of it in particular. And they were then constantly cited in speeches and interviews by British ministers such as Douglas Hurd and Michael Heseltine, and EC Commissioners such as Sir Leon Brittan and the Commission President M. Jacques Santer. For instance, in the House of Lords in the summer of 1995, foreign minister Baroness Chalker made tremendous play with the CBI survey on the Single Market, which showed, she claimed, that 71 per cent of British firms 'were enjoying greater trading opportunities with Europe, due to the Single Market'.

It all sounded highly impressive, until one looked more carefully at what this figure was based on. For a start, although the CBI questionnaire on the Single Market had been sent to all its members, more than 8,000 companies, only 579 replied. The survey was thus based on only a 7 per cent, self-selecting response; in terms of the whole of British industry, a tiny minority of a tiny minority. Lady Chalker's '71 per cent of British firms' came from the survey's first question, asking companies whether, compared with five years earlier, they were experiencing 'greater trading opprtunities', both exports and imports, with the rest of the EU. 71 per cent replied 'yes', 27 per cent said no. But when those who answered 'yes' were asked their reason, only 27 per cent said that it was 'a direct consequence of the opening up of the Single Market'. The largest group, 41 per cent, said this was simply because their company had made greater efforts to sell in the EC. In fact answers to the next two questions showed that almost exactly the same number of companies were making efforts to sell outside the EC (78 per cent) as inside it (79 per cent). In other words, the firms were generally trying to increase their business, which was not exactly surprising.

Where the survey became more interesting, however, was when more detailed questions were put on the Single Market. It appeared that a substantial minority of companies in fact had very serious concerns about it. More than a quarter complained of the 'over-zealous implementation of EC legislation by UK authorities'; 28 per cent said they were faced with 'unfair competition' due to 'the failure of governments to enforce EC legislation'; more than a fifth complained of 'illegal state aids or subsidies in other EC countries'. All of which hardly amounted to the paean of unbridled enthusiasm for the Single Market those politicians liked to pretend. But it was noticeable how carefully the CBI angled its own summaries of the survey, playing up anything which might seem to favour the Single Market, while playing down its members' real concerns almost to vanishing point.

Even more startling was the use made of the CBI's second survey, on the Single Currency. Again the pro-EC establishment went into overdrive, citing this as evidence that British industry was enthusiastically in favour of a Single Currency. For instance, in a prominent lecture in the City of London in November 1994, the EC's Trade Commissioner Sir Leon Brittan claimed the survey had shown that 'a majority of CBI members were in favour of Economic and Monetary Union'. 'It is not surprising', he concluded, that 'those most involved in business want Britain to have the advantage of a single European currency.' Certainly this was the spin the CBI's Director General Howard Davies wished to put on the survey, when he claimed that a single currency was what 'most CBI members want', favoured by 'a large majority'.

Again, on what were such statements based? This time the CBI sent out questionnaires to only 624 selected member companies or their chairmen. Even of these only 206 bothered to reply, and in answer to the main question, as to whether they supported Britain joining a single currency, only 28 per cent, just 59 replies, were positively in favour. 72 per cent were either actively hostile or merely lukewarm. So how did Mr Davies, Sir Leon and countless others manage to twist this round into 'a large majority' of CBI members being in favour? They did this by taking the largest group, 56 per cent, who were prepared to agree that EMU could help business in the long run but 'was not a necessity', and adding them to those positively in favour. By this sleight of hand, they were able to claim that '84 per cent of CBI members are in favour of a single currency', which was exactly how the survey was reported by the BBC and by presenters of the Today programme – without their researchers bothering to question how the views of fewer than 60 companies were finagled into representing the view of 'most firms in British industry'.

One of the most dramatic of the survey's findings was the response to a question on Europe's political future. A staggering 88 per cent of respondents said they were opposed to 'deepening integration'. But was this not a contradiction? Was not 'economic and monetary union' easily the most obvious expression of that 'deepening integration' which nine out of ten said they were opposed to? Again it was world of mirrors time. It would have been rather more honest of the CBI to headline its survey 'Huge majority of CBI members opposed to a united Europe'. But this, of course, was not the game the CBI leadership was playing with its surveys, and a year later they came up with another.

As usual, the CBI stretched itself to the limit in trying to put a pro-EU spin on its findings. The press release shouted 'British Business Backs Europe and Calls for End to Squabbling'. 'The vast majority of UK firms thinks EU membership gives major benefits to British business' the release went on, which seemed to sit rather strangely with the figures in the survey itself, showing that slightly more firms said the Single Market had brought them no benefit, or remained neutral, than those who said they had benefited. But to an outside observer, the most interesting finding of this third survey was the way it showed significant shifts of opinion since the previous year.

Particularly interesting was a big jump in the concern firms expressed over their experience of the Single Market in practice. In 1994, for instance, 26 per cent of the firms questioned had said they were suffering from 'over-zealous enforcement of EC legislation' by the UK Government. In 1995 this figure had risen to 44 per cent. Those who were experiencing 'unfair competition because of the failure of other Member States to implement EC legislation' had risen from 28 to 41 per cent. These were fairly major areas of criticism, and if the CBI had been concerned with representing the interests of its members, they would have been given top billing. Instead they were buried away on an inside page, and the CBI's comment was merely that, since the previous year, 'answers show little shift in emphasis'.

But of course these polls were never intended to represent the real interests of CBI members. Their real function was evident from the way their findings were then trotted out interminably by the pro-EC establishment to show that British industry was right behind the EU, Single Market, Single Currency and everything else. The purpose of carrying out these polls was precisely to help provide the 'correct answers' which could then be quoted ad nauseam in speeches by spokesmem for the System like Secretary Hurd, Commissioner Brittan and President Santer, to help create the illusion that British industry was near-unanimously behind it. And in this they were dramatically successful. So far as the BBC and much of the press was concerned, the surveys showed beyond question that the majority of British industry was solid for the Single Currency and over the moon about the benefits of the Single Market; and in this respect the CBI's 'findings' went on being deferentially quoted and requoted by the media as if there was no other side to the story. There was very significantly less coverage, for instance, when in 1996 2,000 members of the other main business organisation, the Institute of Directors, voted by an overwhelming majority at their annual conference against the single currency. Remarkably little attention was paid in 1996 to a survey of its clients by the Institute of Chartered Accountants, showing that Britain's medium-size firms now named 'European Union legislation' as the biggest single obstacle to expansion of their business. Even less notice was taken in 1995, when the Federation of Small Businesses, representing 70,000 firms, voted at its annual conference for Britain to leave Europe altogether. Compared with the CBI, in the eyes of the EU-bedazzled media like the Today programme, these were all nothing more than a tiny minority of unimportant and unrepresentative dissidents.

The farce of 'consultation'

The use made of these CBI polls to dazzle the media was only the most conspicuous example of the way the System relied on puppet 'front organisations' to promote its cause. One of the most highly developed features of the Britain's new system of government was the way it used trade associations like the CBI and the National Farmers Union to keep their members quiet, and to convey to the outside world that one industry after another was solidly behind the EC, whatever new regulations and bureaucracy the System might wish to impose.

It might not have been surprising to find the NFU so fanatically enthusiastic about the EU, since many of its members derived such a colossal cash bonanza from Brussels subsidies. This was considered to justify even the fearsome blizzard of bureaucracy farmers consequently had to endure. But it was very noticeable how the NFU represented the interests of the larger farmers, in alliance with those of the chemical companies and the supermarkets, while hundreds of thousands of smaller farmers struggled to earn a living, either with much smaller subsidies or none at all, and with very little support from the top officials of the NFU. Again, in its war against the smaller slaughterhouses, MAFF leaned heavily on the support of the ultra-loyal Federation of Fresh Meat Wholesalers, representing the large industrial abattoir companies which had everything to gain from seeing their smaller competitors go to the wall under the regulatory onslaught. This meant that, whenever the policy came under fire, MAFF officials could reassuringly cite the views of the Federation as showing how the industry was right behind it, even though most individual firms were desperately and angrily opposed. As Britain's fishermen faced growing disaster through the crisis created by the Common Fisheries Policy, MAFF similarly relied on the loyalty of the main fishermen's organisations, the National Federation of Fishermen's Organisations and the Scottish Fishermen's Federation, whose leaders were ultimately prepared to accept almost any indignity Brussels and the ministry officials heaped on them. But eventually many individual fishermen decided they could take no more. By 1996 the most significant development in the fishing industry was the way thousands of fishermen, including many of their more articulate spokesmen, were flocking behind the banner of the Save Britain's Fish campaign, pledged to take Britain out of the CFP. This left the alliance between MAFF and the official organisations increasingly high and dry, as the membership drained away to support SBF. But MAFF ministers and officials continued to cite the views of the NFFO and SFF as if nothing had happened, as if they alone still represented Britain's fishing industry; because this was the way the System worked.

The System's ideal was that every industry should have its tame trade organisation, usually representing the larger members, working closely with ministry officials, never stepping out of line, always happy to come up with a statement endorsing Government policy. What the System hated more than anything else was a breakaway trade association, such as was developing in the fishing industry with SBF, because this was beyond the officials' control. A similar development emerged in the meat industry, when the Quality Meat and Livestock Alliance was formed by 200 abattoir owners to fight the ministry's war on slaughterhouses. It happened in the egg industry when 800 smaller producers set up the United Kingdom Egg Producers Association. The one thing the System could not tolerate was an association which genuinely tried to represent the interests of its members, and which refused to collaborate with whatever regulatory overkill the officials threw at them. But it was noticeable how each of these breakaway groups had only been set up in desperation, when the System was threatening to wipe out large sections of their industry.

One reason why the officials so valued the more compliant trade organisations was that it enabled them to carry out one of the System's more bizarre rituals, the procedure known as 'consultation'. Whenever new regulations were drafted, these were sent to the industry affected, asking for its comments. This was a cardboard sham. Hardly ever did the 'consultation' process result in changing a word of the regulations as drafted. Often the officials would only send out some complex piece of legislation for 'consultation' within

170

a week or two of it passing into law. The record was held by the Sea Fish (Conservation) Bill in 1992, when the 'consultation' deadline for fishermen to express their views to the ministry was 14 June, although the Bill had already passed its Second Reading in the Commons six days earlier. Nevertheless the charade did serve a purpose. It meant that, whenever the new regulations subsequently created problems, the ministerial word processors could churn out letters claiming that the industry's views had been 'fully consulted' when the regulations were drafted. This formula, used on countless occasions, provided the best possible answer to any criticism. It showed that whatever disasters might result, the industry was in no position to complain, because it had 'approved' the regulations before they became law. Once again, it was pure world of mirrors.

Grants and the ring of stars

Off Lickers Lane in suburban Knowsley, Lancs, a scruffy patch of open space contains some weedy saplings surrounded by hideous metal and concrete fences. In the centre of Naples and outside Patras in Greece, traffic jams are caused by motorway schemes left half-finished. From the church tower of a Sussex village holding an arts festival flies a flag in blue and gold. What these, and ten thousand other projects all over the EU have in common is that each carries a telltale logo – the 'ring of stars' which shows the project has been part-subsidised by money from Brussels.

All over the EU by the mid-1990s, people were becoming familiar with this 'ring of stars' indicating projects which had been 'funded by the EU'. Rather less well known, however, was the peculiar pressure exerted to ensure that, whenever taxpayers' money was handed back for such purposes, proper due was paid in terms of publicising the EU's 'gift'. Far from being just an altruistic way of directing money at socially desirable projects, under the EU's 'Social Fund', Structural Fund' or 'Regional Fund', the way these billions of pounds in grants were handed out played a crucially important role in the EC's drive to promote its own image.

In 1994 Britain's universities received a letter from a body called 'Higher Education ESF Services'. This turned out to be a department of John Moores University in Liverpool which co-ordinated the dishing out of money sent back from Brussels for grants to universities, under the 'European Social Fund'. Much of this money went on projects which themselves had a 'European dimension', like those conducted under the EU's ERASMUS programme. But the letter also explained that the Department of Education was preparing a report to the European Commission on 'activities funded by the ESF in the UK', and particularly wanted to see 'examples of advertising, publicity and promotional materials' used to recruit for such projects. The Commission was 'becoming increasingly concerned', the letter went on, 'at the lack of impact the ESF has on the consciousness of the general public'. The 'EC sees advertising etc. as a means of informing individuals in each Member State of the direct benefits available from membership of the EU'. Then came the clincher. 'The receipt of future ESF support' would be 'influenced by the amount of publicity given to ESF projects.' Access to Euro-funds 'could be dependent on the extent to which individual institutions promote the receipt of grant aid'. In other words, if British universities wanted to lay hands on any of the cash British taxpayers had handed over to Brussels in the first place, this would very much depend on how much publicity they accorded to the EU for its generosity.

This was by no means the only obstacle to obtaining a grant from the EU. Martin van der Weyer wrote a hilarious, nightmarish account in the *Spectator* (9 September 1995) of the months he spent stumbling through an unending bureaucratic labyrinth trying to obtain a small grant for converting an old building in Helmsley, Yorkshire, into a community arts centre, under the 'Objective 5(b)' procedures of the EC's Structural Fund. At one point he was faced with the 193-page Single Programming Document, 'the bible of Objective 5(b)', which informed him that Helmsley was 2,500 kilometres from Thessaloniki, and wasn't in Yorkshire anyway, but in a region of England known to Brussels as 'the Northern Uplands'. At another he had to complete a dense twelve-page form asking among other things how many 'kilometres of railway track' would be built by his project. In the end, after hundreds of hours of paperwork, telephoning, form-filling and meetings, his arts centre project was rated so low by the officials of DG X in Brussels on such factors as 'energy saving' and 'partnership synergy' that it was dismissed out of hand. Only then did the Whitehall official who had advised him through the whole process tell him that a project like his would never have had a chance of getting an Objective 5(b) grant anyway.

At least Mr Van der Weyer never had to erect a large hoarding outside his arts centre showing the 'ring of stars'. But those who were successful in winning grants invariably found there was no condition on which the Brussels officials were more insistent. When the Sussex village of Mayfield was given a small EC grant for its 1996 music and arts festival, a promise was extracted that the EU flag would be flown on the church tower, not only during the 1996 festival itself but at subsequent festivals and on 'Europe Day', which fell like a saint's day on 9 May each year.

The recipients of grants often found there were other unforeseen snags to the system. When the 1994 World Disabled Sailing Championships were held in Rutland, application for a grant towards expenses was made to the EC's 'Foundation for International Co-Operation of Projects and Other Activities for Humanitarian Affairs'. Eventually 'FIPA' agreed to give 7,130 ecus (around £5,900), but only on condition that the EU's support was mentioned in all literature and promotions advertising the event. Audited accounts should then be supplied within four months, and only then would payment be made. The charity therefore had to borrow the money to cover the contribution eventually anticipated from the EU. After the event accounts were duly supplied. But only six months later did a cheque finally arrive, for a sum smaller than the grant agreed. This, the officials explained, was because 'EU rules needed clarifying before the final balance could be paid'. The organisers of the sailing championships had honoured their part of the bargain by paying tribute to the EU's generosity in all their advertising and programmes. But so many problems had the small grant given rise to that one organiser could not resist writing to his MEP that 'as the only direct personal contact I have had with the EU, it supports my worst fears. In simple terms it endorses my view that for Great Britain to remain part of your organisation will be an unmitigated disaster for us all.'

A much more fundamental way in which these funds were used to further the EU's interests could be seen in the system whereby money was handed out to local authorities in a deliberate drive to build up 'regional identity'. The purpose of this was to promote a direct relationship between the 'regions' and Brussels, by-passing central governments. Lying behind it was the idea, fostered by the creation of the 'Committee of the Regions' under the Maastricht Treaty, that the Europe of the future would be not so much a union of countries as a 'Europe of Regions', in which each region would enjoy its own direct links with Brussels and in which national governments would play an ever more marginal role. If these Brussels-promoted 'regions' could cross national borders, as we saw reflected in that newspaper published jointly in Kent, the Pas-de-Calais and southern Belgium, so much the better, because this would assist in the erosion of purely national identities. But even within national boundaries, oceans of Brussels money were directed to furthering this cause. Drivers down the main north-south motorway in Greece could see a huge sign near Volos, bearing the 'ring of stars', welcoming them to the European 'Region of Continental Greece'. In County Hall, Chichester in September 1995, 121 hand-picked delegates from local councils, education authorities, the police and the fire service attended a day-long conference organised by the European Commission, urging them to build up a new identity for the 'South-East Region of England'. The public and press were rigorously excluded from a hall lavishly decorated with Euro-flags and flower arrangements in blue and gold, as delegates were treated to champagne and briefings from Geoffrey Martin, the 'Permanent Representative of the European Commission' in London, a local member of the European Parliament, a representative of the CBI and other spokesmen for the System. And in no way was the attraction of developing this new sense of 'regional identity' more persuasively dressed up than in the idea that it would give more effective access to grants from Brussels.

But it was all a chimera. All this money so 'generously' handed out by Brussels was only a small part of that taken from British taxpayers in the first place. And an even more insidious way in which the system was based on sleight of hand was described to us by someone intimately familiar with it from his work in local government. The real problem, he pointed out, was that, since most of the money dished out by Brussels was received by public bodies anyway, this could actually end up leaving taxpayers with an enormous concealed debt. 'An application for an EU grant', he explained, 'takes a full team of expensive local government employees approximately six months to assemble and submit, not always succcessfully the first time. The costs are borne by the taxpayers and are non-recoverable. Then the allocation of Grant is made, usually £X million over several years.' Because the money is only handed over in stages, however, the local authority then has to borrow much of it to proceed with the project, thus running up hefty interest charges, again not recoverable. But the real hidden trap is sprung when central government next comes to allocate funds to the local authority, because it then makes a deduction to take account of the money from the EU. This usually knocks off a sum equivalent to 80 per cent of the grant. So, when all this is allowed for, 'the actual amount of benefit to the locality is very small. But this does not stop the EU from sticking that horrible little blue logo on everything and pretending us they are giving us something – when in fact all that is taking place is a concentration of funds on one high profile project, while at the other end reduced government funding forces cuts in local services for reasons no one explains.'

It was certainly striking how much spokesmen for the System, like members of the European Parliament, liked to highlight these grants from Brussels as one of the chief blessings of belonging to the European Union. On closer examination, however, they turned out to be just another instance of the world of mirrors.

The myth of the Euro-myths

One of the System's more bizarre propaganda campaigns was its attempt to discredit criticism of the EC in Britain by publishing regular lists of what it termed 'Euro-myths' – stories printed in the British press about Brussels directives which it claimed were not true.

This began in 1993 with a speech by Foreign Secretary Douglas Hurd, reprinted as a leaflet by the Foreign Office. It was then picked up by the European Commission which in 1994 was reported to have set up a special 'response unit' in Directorate-General X in Brussels to combat the perpetration of 'myths' in the British press. In 1995 the campaign came to a head when the Foreign Office published a booklet entitled 'The European Community: Facts and Fairy Tales', with a foreword by Mr Hurd; while at a conference in Torquay Geoffrey Martin launched a lavish booklet published by the Commission entitled 'So You Still Believe What You Read in the Newspapers?', 50,000 copies of which were sent out to MPs, journalists, businessmen, libraries and members of the public.

The central tactic of the Foreign Office/Commission campaign was first to catch the eye by highlighting silly tabloid-type 'Euro-scares' about 'square strawberries' or 'EC to ban Valentine cards', which were only too easy to knock down as untrue; but then subtly to mix these in with genuine examples of Euro-legislation which were seriously damaging. The intention was to convey the impression that the genuine stories were just as 'mythical' as the tabloid fictions. The campaign's real purpose was to make out that all this talk of Britain suffering from membership of the EC was just fanciful rubbish and 'mass self-deception'.

We examined the Commission's booklet with particular interest, because nearly half the 40 examples of 'Euro-myths' it cited were based on stories we had reported ourselves. We could therefore recognise only too clearly the various techniques the officials fell back on in their efforts to discredit them.

A favourite tactic was to dismiss as a 'myth' any example where the real problem arose not from a directive itself but from the way it was implemented by the UK Government. A typical instance was the disaster which had faced Britain's herbal medicines industry in 1994 because of the crazy misreading of a directive by British officials. Because blame for this threat did not lie directly with Brussels, and the disaster had in the nick of time been averted, the Commission was able to wave this aside as a 'Euromyth', while completely failing to mention that the threat had at one time been perfectly genuine.

Another tactic was to dismiss as 'myths' stories which were true at the time they were reported, but where the situation had subsequently changed. It was easy in 1996 to deny that Brussels planned to impose a complete ban on double-decker buses since, after this was publicised in 1994, this particular proposal had been dropped. But the Commission had to use weasel words to conceal the fact that Britain's bus industry still faced the probability of restrictions which would entirely change British bus design at a cost of billions of pounds. 'It is true', the booklet coyly conceded, 'that a continental-style Eurobus will form the basis for the Directive', but such 'arguments are only to be expected in a highly technical field.'

A third tactic was so to misrepresent the basic facts of a serious story as to make it virtually unrecognisable. One example was a grotesque travesty of the Lanark Blue cheese case, which was presented as nothing more than a tabloid-style scare that 'many traditional soft cheeses, including Stilton, Brie and Lanark Blue, are likely to disappear due to EU rules relating to listeria'. The booklet then made the wholly fictitious claim that the EC directive's ban on *Listeria monocytogenes* in cheese was only 'provisional, pending the outcome of work by the United Nations'. Another instance was the way the Commission wriggled out of the absurd consequences of the EC forestry directive, which had led 80 per cent of all acorns sold in Britain having to be imported. This was now presented as some kind of benevolent concession by Brussels, 'allowing the UK to import acorns from abroad, notably from central and eastern Europe'.

A fourth Commission trick was simply to rephrase the problem in such a distorted fashion that it was then easy to dismiss a charge no one had actually made. An example was the £3-4 billion bill UK taxpayers were having to pick up for the strengthening of tens of thousands of road bridges, to comply with a ruling under EC directive 85/3 that even minor roads must be capable of taking 40-tonne lorries. The Commission trivialised this into some supposed demand for the strengthening of 'railings and parapets on motorway bridges to bring them into line with EU standards'. Since this 'demand' was entirely imaginary, it could easily be dismissed. The Commission did go on to say that, however, that 'councils may be strengthening bridges in anticipation of the trans-European road networks, a project gaining momentum and which aims to tie the regions of the EU closer to one another for the benefit of industry and travellers'.

What delighted us about the Commission's efforts was that, of the 16 out of 40 examples taken from our own reporting, the officials were unable to disprove a single one. Indeed, so thankless was their task that they even ended their booklet with a section entitled 'True Myths', shamelessly listing eight examples of stories about EC legislation which they had to admit were completely true. These include several we had reported, such as the subsidies Brussels was giving the Canary Islands to breed rabbits, which the Commission now defended as a scheme 'to assist in the diversification of the Canary Islands economy'. It would have been hard to find a more bizarre example of the world of mirrors than this attempt to discredit critics for the crime of peddling 'myths' which were actually true.

Nevertheless the most revealing feature of the Commission booklet was how many of the genuine catastrophes being created by the Euro-system it simply omitted altogether. There was no mention, for instance, of the mass-closure of abattoirs; or the chaos inflicted on small electronics and engineering firms; or the billions of pounds the British were having to pay in higher water bills to comply with absurdly exacting standards required by EC water directives; or the billions of fish destroyed each year by the CFP's 'conservation' rules.

This did not, however, prevent many MPs, MEPs and journalists on newspapers like the *Guardian*, the *Observer* and the *Independent* from eagerly recycling the booklet's contents in articles, letters and speeches for months to come. In their blissful ignorance, they fell for precisely the line the Commission wanted them to. This was to put across the message that all stories about Brussels directives were on a par with the silliest tabloid front page about straight bananas. Any criticism of the European Union in the British press must be dismissed as nothing more than 'xenophobia' or 'hysteria'. Repeatedly these two words were hammered home, even where they were most laughably inappropriate. That Brussels message was getting across.

'So You Still Believe What You Read in the Newspapers?' may in truth have been little more than a farrago of half-truths and amateurish inaccuracies. But in purely propaganda terms the officials of DG X could be pleased by their work.

Fellow travellers in the media

Certainly the System devoted vast amounts of effort and money to putting across the image of itself it wanted. And there were ways in which that money could be used to good effect to ensure that reporting of the System's activities in the media struck exactly the note which was wanted. That proposal of the 'Committee of Wise Men' in 1993 that funds should be made available to ensure that the media took a 'positive line' had not gone unheeded. As the Belgian journalist Gerard de Selys explained in an article, 'The Propaganda Machine of the Commission' in 1996, 'many of the 765 journalists accredited to Brussels are offered very generous gifts in the form of reports for which they are paid, and for which tidy sums are also paid as expenses. Alternatively, they are offered regular or occasional work for one of the many publications produced essentially by the Commission. For some of them, this work can double or treble their salary.'

But it was equally true that influential sections of the British media were only too happy to fall in with the party line without any such discreet 'encouragement'. Despite the paranoia which led the officials of the Commission and the Foreign Office to compile their little lists of 'myths' and 'fairy tales', most mainstream journalists were just as scornful of 'hysterical Euro-bashing' as they were themselves, and this was particularly true of the main current affairs programmes of the BBC. The System had no more reliable allies than programmes like Today and Newsnight, which liked to portray any criticism of Europe as just the preserve of a small minority out on the political margins. If Panorama made a programme about the Common Fisheries Policy, it would inevitably follow the Brussels party line that the basic problem was all just a matter of 'too many fishermen catching too few fish'. Any British fishermen who objected to the CFP were only complaining about rules that were sensible and necessary. If the CBI put out spurious claims about industry's support for a Single Currency, it could at least be assured that the presenters of Today or Newsnight would accept their validity without question; because, without knowing it, they had become sucked in to become a vital part of the System themselves.

There were two main reasons why most leaders of opinion in Britain so long remained happily uncritical of the consequences of Britain's involvement with Europe. The first was fashion. For twenty years, it was the received view of the opinion-forming classes that 'Europe' was generally 'a good thing'. All the main political parties were in favour of it. No significant part of the intellectual establishment offered any alternative view. It was remarkably difficult for most people in politics or the media to think outside that cosy, reassuring consensus. And if they didn't, why should anyone else?

But a second reason, allied to the first, was the quite remarkable state of ignorance in which most otherwise well-informed people remained about the impact 'Europe' was having on Britain's politics and way of life. Except to those in some way inside the System, and benefiting from it, 'Europe' was on the whole regarded as immeasurably boring, abstruse and remote. It was just not something most intelligent people needed to think about. It was all far too complicated and technical to be worth getting involved in, certainly not in any detail. This was why it provided such a perfect field for the cleverdick tendency now so dominant in the media, represented by journalists like Jeremy Paxman or John Humphrys, those who liked to appear knowing about everything without actually knowing very much about anything.

So Britain entered on the most far-reaching political transformation in her history with most of her politically-aware classes in a state of near-total anaesthesia.

When in 1992 we ourselves began reporting in detail on the bizarre and devastating impact this new System was beginning to have on so many British industries, we received thousands of letters from people running businesses, expressing almost incredulous relief that at last someone was taking an interest in this weird new nightmare world which was creeping up on them. For most in the ingrown, hothouse world of the media, whose professional lives were largely unaffected by the workings of the System, it was as if these desperate concerns were just something to be viewed from down the wrong end of a very long telescope. As one very grand ex-editor once put it in a newspaper office discussion on Europe, 'Why do we have to worry about all these small businesses closing down. Why can't we just concentrate on the big picture?'

But, almost month by month through the years of the mid-1990s, the picture began to change. Out in that world of which the media were so happily oblivious, more and more people were beginning to wake up to just what an extraordinary thing was happening to Britain. Eventually, even inside the hothouse, the penny began to drop. The System had managed to keep the country in a state of anaesthesia for long enough. The moment was approaching when its bluff would at last have to be called.

15. Britain Awakes to a Nightmare

I was under no illusions when I took Britain into the ERM. I said at the time that membership was no soft option. The soft option, the devaluer's option, the inflationary option would be a betrayal of our future; and it is not the Government's policy.

John Major, 10 September 1992, six days before Britain left the ERM

In the years after 1992 a historic change came over British perceptions of the European Union. For four decades, even during the first 20 years after Britain joined, national debate over 'Europe' had been conducted almost entirely on a theoretical level. It was dominated by hypothetical abstractions, in particular by projections of what might happen for good or ill in the future. Although, since 1973, the influence of the new system of government on British life had imperceptibly grown year by year, for most people 'Europe' was still something far away and remote. They were not aware that it had any direct influence on their daily lives. This was despite the fact that Europe's real impact on British life was already in many respects enormous, from the way it increased the cost of food in our shops to the astonishingly disruptive effect the European issue had on domestic politics. In just a short period at the beginning of the 1990s, for instance, divisions over Europe played a key part in the forced resignations of a Chancellor of the Exchequer (Lawson), a Foreign Secretary (Howe), a Secretary of State for Trade and Industry (Ridley) and the Prime Minister herself (Margaret Thatcher).

This sense of the remoteness of Europe remained right up to the time of the General Election in April 1992, when John Major's Conservative Party became the first party in Britain's history to win over 14 million votes. Europe was scarcely mentioned in that election campaign, even though it was only two months earlier the Government had signed the 'Treaty on European Union' agreed at Maastricht the previous December, committing Europe to a far greater degree of political and economic unity than ever before; and even though, since October 1990, the British economy had been locked by the EC into the monetary straitjacket of the ERM, which had played a key part in inflicting on Britain's economy one of the sharpest and most devastating recessions it had ever experienced.

The Maastricht steamroller

Scarcely was Mr Major's election triumph over, however, than the European issue began to creep out of the shadows, to dominate British politics over the next few years in a way it had never done before (it might be recalled that in

1972 Richard Nixon had likewise won the greatest popular vote in his country's history just before the Watergate scandal erupted to overshadow the rest of his Presidency). One of the first tasks of the new House of Commons was to give its formal approval to the Maastricht Treaty, and although in principle this was forced through in May 1992, the way it was done provoked a new kind of alarm over where the 'European process' was taking Britain's parliamentary democracy. Despite the fact that the new treaty, designed to establish 'ever closer union' between the nations of Europe, was technically a series of amendments and extensions to the two earlier treaties, Rome and the Single European Act, and could not be properly understood except in the context of what it was amending, the Government astonishingly decided that MPs could not have sight of the Treaty in full until after they had voted it through. Foreign Office minister Tristan Garel-Jones decreed that it would be 'presumptuous' to publish the Treaty until after every country had ratified it. The Foreign Secretary Douglas Hurd even admitted that he had not read the Treaty before signing it. The ruthless behind-the-scenes pressures applied to many Tory MPs to whip them into line were to be sustained for months to come, as the more controversial points of the Treaty gave rise to days and nights of bitter discussion in Committee. An organised team of highly alarmed backbenchers, co-ordinated by Bill Cash and Michael Spicer, subjected the Treaty to line-by-line examination, bringing to light many of its more disturbing implications which even Government ministers had not noticed before. But this only made the Tory whips even more anxious to suppress further discussion of the matter. And of course the truth was that the views expressed by MPs were not really of the slightest significance. They had no power to change the Treaty in any way. It was like a last ghostly charade of parliamentary sovereignty, as the House of Commons wrangled over an agreement to surrender another large chunk of its powers, but which it had already irrevocably voted to accept before the discussions began.

On 2 June 1992 the role of democracy in the 'new Europe' was called even more startlingly into question when the Danes voted by a narrow referendum majority not to ratify Maastricht. The terms of the Treaty of Rome were crystal clear on what this meant: under Article N, if even only one Member State failed to ratify a new treaty according to the laws of its own constitution, that treaty automatically became null and void. But immediately this solemn agreement was brushed aside. The other Member States, with the full support of Britain's Foreign Secretary, began looking for ways to move the goal posts, to force the treaty through regardless. The Danes were reviled in the most condescending terms. In the words of Portuguese foreign minister Sr de Pinheiro, 'there is something rotten in the state of Denmark'. Either Denmark should simply be expelled altogether, or at least ordered to hold a second referendum and this time to get it right. As Sr de Pinheiro charmingly put it, 'Only donkeys don't change their minds.' Over the following months referendums were held in other countries. The Irish, who for every punt they paid into the Brussels fruit machine were given back six, voted firmly in favour. The French, despite overwhelming pressure from their political establishment and media, approved Maastricht by only the narrowest of majorities, a little over 1 per cent. And eventually, after threats of dire political and economic consequences if they did not come into line, the Danes narrowly voted the treaty through on a second referendum. But this episode provided a haunting glimpse of the lengths to which the leaders of what we now had to call 'the European Union' were prepared to go, to ensure that nothing would stand in the way of their political Grand Design.

The ERM disaster

In the early autumn of 1992 the British people were given a dramatic object lesson in the realities of another part of the Grand Design. Since the early 1970s, nothing had been more central to Europe's drive towards full eventual political and economic union than the various experiments in locking together their currencies in a succession of exchange-rate straitjackets, as a prelude to eventually merging them in a single currency. Once this was achieved, the drive to full political union would be irreversible, because a single monetary system would mean every Member State having to surrender ultimate control of its economy to the 'centre'. A further major step along this path had been taken with the complex provisions of the Maastricht Treaty to achieve full 'economic and monetary union' by the end of the decade, although on paper Britain retained the option not to participate in the third and final stage of this process. But in the late 1980s, Britain had already fallen under the shadow of the transitional phase of this grand plan, the Exchange Rate Mechanism or ERM. Chancellor Lawson had kept Britain's interest rates artificially high to keep the pound 'shadowing' the Deutschmark, and in October 1990 his successor as Chancellor, John Major, against the instincts of his prime minister who was to be brought down only a month later, had taken Britain into full ERM membership.

The consequences were catastrophic. Already the economy was slowing down. High interest rates had devastated the housing market, leaving millions of homeowners who had bought in the boom market of the late 1980s stretched to breaking point to pay their mortgages. Now in the name of bringing down inflation and maintaining the pound at an artificially high level against the Deutschemark, Britain plunged into an even deeper and more destructive recession than that of the early 1980s. Hundreds of thousands of businesses went under. Unemployment soared by 1.2 million, or 72 per cent in little over a year. GDP fell by nearly 4 per cent. Although other factors contributed to this brutal awakening from the boom years of the 1980s, the measures forced on Britain by the ERM administered the coup de grâce. And nothing exposed more clearly how unworkable this grandiose theory was in practice than the way in the late summer of 1992 the markets brought the ERM level of the pound under increasingly intolerable strain.

By early September, despite the absurdity of the Bank of England borrowing £10 billion in Deutschemarks in a futile effort to buy up its own currency, the pound was on the floor of its permissible value. Yet so obsessed was the prime minister with the idea that the ERM was the cornerstone of his entire economic strategy, that on 10 September he assured the Scottish CBI in Glasgow that allowing the pound to slip below that floor was the very last thing he would do. With all the obstinacy at his command, he launched into a scornful attack on what he called 'the soft option, the devaluer's option, the inflationary option' which would be 'a betrayal of our future'. If Britain devalued the pound, nothing was more certain than that inflation would follow. Mr Major congratulated the CBI on its loyal insistence that the current level of sterling in the ERM was one which could enable British industry to 'compete successfully'. He extolled the wonders of the forthcoming Single Market and the 'level playing field'. But above all he pledged that devaluation of the pound was simply 'not the Government's policy'.

Less than a week later, on Wednesday 16 September, the City of London saw one of the maddest days in its history. Speculators launched another massive, concerted attack on sterling, forcing Chancellor Norman Lamont first in panic to raise interest rates twice in one day, to 15 per cent, and then to cave in completely. From outside the Treasury, he announced to the waiting media that Britain was withdrawing from the ERM. Within days the pound had been 'devalued' by 17 per cent, thanks to the realities of precisely that free market in which British ministers still claimed to believe, but which they had so wilfully decided to ignore. The bizarre economic strategy into which Mr Major had been beguiled by the spell of Europe was in ruins. And over the next four years, precisely because he had been forced into the very step he had pledged the world he wouldn't take, the British economy enjoyed a steady recovery which transformed it one of the strongest and most buoyant in Europe, with the lowest inflation rate for 40 years. 'Black Wednesday' passed into folklore as 'White Wednesday'. It only did so because, in the nick of time, Britain had escaped Houdini-like from the crippling straitjacket of one of the most cherished elements in the EC's Grand Design. But Mr Major himself never dared to admit as much and this, as much as the episode itself, dealt a crippling blow to the credibility of his government.

For the British people it was a landmark moment. It was the beginning of their awakening from two decades of somnambulism. They were at last beginning to see just how far apart was the high-sounding theory of 'Europe' from its reality, and the extent to which the whole ramshackle edifice was only kept in being by a world of mirrors.

Reality breaking in

The price Britain paid for her two year 'experiment' of remaining in the ERM was colossal. According to an estimate by three academic economists (Burkitt, Baimbridge, Whyman, *There Is An Alternative*, 1996), the overall cost in terms of lost GDP, lost jobs and lost businesses amounted to £70,000 million. This made it arguably the greatest peacetime disaster ever consciously imposed on the British economy, quite apart from the personal misery suffered by so many through the experience of living through that surreal episode. This was what Mr Major and his ministers had been prepared to inflict on the British people as the price for their obsession with the European dream.

Around the same time, however, the British people were just beginning to recognise all sorts of other ways in which the impact of 'Europe' on their lives was very different from the rose-tinted picture they had been given by wishful-thinking politicians. In the run-up to the Single Market, due to start on 1 January 1993, one sector of Britain's economy after another was suddenly becoming aware of the deluge of new regulations which this further great step forward to a 'Single Europe' was about to inflict on them. Again there was all the difference in the world between the theory of this 'liberating moment' when 'the barriers are coming down' allowing businesses to 'trade freely' throughout the EC, and the deadweight of new bureaucracy it so often meant in practice. In the week of 'White Wednesday', we published in the *Daily Telegraph* the article 'Who's That Lurking Behind the Brussels Book of Rules?', drawing attention to how much responsibility for this damage rested with the peculiar way in which Britain's own bureaucracy was interpreting the legislation handed down from Brussels. Farmers faced their own version of this onslaught in the avalanche of red tape accompanying the supposed 'reforms' of the Common Agricultural Policy also due to be introduced in 1993, such as the immensely cumbersome new IACS or 'Integrated Administration and Control System'. Britain's fishermen were faced by the horrific implications of the CFP's 'Multi-Annual Guidance Programme' agreed in Brussels in December 1992, under which Britain, having contributed four-fifths of the 'EU's' fishing waters, was now expected to reduce her 'fishing effort' by a fifth, to accommodate all the other countries whose fishermen now had the right of 'equal access' to those seas around her shores.

Suddenly, in short, people in Britain were waking up to the practice as opposed to the theory of 'Europe', in quite a new way. And one consequence of this, as we could observe through the regular flood of correspondence we received from people running businesses of all kinds, was how those directly affected gradually came to recognise that what was hitting them and their own industry was only part of a much wider disaster. In 1992, when we began our reporting, almost everyone we spoke to, fishermen and scrap metal dealers, electronics firms and abattoir owners, farmers and chemical companies, imagined that the new problems they were facing from mad officialdom were something unique to their own type of business. But the penny was dropping. Over the next few years, each of these groups came to see that they were only one among many victims; and that the multitude of different nightmares they were faced with were all in the end the work of the same monster.

Trouble in the Tory Party

Anyone who followed the course of British politics through the middle period of the Major Government between 1993 and 1995 might have observed two quite different political battles going on in those years. The main conventional battle between Government and Opposition was strangely grey and unreal. Despite an unending succession of blunders and minor ministerial scandals giving the impression of a government of remarkable ineptitude, the Labour Party seemed curiously muted and unable to press home its advantage. The sound and fury generated in parliamentary debates seemed more than ever synthetic and thin. Despite a vast lead enjoyed by Labour in the opinion polls, and huge swings against Government candidates in a succession of crushing by-election defeats, there was little sign of any real groundswell of popular enthusiasm behind the opposition parties. Beneath the outward rituals of party skirmishing, it became harder and harder to know what issues of fundamental principle really divided the three main parties at all.

15. *Britain Awakes to a Nightmare*

On the other hand, the battle really beginning to generate passion in these years was one which was developing largely off the conventional political stage, although it did arouse passion and drama in parliament out of all proportion to the number of MPs involved. This was the growing wave of anger felt largely inside the Conservative Party itself over Europe. In parliamentary terms this had first manifested itself in the debates over Maastricht, which only came finally to an end with the ratification of the Treaty in June 1993. But this episode, and particularly the brutal methods used by party managers to keep MPs in line, had left a legacy of bitterness which did not dissipate. The sense of frustration and anger aroused among MPs over the European issue eventually erupted in more dramatic form with the emergence of the 'Euro-rebels', a group of nine MPs who felt so strongly over what Europe was doing to British politics that for a while in 1994 and 1995 they were happy to forfeit the Tory whip. MPs such as Teresa Gorman, Sir Richard Body, Sir Teddy Taylor, Christopher Gill and Richard Shepherd became familiar faces on television as some of the best-known Tory backbenchers in the land. But the much-publicised activities of the 'rebels' were only the most extreme expression of a growing 'Euro-scepticism' shared by dozens of more overtly loyal Tory MPs, including the three members of his own Cabinet whom Mr Major described in an unguarded moment in July 1993 as 'the bastards'. And this in turn was only the tip of a tidal wave of feeling building up among Conservative Party supporters in the country at large. So great was the frustration and bitternesss felt by many of the normally loyal membership that this created a sense of grassroots alienation from the leadership quite without precedent in the Party's history. Formerly diehard party workers departed in droves. Donations and subscriptions collapsed. Only the most ferocious efforts by Party managers to suppress public evidence of what was going on succeeded in obscuring the full scale of the Tory Party's internal disaster from general view.

One of the most significant developments during these years was the degree to which critics of the 'Euro-system' were now becoming very much better informed about the way it worked. One of the greatest assets the System had enjoyed until now was that its convoluted operations were so complex and riddled with bureaucratic technicalities that to outsiders they had been virtually impenetrable. Even its most fervent supporters often knew remarkably little about how it operated in practice, and certainly they had astonishingly little idea of how all the countless different components of the System pieced together. But now at last those layers of mystery were gradually being stripped away. An ever clearer picture was emerging of how this labyrinthine new System of government really worked; and the more that was revealed, the more clearly it could be seen just how out of control the System had become. Every piece of new evidence which emerged underlined yet again that astonishing contrast between the high-flown theory, based on wishful thinking, and an increasingly alarming reality.

What was particularly telling was that the System's critics were often now beginning to see much more specifically how it was not working than those ministers and officials who, still bemused by the theory, were trying to defend it. No longer were the System's spokesmen able to make their airy pronouncements and hand down their diktats unchallenged. Increasingly they were being forced to move into a defensive, often petulant mode which only reinforced the impression that there was something very odd indeed about this ramshackle system they were defending. Behind closed doors, even at the heart of the Europhile establishment there was deep unease at how far the Euro-train seemed to be careering off the rails. In the spring of 1995 a senior Tory member of the House of Lords, Lord Renton, visited Rome as President of the Statute Law Society to attend a high-level conference on 'Legislation in the EC'. Among the speakers were some of the EC's top lawyers, including Dr Rolf Wagenbaur, head of the Commission's Legal Service. When Renton returned home he sent a confidential report to John Major and Douglas Hurd. The lectures and discussions had 'revealed a most unsatisfactory state of affairs with regard to EC legislation'. The appalling problem of trying to get 15 countries with different languages and legal systems to agree on legislation had resulted in the 'astonishing complexity and obscurity of the detailed contents of directives and regulations'. Delegates had stressed that 'improvements' must be made if EC legislation was 'to become respected and enforceable'. It was 'notorious' how 'the governments and people of Greece, Italy, Portugal, Spain, France and even Belgium frequently fail to comply with EC laws, even when they have ratified them'. The same was true of the rulings of the European Court of Justice. At the end of 1993 'there were 82 outstanding cases where Member States had not complied with judgements given against them and nine in which a second judgement had also been disregarded'.

Lord Renton ended his report by recommending that, particularly if the EC was to be enlarged, the existing Treaties should be scrapped and replaced by an entirely new one. This should drastically cut down the areas of EC law-making, including a completely reformed and much simplified CAP. 'A vast quantity of legislation covering other matters should be repealed and not re-enacted'. Otherwise, 'if nothing on these lines is done', the 'Community will become increasingly unworkable and chaotic'.

Such was what the Prime Minister and the Foreign Secretary were being told behind the scenes by a senior Conservative judge. But of course the kind of reforms Lord Renton was suggesting were unthinkable. And certainly there was no way the Government could give public voice to such outspoken criticisms. The party line was still that Britain wanted to be 'at the heart of Europe' and there – although her Government would always be ready to press for 'sensible' reforms, the kind other Member States might accept – Britain intended to stay.

Establishment on the run

Almost month by month, however, the terms of the debate were changing. One landmark moment came when, at a packed fringe meeting of the Conservative Party Conference in October 1994, ex-Chancellor Lamont admitted that 'when we come to examine the advantages of our membership of the European Union they are remarkably elusive. As a former Chancellor I can only say I cannot pinpoint a single concrete economic advantage that unambiguously comes to this country because of our membership of the European Union.' After a trenchant summary of the EU's economic failings, and of its relentless drive towards economic and political union, he stated, 'If Britain were not a member of the European Union today, I do not believe there would be a case to join.' He even put down the marker that, although of course he was not suggesting that Britain should contemplate anything so extreme as withdrawal from the EU altogether, 'the issue may well return to the political agenda'.

So far were events subsequently to move that it may today be hard to recapture just how startling it seemed in 1994 that any politician could even mention the possibility of British withdrawal from the EU. It was like the breaking of a taboo. So absolute had become the consensus between the political parties that Britain was irrevocably part of the European Union, so overwhelming was the conventional wisdom that it was wholly in Britain's interests to be in, that for several years the possibility of British withdrawal was something no politician would have dared refer to. The mere fact that a former Chancellor had dared to speak the unthinkable opened a first chink in a door everyone assumed had been locked forever.

In 1995 came more landmarks. One in March was the popular response to the 'fish war', when the Canadian Government arrested one of several Spanish trawlers which had been shamelessly flouting conservation rules negotiated between the EU and Canada. What particularly hit a symbolic nerve with the British people was the sight of the British Government and Britain's senior Commissioner in Brussels, Sir Leon Brittan, automatically lining up in support of the Spaniards and against the Canadians, so recently one of our closest Commonwealth friends and allies. When Fisheries Commissioner Mrs Bonino made her astonishing outburst that it was the Canadians themselves who were 'lying' and indulging in 'piracy' (although subsequent evidence abundantly confirmed that it was the Spaniards who had been cheating and lying), the protests which erupted were so fierce that ministers were forced into a quick retreat. But the speed with which Maple Leaf flags then sprouted round Britain as a gesture of solidarity with the Canadians was a reflection of a more general anger. First, the episode was a shocking reminder of just how far Britain had been led by Europe into betraying her links with those Commonwealth countries which had been much closer to her than any continental country could ever be. Secondly, it reflected the extent to which the British had lately been waking up to the bizarre disaster of the Common Fisheries Policy. No European issue was beginning to generate so much passion as the story of how the politicians had for so long managed to conceal the secret deal to sell out Britain's fishing waters in 1972; and, equally, the consequent catastrophe now facing Britain's fishermen, as Brussels forced them off the seas in favour of an increasingly predatory armada of Spanish and other foreign trawlers.

A second landmark that July was the curious episode of the Tory leadership contest. So frustrated had Mr Major become by the hopeless task of trying to bridge the ever wider gulf between the two wings of his party on Europe without vanishing down the abyss between them, that he took the unprecedented step of resigning as Party leader, inviting his opponents to challenge him openly. He had not expected one of his own Cabinet ministers, John Redwood, to take up the gauntlet. The battle which followed was fought largely in code, because Redwood was careful not to step too far out of line with the policies of a government of which he had been a member. But the code could be clearly deciphered in the names of the MPs who flocked most enthusiastically to his banner, led by Norman Lamont and the nine 'Euro-rebels'. The real argument was over the increasing futility of the party's official line on Europe. And the significant thing was the scale of Redwood's 89 votes. Had the pro-European Michael Heseltine not swung his twenty or more supporters behind Major at the very last minute, Redwood's support would have been enough to force the Prime Minister to resign. It would have been the second time in only five years that the issue of Europe had brought down a Tory Prime Minister; except that in 1990 it was the pro-Europeans who were on the offensive, driving a Euro-sceptic leader out of office, while this time the balance had shifted the other way. It was now the sceptics who had the initiative. In the peculiar circumstances of that election, it would indeed have been surprising if Mr Major had not survived. But his victory had not been so overwhelming that his boast 'the boil has been lanced' carried much conviction. The underlying message was that Redwood had put down a powerful marker for the real showdown between the party's two wings, which could not be fought out until after another General Election.

A landmark of a quite different kind was the appearance in September of an extraordinary book. Bernard Connolly's *The Rotten Heart of Europe* was simply the most devastating picture of the Brussels System of government yet published. And what gave it its real power was that it was written by an insider. Its British author was a comparatively senior Brussels official, head of a unit in DG II working on the ERM. In scarifying detail, he presented the history of the various attempts since 1978 to lock the European currencies together in preparation for an eventual Single Currency. What made his narrative so horrifying was the picture it gave of the obsessive determination of the French and German officials repeatedly to force everyone into these experiments, each hoping to serve their own national interests. Every time the experiment had crashed in ruins, wreaking havoc, as in Britain in 1990-2, only for the officials then to persist with their crazed dream in some revised form. Obviously this was as stark a warning as anyone could wish for as to the likely outcome of the greatest such experiment of all, the planned Single Currency itself.

More generally Connolly's book provided a perfect model of the Euro-system's approach to almost everything, its remorselesss attempts to fit the world into some clumsy bureaucratic straitjacket which did not match up to reality. The ERM, he wrote, was not just 'inefficient', it was profoundly 'undemocratic', a 'confidence trick' designed to subordinate the 'economic welfare, democratic rights and national freedom' of Europe's citizens to the will of a political and bureaucratic elite, hellbent on creating 'a European superstate'.

Perhaps the most powerful aspect of *The Rotten Heart of Europe*, however, was the chilling picture it painted of the true ethos of the Euro-system, behind those frozen smiles for the cameras and the parroted slogans about 'co-operation with our partners'. What came across above all else was the relentless backstairs rivalry and plotting, the endless deceptions and secret deals, the ruthless pursuit of power, the distrust, the spying, the bullying, the fear that stalked the corridors of those Brussels office buildings, the sheer nastiness of it all. And this was the reporting not of some rabid Euro-sceptic, but of someone once a keen supporter of the system, one of its faithful servants, who had only become disillusioned by discovering at closest quarters that horrifying gulf between theory and reality. What finally impelled Connolly more than anything to publish his book was the incredible web of lies and dishonesty which pervaded the system:

> It is one of the astonishing things about the ERM and EMU that what needs to be revealed is not 'the facts' but their manipulation and distortion. The more blatantly obvious the falsehood, the more insistently its perpetrators repeat it. My own decision to write this book ... was born first of incredulity at the hundreds of 'black is white' statements made about the ERM, and then of anger at the treatment given to anyone who tried to point out the lies.

Connolly went on to compare the intolerance of any dissent within the European Commission to the attitude towards dissidents in the old Soviet Union. Of course Brussels did not consign its dissidents to psychiatric hospitals. But there was the same almost psychotic inability to permit even the faintest deviation from the 'party line'. As he ended his 400-page book: 'the propaganda steamroller attempts to flatten analysis. For analysis can only mean dissent. And dissent cannot be tolerated.' As if only to prove his point, the moment the book was published the Commission officials put it round that he was 'unbalanced' and 'psychologically unstable'. He was quickly dismissed from his post. To Brussels Mr Connolly had become an 'unperson'.

At least, however, Connolly had managed to bring out his extraordinary message to the world. And to that minority of people who read it, the impression it conveyed came as a stunning shock. Never before had anyone provided such a vivid insight into what the heart of the Euro-system really looked from the inside. It was the nightmare vision of a madhouse, of a world in which truth had been stood on its head, where all reason was gone, where grey armies of officials and politicians, looking outwardly like normal rational human beings, had become so possessed by their delusions that they had been reduced to gibbering, conniving lunatics. No one who had not read this book could have believed to just what lengths that once-noble European dream had carried its acolytes, the scheming and deception to which they were prepared to resort in pursuit of their crazed obsessions. But over the year which followed the British people were to be given a series of rather more public demonstrations that Mr Connolly was not exaggerating.

16. Currency, CFP, Court and Cows –
The Showdown Approaches

Building the Single Currency is like building the mediaeval cathedrals. It will be as big. It will be as beautiful. It will last as much.
> Chef de Cabinet to Yves Thibault de Silguy, Commissioner in
> charge of preparations for Economic and Monetary Union,
> BBC Radio 4, 24 August 1996

What will people eat when all the fish are caught and all the cattle slaughtered?
> Maxim Gorky, *Three of Them*

As 1996 began, the issue of Europe was pushing John Major's Government into an increasingly tight corner. Long gone was the time only twelve months earlier when a British Foreign Secretary could blithely greet a New Year, as Douglas Hurd had done in January 1995, by sending out a 'briefing note' to Tory constituency associations reminding them of all the glorious benefits 'the European Union' had brought to Britain. These, according to Mr Hurd, ranged from 'the priceless gift' of 'nearly 50 years of peace' (although it was news that the 'European Union' had been around in 1949 when NATO was born) to the wonders of the Single Market, which now enabled Britain to sell no less than '53 per cent' of her exports to the EU (no matter that the Government's own Central Statistics Office showed the true figure to be only 44.6 per cent).

In that intervening year the mood in Britain, as reflected not just in parliament but increasingly vociferously in the Tory press, had changed so dramatically that such soothingly specious bromides from a British Foreign Secretary would no longer really seem (to use one of Mr Hurd's own favourite words) 'helpful'.

Britain the odd man out

Looming up in particular at the start of 1996 were two horrendous problems. The first was the shadow of the next 'Inter-Governmental Conference' due to begin before the end of the year, a succession of meetings to negotiate the next major European treaty, the successor to Maastricht. It was already clear that the other Member States, led by the Germans and the French, were planning to use the new Treaty to move the EU another big step towards full political and economic union. It was equally clear that Britain was completely the odd man out in this process. It was one thing to reassure the British people

188

that the IGC was not very important, just a tidying up of loose ends, a '5,000 mile service' of Maastricht. But when this was measured against the ambitions of the rest of Europe, such as the plans for a common foreign and defence policy, so obviously designed to weld the 'Union' even more irrevocably into one super-state, it became only too obvious that Britain was on a completely different tack.

The result of trying to appease all the various pressures, from both sides of the European divide, was that the British Government's approach to the IGC, expressed in a White Paper in March 1996 and other statements, turned into a curiously consistent fudge. Again and again, on almost every issue, it was trying to placate the Euro-sceptics by promising to make firm demands for reform in directions they might approve. Britain would call for a drastic reduction in the flow of Brussels legislation. She would call for a drastic reduction in the powers of the European Court of Justice, which had become too 'political'. She would call for drastic reforms in the 'damaging' and 'irrational' Common Agricultural Policy. Under the Common Fisheries Policy, she would 'seek' treaty changes to end the scandal of 'quota hopping'. All this and more was intended to give the impression that Britain was going to insist on trying to ensure that the IGC resulted in a more 'open', more 'flexible', more 'rational', less 'intrusive', less 'centralised', less 'political' Europe, of a kind the sceptics might find more to their liking.

The only snag was, as the Government well knew, there was not the slightest chance that any of Britain's demands would be listened to. Indeed most of these items would probably not even appear on the agenda, because the other Member States had wholly different matters on their mind. What they were concerned with was taking the next steps towards building that 'ever closer Union' promised by Maastricht. And this, of course, was the very last thing Mr Major would wish to admit openly to the British people.

The flightless bird: EMU – deadlock no. 1

The other great problem looming up as 1996 began, closely allied to the first, was 'Economic and Monetary Union' or EMU, so often inadequately summarised as just a Single Currency. On this issue the moment was fast approaching when Britain would have to come off the fence on which Mr Major had been sitting ever since 1991, when at Maastricht he negotiated his famous 'opt out', the possibility that Britain would be able to avoid joining in. Nothing more pointedly conveyed the essence of Major's style of leadership than the way, for four years, he had sought to muffle all attempts to debate the question of whether Britain would enter the Single Currency by saying he would neither 'rule it in' nor 'rule it out'. For the French, the Germans, the Commission and other countries, the move to economic and monetary union agreed at Maastricht was the central thrust of their drive towards the complete integration of the Community into a single state, of which the further additions planned at the IGC, such as a common foreign and defence policy, were only corollaries which must logically follow. Mr Major's refusal to discuss the Single Currency issue had been a crucial part of his strategy to divert British attention from what was really going on in the rest of Europe.

It was true the System had ensured that steady pressure of a non-political kind was maintained to soften up the British for an eventual decision to enter EMU. A key part of this was the propaganda drive co-ordinated through the CBI, to convey the impression that British industry and businesses were demanding that Britain should join, and that to be left out would be economic disaster. The pro-EU lobby organised a steady stream of supposedly independent 'reports' and round-robin letters to the press from 'leading businessmen' and political fellow-travellers to keep the issue in the news. In particular this gave a cue for sycophantic coverage by the BBC, which appeared to have taken an editorial decision to boost the Single Currency whenever it found an opportunity. But it was also noticeable how careful were the lobbyists never to discuss in detail the colossal implications of what 'economic and monetary union' would mean in practice. In general the strategy was to play these down as much as possible, by implying that it was little more than a technical issue concerning money. The line was that a Single Currency would greatly help businessmen by cutting out their 'transaction costs' when selling in the Single Market. More popular BBC programmes were used to emphasise the convenience to holidaymakers of not having to bother with changing money when they flew to Benidorm.

The general idea, on which both Government and lobbyists were agreed, was that the political decision as to whether to go in or not should be left to the last possible moment. This would reduce to a minimum the opportunities for a properly informed national debate, with all its potential for political embarrassment. Nevertheless one snag of this strategy was that it still gave time for those outside the System to look carefully at all the implications of what 'economic and monetary union' would mean in practice – and these were mind-boggling.

For a start, by concentrating on the Single Currency, the spokesmen for the System had quite deliberately been trying to divert attention from the full title of what was being proposed. It was not just 'monetary union'. Even more significantly, it was also 'economic union', a merger of all the economies of the Member States. This would mean not just the abolition of the pound, the deutschemark and all the rest. This would be a serious enough step, since it would mean that the control and management of all money in the EU would pass to the unelected officials of the new Central European Bank in Frankfurt. As laid down at Maastricht, Britain's entire gold and foreign currency reserves of £26,000 million would be physically moved to Frankfurt. The crucial power to set interest rates throughout the Union would be exercised by the central bank. But far more serious even than this would be the fact that, with 'economic union', the whole economy of the EU would now be co-ordinated and controlled centrally, by a new 'European Economic Authority'. Control of Britain's economy would be handed over to this body, to be exercised not necessarily in Britain's interests, but in those of the EU as a whole. Full economic and monetary union, as the System's supporters on the Continent, such as M. Jacques Delors, made clear, would inevitably mean that the power to impose taxes – the essence of political sovereignty down the centuries – would in large measure be handed over from national governments to an unelected central authority. this in turn would mean that, where there was economic imbalance between different parts of the EU, huge sums raised in taxes from richer or more successful areas of the Union could be transferred to less prosperous 'regions' (they would no longer be called 'countries') to correct these imbalances.

In short, the coming of full 'Economic and Monetary Union' would mean the most complete surrender of sovereignty any country could contemplate, short of being physically occupied by an enemy power. And as usual there were all sorts of ways in which, for reasons of national peculiarity, Britain would suffer more than other countries. She, for instance, had a much higher proportion of mortgage-owners than other nations. Their repayments would now be determined in Frankfurt according to the interests of the 'Union' economy as a whole, so a householder in Weybridge might have to pay £250 more a month because of fears of inflation in Germany or Greece.

Even more serious would be the consequences of merging all the Member States' national debts and other liabilities. EMU would mean that no government in the EU would any longer enjoy the status of a 'sovereign borrower', which enables a government to borrow at advantageous rates of interest because their debts are backed up by that government's full authority. Under EMU the only 'sovereign borrower' in the EU would be the new Economic Authority. And Britain would suffer particularly from this, because she enjoyed a comparatively low national debt, and would now have to share liability for all the other national debts, many of which were proportionately very much higher. Worse still, because her insurance system was much more sophisticated than any other in the EU, Britain also enjoyed by far the highest level of properly funded pensions. But now, under EMU, she would have to share liability for all the pension liabilities of the other countries as well, many of which, notably in Germany, were hopelessly inadequately funded.

Adding together Britain's national debt with those future pensions liabilities which were not funded, the total of debt for every man, woman and child in Britain in 1996 came to £9,000 per head. But if, with the coming of EMU, those liabilities were merged with those of the rest of the Union, including countries like Germany and France with huge unfunded pensions liabilities, that unfunded debt per head would soar to £39,000. And within these horrifying figures lurked an astonishing historical time bomb. Statistics showed that, by the early years of the 21st century, Europes's pensioners would outnumber those in work. It would no longer be possible to go on funding pensions out of income. Europe would suddenly be faced by a colossal nightmare, when the bill for not having made proper provision to fund millions of pensions would have to be paid. And if Britain was now forced to contribute to that debt, despite having made better provision than any other country, not only would her taxpayers find themselves having to stump up vast sums for the unfunded pensions of German postmen or Spanish fishermen, but at the same time all Britain's own carefully husbanded pension fund would simply be swallowed up in the same gigantic black hole.

What made it yet more extraordinary that Britain could still be contemplating such a colossal leap in the dark was the evidence piling up on all sides in 1996 of the immense social and economic damage being inflicted on other EU countries by their attempts to conform with the 'Maastricht convergence criteria' laid down as an essential pre-condition for the merger of their currencies. Their economies were stagnating. Unprecedented cuts in public spending and other fiscal restraints were provoking strikes and unrest.

Average unemployment had already soared to 11.6 per cent, in some countries much higher. Typically the System's response to this was simply to suggest that the rules should be changed. Those 'Maastricht criteria', strict adherence to which had once been deemed so vital to the success of the whole enterprise, could be 'relaxed' or 'modified' to allow as many countries to enter as possible. The most important thing, after all, was that EMU should be kept on course, because it was so central to the political union which was to follow.

Nevertheless the one country in the EU where the economic indicators were now brightest, with unemployment falling, inflation at a 40-year low, steady growth and rising exports, was Britain. And this remarkable degree of success owed more than anything else to that day in 1992 when, over Mr Major's metaphorical dead body, Britain had escaped from the suffocating stranglehold of the ERM, the Single Currency's precursor. Since that day, when she became free once more to allow her currency to find its natural level on the world market to the huge benefit of her exporters, and to lower her interest rates to boost business and to leave mortgage-holders with more to spend, Britain's economy had been liberated, to grow and thrive. But inevitably the response of the officials in Brussels, Paris and Frankfurt was not to suggest that others might follow suit. It was to look for ways in which Britain could be forcibly shackled back into the dismal prison house they were building for themselves. At the EU's Verona summit in March 1996, when the decision was approved to give the new currency the delightful name of the 'Euro', there were complaints that Britain was only now prospering because she had deviously resorted to what they called 'competitive devaluation' (how revealing that they could not recognise a true free market when they saw one). This, it was argued, was clearly in breach of 'the rules of competition in the Single Market'. If any country, like Britain, was so un-'*communautaire*' as to stay out of the Single Currency, then it might have to be punished. Every time its currency 'devalued', it would have to be made to pay the price, with fines running into billions of pounds. What else was that 'level playing field' about, if it wasn't that everyone must be made to share the same misery?

The great fish disaster: CFP – deadlock no. 2

By the spring of 1996, it was becoming clear that, on four issues in particular, Britain's relations with the rest of the EU were heading straight for deadlock. The first of these was the mounting pressure to force Britain into EMU whether she liked it or not. Britain's Maastricht 'opt-out', it was argued, should simply be overruled. What were solemn agreements between EU 'partners' for, except to be broken when the majority wanted it?

The second issue on which Britain and Brussels were on a collision course was the CFP. On 1 January a new armada of Spanish trawlers had entered the British and Irish waters west of the British Isles. This was a full six years earlier than Spain had accepted in her Treaty of Accession in 1986. But she had managed to get this clause in her treaty torn up by the simple device of threatening to veto the entry of Austria, Sweden and Finland into the EU unless she got her way. The ships now entering Western Waters and the Irish Box were modern and powerful, heavily-subsidised with funds from EU taxpayers, including the British, and they were soon outcatching most of the smaller, older British and Irish boats, not least because of their disregard of the rules. But all this only helped to dramatise further the extraordinary way in which Spain was now becoming the greedy cuckoo in the CFP nest, leaving Britain and her much smaller fishing fleet easily the most obvious loser (although Ireland was not far behind).

What made this such a peculiarly explosive issue in Britain was the relentless fashion in which the Commission in Brussels seemed to be doing everything in its power not only to promote the Spanish cause, but to heap humiliation on the British at the same time. The Fisheries Commissioner Mrs Bonino sternly warned the British Government that it faced enormous fines from the European Court of Justice for failing to reduce the British fishing fleet by 19 per cent, as agreed in 1992. To lend plausibility to her case she repeatedly made the astonishing claim that the British fleet had 'more than doubled' since 1986, from '116,000 tonnes to 239,000 tonnes', when as we saw in Chapter 7, the true figures for those years, accepted by the Commission itself, were 206,000 tonnes and 211,000. When the British Government tried to correct her figures, Mrs Bonino contemptuously exaggerated them still further, now claiming that the current size of the British fleet was '247,000 tonnes'.

Mrs Bonino and her fellow officials were equally contemptuous when it was pointed out that the only reason the British fleet had increased at all was that 40,000 tonnes of it now consisted of Spanish and Dutch-owned 'quota hoppers', flying the Red Ensign only as a mere legal formality to qualify for a huge share of Britain's fishing quotas. By chance this equated to 19 per cent of the British fleet, the exact percentage by which Mrs Bonino was insisting Britain must reduce her fleet. But not a single 'flag boat' would be taken off the British register (indeed their numbers were rising by the month) because, as Mrs Bonino enjoyed rubbing in, the practice of 'quota hopping' had been upheld by the ECJ in the Factortame case as perfectly legal under EU law.

Indeed further salt was now rubbed into Britain's wounds by the ECJ's latest ruling in the still ongoing Factortame case, that the Spanish trawler owners were now entitled to claim damages from British taxpayers in the British courts amounting to well over £80 million. This was to compensate them for the 15 months when they had been forced to stop fishing until the ECJ had ruled Britain's 1988 Merchant Shipping Act illegal. Meanwhile British taxpayers were also having to pay £125 million to enable Spain to fish in Third World waters, until enough British boats had been 'decommissioned' to make room for them to enter British waters. In the summer of 1996, Britain's fishermen faced demands for yet another massive cut of 40 per cent, on top of the 19 per cent target they still had to meet. And as a final coup de grâce, as we saw in Chapter 7, Mrs Bonino's officials then came up with their cunningly double-edged new 'conservation measures', designed quite deliberately both to deprive yet more British fishermen of their right to earn a living, and to permit the Spaniards to evade the rules altogether.

The truth was that all these were merely steps along the way towards the realisation of another EU Grand Design, the fisheries equivalent of the Single Currency. This was the plan, based on Commission Regulation 3760/92, to merge all the fishing fleets of Europe by the year 2003 into one 'Union fleet', fishing 'European Union waters' under the central control of Brussels. From that date, it came to light in 1996, all the existing arrangements under the Common Fisheries Policy would be scrapped. All waters up to the shoreline would pass under Brussels control. National quotas would be abolished, and fishermen would only be permitted to fish under a Special Fishing Permit, allocated individually, telling them exactly where they could fish, what they could catch and how many days they could stay at sea. And an integral part of this plan was that permits would be handed out on the basis of how well each country had complied with the earlier requirements to cut back their fleets. Spanish fishermen, because they had met their targets, would get a prime share of these permits, while those of Britain, which had failed to meet much higher targets, would receive many fewer.

Such was the barely credible denouement to the story which had begun 25 years before with Edward Heath's secret surrender of Britain's fishing waters, as the price for his being able to lead Britain into Europe. Throughout those years no one had acted as a more tireless defender of the CFP than the officials and ministers of MAFF, acting under instructions from the Foreign Office. Not once had a British minister been allowed to utter any word of public criticism of the deal which had cost Britain billions of pounds in squandered assets and lost tens of thousands of jobs. Even when it became clear that the CFP was leading directly to an immense conservation disaster in the waters round Britain's shores, first by forcing fishermen to discard billions of fish a year, then by allowing in Spanish fishermen who treated the rules with contempt, MAFF spokesmen dutifully continued to defend the CFP as being 'in Britain's interests'. They continued to parrot the Brussels mantra that the only problem was that of 'too many fishermen catching too few fish', when they knew this was merely an excuse for demanding yet more cuts in the British fleet. But finally the pressure on those MAFF ministers had become so intense, from Save Britain's Fish, from Tory MPs, from the press and from Tory supporters in the country, that at last they knew they had to make at least a gesture of protest. They still refused to utter a word of complaint about the CFP itself, for which the Government dutifully pledged renewed support in its IGC White Paper. They maintained deadly secrecy about the permit system which would spell the final death-knell of most of Britain's fishing industry, and which they had known about since 1994. Instead they chose to focus on 'quota hopping', as if this was the only real problem. Ministers insisted they would 'seek' changes in the Treaty to bring this outrage to an end. But all this did was land them with another issue on which Britain faced complete deadlock with her European 'partners'; because there was not the slightest chance that she would get her way.

The 'political' court: ECJ – deadlock no. 3

A third issue on which Britain was heading for the buffers with Europe in 1996 was the role of the European Court of Justice. Few organs of the Euro-system had provided more constant irritation to the British in recent years than the ECJ, even though this was often wrongly confused with that other super-irritant, the European Court of Human Rights, which did not belong to the EU. Scarcely a month went by without some judgement of the

ECJ being splashed angrily over the tabloid front pages, invariably because it seemed to convey some 'fresh snub' to Britain, either in overruling Britain's government or parliament, or because it embodied some gem of politically correct absurdity. A classic example of the first was the Factortame case, pronouncing that EC law was superior to a British statute and then giving the Spaniards leave to claim vast damages from the British taxpayers. A notorious example of the second was the ECJ's ruling that Britain was not complying with EC sex discrimination laws by denying part-time workers the right to join company pension schemes. The Court's finding that this was illegal was, incredibly, based on the fact that most part-timer workers are female; therefore to deny them the right to join pension schemes constituted discrimination against women (this judgement opened the door to backdated compensation claims predicted to total at least £7 billion). Another not dissimilar ruling was that which allowed hundreds of ex-servicewomen to claim sums totalling millions of pounds from the British Government because they had been dismissed for becoming pregnant while serving. The women had known when they joined the forces that it was a strict rule that pregnancy would lead to dismissal. But the ECJ had overruled this longstanding condition of service on the grounds that it was illegal under a directive giving equal employment rights to men and women.

What the British people had only lately been taking on board was not just that the ECJ, as the supreme legal authority in the European Union, was now superior to any court in the UK, including parliament; they had also learned to their alarm that the role of the ECJ was not really judicial at all. It was political. In this sense it was wholly unlike any traditional British court, at least since Charles I's Star Chamber. Its judges were political appointments by the Member States, and of the 15 judges in 1996 it was said that only four had the legal qualifications which would have entitled them to act as judges in Britain. The chief function of these dignitaries, in their hideous concrete building in Luxembourg, was not just to uphold the supremacy of EU law, but to reinforce and enlarge it. Wherever they could use a case to uphold the Commission's powers or to justify an extension of them, they did so. This was why one of their most famous judgements was the so-called Frankovich case, which gave individuals the right to compensation from their own Government if it had failed to implement a directive.

Another judgement which particularly irked the British Government was that which upheld the typically devious tactics employed by Commission officials to force Britain to comply with a directive setting a maximum of 48 hours in the working week. In the negotiations for the Maastricht Treaty, the British Government had particularly prided itself on winning a second 'opt-out' from the Social Chapter, setting the framework for Brussels to impose a whole new raft of legislation extending the rights of workers against their employers. When the Commission wanted to introduce its directive limiting the working week to 48 hours, which had enormous implications for anyone running a business, this should strictly speaking have been done under the Social Chapter. But it was observed that the directive would then not apply to Britain, which would therefore win a 'competitive' advantage over her 'partners'. The Brussels officials therefore decided to introduce the measure as a 'health and safety' directive, under Articles of the Treaty which did apply to Britain. When Britain took her case to the ECJ that this was an improper use of Treaty powers, the Court predictably ruled in favour of the Commission, because this was precisely its function in the System.*

So great had Britain's frustration become with this 'political' role of the ECJ, and with the fact that in any familiar British sense it was only masquerading as a court of law at all, that a paper demanding a drastic revision of the Court's role, and a scaling down of its powers, was added to the 'demands' the British Government hoped to make at the IGC. But once again Britain was whistling in the wind. There was not the slightest chance that other Member States would accept the ECJ's transformation into something nearer a traditional Anglo-Saxon type of court, because this was entirely alien to them. The Commission would not accept it because the Court was one of its most valued allies in upholding and extending its powers. Yet again Britain was the odd man out, heading straight for the buffers.

Mad cows and even madder politicians: BSE – deadlock no. 4

The fourth issue over which Britain found herself completely at odds with her 'partners' in 1996 was the most unexpected and bizarre of all. Suddenly exploding into the centre of the stage, the BSE crisis was like a comprehensive demonstration of all the failings of that new System which in recent years had quietly, inexorably, been taking over the government of Britain. It set in train a catastrophe which had many of the ingredients of an immense tragedy. And it reduced Britain's relations with her European 'partners' to their lowest point in 25 years.

We cannot appreciate the extraordinary nature of the crisis which so came to dominate Britain's relations with the EU in 1996 without first understanding how completely it was spun out of nothing. BSE, Bovine Spongiform Encephalopathy, was a very nasty disease first officially identified in British cows in 1985, although there was abundant evidence that it had been around for several years at least before that. Just why the disease reached epidemic levels in Britain rather than anywhere else in the world remains to this day a mystery. The official theory was that it was due to the cows being fed with

---

*Not the least sinister influence of the ECJ was the effect it had on British judges, aware that it had now become, in many area of law, the supreme court of appeal. This made many British judges keen to interpret EC law in as zealous a spirit as possible, knowing that otherwise their judgements might be appealed against to the ECJ, for not having paid proper deference to the intentions of Brussels. An example was the judge who in July 1995 awarded two Manchester women damages of £3,000 against a travel company on the grounds that, while they had been on holiday in Tunisia, they had been subjected to 'sexual harassment'. The staff of the hotel where they had stayed had 'written them love notes', made 'obscene gestures' and 'stroked their backs when they were being served meals'. The judge (who ruled that his name, along with those of the women themselves and the whereabouts of his court, should be kept out of the papers) found that the package tour operator was liable to pay damages under the terms of the EC's Package Holiday directive, 90/314. This made tour operators liable for 'the proper performance of the obligations arising from a contract', even if, as in the Tunisian case, the failure to fulfil these obligations was due to factors over which the operator could have no control. If the judge had not been so eager to carry out what he assumed were the intentions of the directive, under British law the plaintiffs could have had no case whatsoever.

the remains of sheep infected by a similar disease called scrapie. But American research failed to bear this out, and it certainly did not explain why vast quantities of identical feed given to cattle on the continent had not led to the same results. The two most obvious factors which might have distinguished British cattle from those in any other country were the possibility of a genetic predisposition inherited through mass artificial insemination; and the uniquely concentrated use in Britain of phosmet, a treatment for cattle parasites based on nerve-gas related organo-phosphorus chemicals and a drug related to thalidomide, which was made compulsory in Britain's dairy herds through the 1980s. But very noticeably neither of these possible causes were ever subjected to proper scientific investigation.

What suddenly turned BSE into a really major political crisis, however, was the suggestion that there might be a way in which this fatal animal disease could be transmitted to humans. And what triggered the crisis were just 24 crucial words uttered in the House of Commons on 20 March 1996 by Britain's health minister, Stephen Dorrell. His statement was based on a message his officials had received from a group of Government scientific advisers, the Spongiform Encephalopathy Advisory Committee (SEAC), concerning what they believed to be several cases of a 'new strain' of the human brain disorder Creutzfeldt-Jakob's Disease or CJD. 'While there is no direct evidence of a link,' Dorrell told MPs, 'the most likely explanation is that these cases may be linked to exposure to BSE.'

What was astonishing about this statement was not just that there was not a scrap of hard scientific evidence to justify it. It was that such evidence as there was pointed in exactly the opposite direction. BSE or 'mad cow disease' had been appearing in British cattle herds for more than 15 years. It was later estimated that meat from at least 750,000 animals had got into the human food chain, most of them between 1986 and 1989. This meant that, if there was any connection between BSE and CJD, with an incubation period of 5-10 years, the incidence of 'new' CJD should now in 1996 be rapidly rising. But the incidence of CJD of all kinds was in fact going down. In 1994 there were 50 cases in Britain, in 1995 40. And to those ten so-called 'new strain' cases, only two more could be added in the following six months. Indeed, it later emerged that SEAC did not even have any scientific justification for describing them as a 'new strain'.

Nevertheless the entirely predictable effect of Dorrell's statement, in the neurotic, health and safety-conscious mood of our time, was to unleash pandemonium. It was like throwing a lighted match into a sea of petrol. Not only was it immmediately apparent that this was set to become the most catastrophic food scare in history, likely to inflict on British agriculture the worst disaster it had ever known. It was soon to plunge Britain's relations with Europe into unprecedented crisis.

In the first few days after Dorrell's statement, hysteria knew no bounds. Newspapers like the *Observer* dripped with crazed apocalyptic visions of Britain in 2015, with thousands of Britons dying a week from CJD, the Channel Tunnel blocked off and Britain totally isolated from the world. Apparently sober scientists solemnly agreed on television that the number of victims might well rise to 500,000. Beef sales plummeted, not just in Britain but all over Europe. And as one EU country after another imposed bans on imports of beef from Britain, it was less than a week before European Commission officials had imposed a total ban on exports of British beef or beef-derived products to anywhere in the world. The ban not only included wine gums made with gelatin but even soap or candles made from tallow.

Faced with such a disaster – Britain's beef exports alone were worth £550 million a year – the immmediate question was how confidence could be restored. Only a week after the EU imposed its ban, Agriculture Minister Douglas Hogg was due to visit Luxembourg for a meeting with other EU agriculture ministers. In view of the disaster now falling on the meat industry all over Europe, how was he to persuade them that the ban should be lifted? The answer Hogg and his officials came up with was to precipitate a new step in the unfolding tragedy as disastrous as Dorrell's statement itself.

Part of the advice the SEAC scientists had given Dorrell was that, because BSE was most likely to appear in older cattle, to be absolutely on the safe side beef from cattle over 30 months old should only be sold for eating after it had been taken off the bone. Not for a moment had the scientists suggested that this meat from healthy cattle would not be perfectly safe to eat. Hogg's officials therefore drew up an emergency regulation under the Food Safety Act, ordering meat from such animals to be withheld from sale until arrangements were in place for its deboning in specially licensed cutting plants. But such was the madness of the time that, on 25 March, the President of the NFU, Sir David Naish, told Hogg that, as a measure 'to restore consumer confidence', the supermarkets wanted meat from animals over 30 months old to be removed from the food chain altogether. Initially Hogg was less than enthusiastic at taking such a draconian step, which flew right in the face of the advice the scientists had given. But when, three days later, the McDonald beefburger chain announced that it would no longer serve British beef, the pressure for the Government to 'do something' to restore 'consumer confidence' became irresistible. Clutching at the nearest straw which might give the impression of resolute action, Hogg activated the 'Naish' plan. Then, fatally, he and his officials seized on this reckless measure and offered it as a possible way out of the appalling mess they were in in Europe.

On 1 April Hogg arrived in Luxembourg, looking woebegone in his shabby raincoat and fedora, for what turned out to be the most humiliating meeting with the European 'partners' any British minister had ever attended. He presented his officials' plan that all 30-month-old British cattle due to be sold should be killed, rendered down into powder and disposed of, probably by incineration. Commission officials and the other ministers listened with barely concealed impatience, but agreed that, if this was what the British Government wanted to do, they would accept it. Since the scheme would be hugely expensive – it would mean destroying an estimated three million cattle over three years, and would cost £2,400 million – they even agreed to 'co-finance' it. Two weeks later a Commission Regulation, 716/96, was issued, arranging for the financing of Britain's 'Cattle Disposal Scheme'. Headlines proclaimed that the EU was generously 'coming to Britain's aid' by providing most of the money. Only the small print of the deal revealed that most of the money would then be subtracted from Britain's budget rebates, so that in the end British taxpayers would be contributing 80 per cent of the total, nearly £2,000 million. But most astonishing of all was that a scheme only offered in the hope that it might persuade the EU to lift its ban was regarded by the other Europeans as completely irrelevant. This was not what they were looking to Britain for at all. If they were even to consider lifting the ban, they wanted a mass selective slaughter of herds directly affected by BSE until the disease was completely eradicated. This British plan to destroy millions of healthy cattle, most of which had been nowhere near BSE, was just a private sideshow.

Thus the unfolding tragedy moved into its third stage. It soon became apparent that the British officials had given no thought at all as to how to carry out their 'Cattle Disposal Scheme'. Astonishingly, they did not even have the legal powers to proceed with their plan. The Food Safety Act only authorised them to prevent food being offered for sale when there was a genuine risk to public health. The Animal Health Act 1981 only authorised them to kill animals when this was to control disease. And the only purpose of this present scheme was to destroy perfectly healthy animals, posing no risk to the public, purely as a public relations exercise to 'restore consumer confidence'. Nevertheless, no MPs seemed to notice this startling fact, and amid scenes of indescribable chaos and confusion, the officials slowly put together a scheme which was in fact largely organised for them by a handful of large abattoir operators in the Federation of Fresh Meat Wholesalers. These were the same firms which had given MAFF such active support in its attempts to close down hundreds of smaller abattoirs in the battle over the meat hygiene directive 91/497. The task of slaughtering 25,000 animals a week was allocated to just 20 big industrial abattoirs, which were to be paid three times the normal commercial rate for killing the cattle. Although after protests another 21 smaller firms were later added to the scheme, more than 350 of Britain's slaughterhouses were excluded, at a time when they were struggling to survive because of the loss of business caused by the BSE crisis. When the largest abattoir in Europe, Manchester Meat Market, offered to take part in the scheme at a third of the rate being given to the select few insiders, its offer was ignored. While the chosen handful of firms enjoyed an unparalleled bonanza – between them they were earning excess profits at a rate of £2 million a week – hundreds of their smaller competitors feared the BSE crisis would finally achieve precisely the result MAFF had failed to achieve earlier, by driving them out of business.

Inevitably, with such mountains of public money being thrown at it, this scheme gave rise to every kind of racket. But what was truly obscene was that, with 25,000 healthy cattle being destroyed each week, huge quantities of the finest and safest meat in the world were going up in smoke for no purpose at all. Although beef sales in Britain were recovering, particularly in country areas, there was no way in which the sight on television of this continual slaughter could help to 'restore consumer confidence'. And any idea that this might make a favourable impression on the continent, where beef sales had fallen much further than they had in Britain (in Greece the BSE crisis added 0.5 per cent to the cost of living in a month), was the sheerest wishful thinking.

At the end of May, Mr Major suddenly gave vent to his Government's growing frustration with the startling announcement that Britain intended to conduct a policy of 'non-cooperation' with the EU until it was prepared to make concessions on lifting the worldwide export ban. For four weeks, the rest of the EU stared in amazement as British ministers and officials solemnly vetoed every item of business which came up. The agenda of one meeting after another ground to a halt, as Britain put a stop to more than 65 proposals for legislation. This so-called 'beef war' was intended to bring Britain's 'partners' to their senses before the next summit meeting in Florence at the end of June. The hope was that they could be persuaded to abandon their proposal for a 'selective cull' of all BSE-affected herds, which the British Government insisted made no scientific sense, and to put forward a firm timetable for the lifting of the ban.

But when the prime ministers announced in Florence the 'deal' they had arrived at, it became glaringly obvious that Britain's policy of non-cooperation had achieved less than nothing. The EU had forced Mr Major to accept the 'selective cull' of up to 147,000 cattle. These were mainly productive dairy cows, whose slaughter would have dealt a devastating blow to many of Britain's dairy farmers. In return the EU had given vague indications that, once this new mass-slaughter programme was under way, further considera- tion might be given to a relaxation of the ban. Mr Major's 'beef war' had been nothing but petulant play-acting, which had made Britain's position in Europe more humiliating than ever.

Through the late summer months the unresolved dispute remained in a state of total impasse. The Government already quietly realised that it would have great difficulty forcing through parliament the new legislation required for any 'selective cull' scheme. The European 'partners', led by the neuroti- cally health-conscious Germans, if anything only hardened their position still further. The only good fortune for the British Government was that, thanks to an almost complete lack of interest from the media, the British people still remained largely unaware of the stupendous shambles surrounding the Cattle Disposal Scheme, although though many better-off households would be contributing hundreds of pounds in taxes to pay for this fiasco. The rendering plants were unable to keep up with the task of boiling down huge numbers of carcases into powder prior to incineration. The backlog of hun- dreds of thousands of animals awaiting pointless destruction scarcely diminished, as thousands more cattle passed the 30-month threshold every week.

Already this vast catastrophe had cost tens of thousands of jobs in and around the meat and dairy industries. It had forced thousands of businesses to the edge of bankruptcy. It had already claimed more victims through desperate farmers committing suicide than the 'new' strain of CJD. But now the tragedy moved into its fourth stage, with the approach of autumn when the grass in the fields stopped growing. All summer farmers had been able to keep vast numbers of animals out in those fields, waiting in the queue for destruction, kept alive meanwhile by nature. But the moment was approach- ing when they would have to start paying to feed those cattle through the winter, at up to £10 a week for each animal. When Stephen Dorrell uttered his 24 fateful words in March, Devon beef farmer Richard Haddock had 1,000 animals worth £1 million on his 850-acre farm. Over the next six months, when he would normally have expected to make £200,000 from sales, because of the chaos surrounding the Cattle Disposal Scheme only three animals had moved off his land. He now had to face the prospect of paying out £10,000 a week to feed his herd, when his income was nil and his bank manager could see no point in lending money to pay to feed cattle which were in effect worthless. Thousands of other farmers were facing the same horrendous crisis, many imagining that they would have no alternative but to leave their animals to starve to death in the fields.

So long as this hidden crisis remained unresolved, there was no way the British Government could agree to the demand for another mass-slaughter which would simply pile more animals into a system already at breaking point. In mid-September Douglas Hogg made another forlorn visit to Brussels to tell his fellow farm-ministers that 'new research' had shown that BSE was dying out naturally, and by 2001 would have disappeared. They should 'rest on the science' and accept that their proposed cull was pointless. The EU ministers stared in disbelief, telling him politely they would 'consider' his new research. But meanwhile there wasn't the faintest chance of their ban being lifted until the last British BSE-infected cow had disappeared off the earth. The British Cabinet decided it had no alternative but to call off the cull unilaterally. The Florence 'deal' was dead. Britain must now go it alone.

*

Britain's decision to walk away from Europe on BSE came only 24 hours after a much-headlined speech in Zurich in which the new Foreign Secretary Malcolm Rifkind warned that the relentless momentum towards economic and monetary union would merely split the European Union into two. 'Jumping blindly towards ever greater integration', he suggested, might only eventually bring about an irreparable catastrophe. It was by far the most outspoken statement any British Foreign Secretary had ever made on the slide towards a European super-state, one in which he implied Britain could have no part. It was light-years away from those days in the 1980s when Mrs Thatcher's fanatically pro-European Foreign Secretary Geoffrey Howe used repeatedly to urge the need for Britain to jump on board the clattering Euro-train as it hurtled ever faster towards some unspecified destination, for fear that Britain might be 'left behind' or 'left out'.

The responses to Rifkind's grim warning, reported under headlines such as 'Euro Fury as Rifkind Joins EMU Battle', were now wholly predictable. Britain's delighted Euro-sceptics welcomed his stark warning. John Redwood cheered Rifkind for 'responding to the clear mood of the country'. The Single Currency was just 'a disaster waiting to happen'. On the other side, the Commission, through Vice-President Brittan, had already lined up a familiar claque of the EU's most faithful fellow travellers, led by an ageing group of veteran politicians of the 1970s and 1980s such as Edward Heath, Geoffrey Howe and Douglas Hurd, to protest that it would be equally disastrous for Britain to rule monetary union out. At the centre of the web in Brussels, the President of the Commission, M. Santer, merely issued a statement that the Single Currency 'now has to be seen as inevitable'. The EU's historical destiny could allow nothing to stand in its way.

The real question now looming larger than ever through all the smoke and fury of this battlefield was – how long could Britain remain part of it at all?

201

Was it not clear that Britain's vision of where events were leading was now so far apart from that of the rest of the 'Union' that there could no longer be the slightest chance of any reconciliation or compromise between them? Had the time not come, in short, as increasing numbers of people were now passionately convinced, for Britain just to get out altogether?

17. The Castle of Lies (I) – 'It Isn't Political'

There are some in this country who fear that in going into Europe, we shall in some way sacrifice independence and sovereignty ... These fears, I need hardly say, are completely unjustified.

Edward Heath, television broadcast, January 1973

Economic and monetary union ... would in effect require political union, a United States of Europe. That is not on the agenda now, or for the foreseeable future.

Margaret Thatcher, House of Commons, 2 May 1989

One of the hardest things to grasp about this entity which today calls itself 'the European Union' is how very odd it is. Nothing remotely like it has ever been seen in the world before. It is not just an economic and a political phenomenon. Just as much, perhaps even more, it is a psychological pheno- menon. Indeed one of its most pronounced characteristics is how hard it is to pin down just what it is at any given moment. This is not merely because it is always in a state of ceaseless change and evolution, but because it is never in any way quite what it seems, or what it pretends to be.

One symptom of this is the way the entity has constantly changed its name. When the United States of America was formed, it was known immediately as the United States of America. It had a constitution, which has evolved and been amended down the centuries. But it has always been possible to define exactly what the USA is and what it is intended to be. No one has ever tried to pretend that it is anything else.

This phenomenon which has grown and taken shape in western Europe in the past 50 years has been altogether more elusive. To begin with, it was known as the 'Common Market'. This at least might have seemed perfectly straightforward, honestly describing what it was, nothing more than a customs union to encourage trade between its members. But examine the Treaty of Rome setting this up, and the preamble cites as one of its chief aims that the 'High Contracting Parties' are 'determined to lay the foundations of an ever-closer union among the peoples of Europe'. So we already have a clear indication that this was something intended to be much more than just a customs union, although it is not specified what that shall be.

Then in the 1970s and 1980s it gradually took on another name, the 'European Economic Community', the EEC, now making more explicit that it was more than just a customs union. Again this was fair enough, since the entity clearly had evolved into more than a mere customs union. Indeed the European Economic Community had been always been the technical term for one part of that entity, to distinguish it from the other 'communities' making it up, the original 'European Coal and Steel Community' which had been the germination of the whole idea, and 'Euratom', the European Atomic Community, which expressed co-operation between the original members on nuclear matters.

In the late 1980s, however, it was subtly conveyed from Brussels that the correct or preferred term was now the 'European Community', the EC, clearly implying that this was now much more than just an economic entity. Again, this might have seemed fair enough, since it clearly had developed into much more than just an 'economic' community. Except that for the first time the terminology was now running ahead of itself, because under the treaties there was actually no such thing as a 'European Commmunity'. There were merely the separate communities, the EEC, ECSC and Euratom, making up a linked agglomeration. In fact it was not until the 'Treaty on European Union' signed at Maastricht in February 1992 and finally ratified in 1993 that the 'European Community' as such was called into being. 'Article 1' of Maastricht solemnly states that 'by this Treaty the High Contracting Parties establish among themselves a European Community'. This was made of the four 'pillars', which were the three original 'communities', plus now a 'common foreign and security policy'.

Thus it was only in 1993 that the entity in fact formally established the name under which it had been informally but systematically referring to itself for some years. But, revealingly, no sooner had this been done, and the 'EC' finally brought ex post facto into being, than it immediately began to call itself something else again. It was now to be referred to as 'the European Union', now implying something much more than just a mere 'Community'. This was because the Maastricht Treaty not only formally for the first time set up the European Community. It also, in a quite separate preamble, declared under 'Article A' that the High Contracting Parties should 'establish among themselves a European Union, hereinafter called "the Union" '. So it was now both a 'Community' and a 'Union' at the same time, according to whether one was consulting 'Article 1' or 'Article A'. But of course the name which the Community preferred, and which it insisted on using wherever possible was 'the Union', because this sounded much nearer to something which was a political entity, that fully integrated United States of Europe which had not yet come into being. The mere repetitious use of the term 'the Union' would accustom people to the idea. It would soften them up. So that when the next big leap forward was made, to a much more complete political integration, they would accept this as something which already seemed so established and familiar, such a fait accompli, that it would be hard to know quite how to stop it.

It was all just another, very important example of the way, wherever you touched it, this System relied to achieve its purposes on creating a world of mirrors.

Indeed if some old Chinese philsopher was to pen a meditation on the history of 'the European Union', he might well term it the Story of the Three Great Deceptions. The first deception was the claim that its real purpose was not political. The second deception, as much a self-delusion as anything, was that what it was seeking to achieve could or would ever work. The third, every time it became obvious that it wasn't working, was the need to pretend that it was. Such are the themes of our two final chapters.

Birth of a dream

The real key to understanding this strange story is psychology, to look at what was going on in people's heads, what drew them to act as they did.

In the 1960s when Britain first contemplated the breathtaking departure from her past that was implied by throwing in her destiny with Europe she was going through a peculiarly traumatic phase of her history. In a remarkably short space of years she had lost the most far-flung empire the world had ever seen. She had ceased to be one of the 'Big Three' of the wartime and immediate post-war years. Her economy seemed to be in irreversible decline. With her newly shrunken role on the world stage, she was suffering not only from a loss of historical identity but from a pronounced national inferiority complex. The British felt they were no longer much good at anything, apart from producing pop singers and teenage fashions. And all this created the psychological hunger for some large new vision, some new destiny which might offer hope of salvation.

Nothing provided a more beguiling image of that alternative future than the spectacle of what was going on just over the Channel on the continent of Europe. Britain's nearest neighbours, who less than twenty years before had seemed utterly devastated by the war, had made an astonishing recovery. In particular Western Germany, thanks to its 'economic miracle' in the 1950s, was now the most prosperous, efficient country in Europe. France, having pulled itself together politically under the leadership of of de Gaulle, was not far behind. Even Italy, until recently comparatively backward and inefficient, was modernising fast. And since the early 1950s these countries, with their three smaller Benelux neighbours, had increasingly been coming together in schemes of economic and political co-operation.

At the time when the first of these schemes was proposed in 1950, the Monnet-Schumann plan setting up the European Coal and Steel Community, it seemed to most British people that this had really nothing to do with Britain at all. In a series of visionary speeches after the war, Winston Churchill had evoked the dream of a future 'United States of Europe', as a way to prevent the catastrophes of the two world wars ever being repeated. But he was always careful to emphasise that he did not see any part from Britain in this process, other than as a benevolent onlooker. 'The Temple of World Peace', as he told his audience at the Albert Hall in 1947, would have four pillars: the United States of America, the Soviet Union, a newly united Europe, and, quite separately, 'the British Empire and Commonwealth', still a world power in its own right.

It is true that a tiny handful of people were already beginning to think that Britain should participate in this process of closer co-operation on the Continent. In June 1950, in his maiden speech in the House of Commons, a new young Conservative MP, Edward Heath, urged Prime Minister Clement Attlee to take a positive approach to the proposed new Coal and Steel Community. Attlee memorably and presciently replied, 'We are not prepared to accept the principle that the most vital economic forces of this country should be handed over to an authority that is utterly undemocratic and accountable to nobody.'

This reflected the basic British attitude which continued to shape her response when the six continental countries moved much closer together with the signing of the Treaty of Rome in 1957, setting up their 'Common Market'. What the 'Europeans' chose to do amongst themselves need not be directly Britain's concern.

Britain 'sees the light'

The change, when it came, took place with such dramatic speed as to be almost akin to a religious conversion. It was in 1960, the year of his 'wind of change' speech in Africa, that Harold Macmillan's Conservative Government suddenly began to reverse all its previous thinking, and in the summer of 1961 Britain applied to join the Common Market. As alarm grew over the continued decline and obsolescence of key sectors of British industry, it was obvious that the booming economies of the Six were now outperforming Britain's, and much of their success was put down to their collaboration in this new venture. The Common Market now suddenly seemed an excellent club to join. If Britain became a member, perhaps she would learn how to share in their success?

Long months of negotiations began in Brussels, led for Britain by Edward Heath, and it became apparent that there were many problems, not least the need for Britain to relinquish much of her traditional trading relationship with the Commonwealth. The Common Market might be a free trade area internally. But the corollary was that this involved putting up a high tariff wall against goods from the outside world to protect producers inside the fortress, above all the farmers who enjoyed artificially high prices for their food. Most of Britain's food imports came in duty free from her overseas Commonwealth partners such as Australia, New Zealand and Canada. All this would now have to change, and it was this that helped to bring home to many in Britain just how much she would actually have to give up, if she was going to throw in her destiny with a wholly new set of 'partners'. It was this feeling which was voiced by the Labour leader Hugh Gaitksell in his famous conference speech in 1962, when he spoke of abandoning 'a thousand years of history'. But to Heath and Britain's growing number of committed 'Europeans', this kind of language summed up precisely what the issue was all about. Britain must cut loose from such nostalgic sentimentality. She must throw off the shackles of the past. She must become 'tough minded' and 'modernise'. It was they, and the 'dynamic' new Europe, who stood for the future, that new role and new wider horizon Britain so sorely needed.

Curiously enough, the man who saw most clearly how much Britain was still wedded to her old identity, her distinctive traditions, her global relationships with America and the Commonwealth – and how profoundly unprepared she was to fit in with the quite different continental ways of doing things – was President de Gaulle. In the celebrated statement in January 1963 in which he foreshadowed the French veto on Britain's application to join, he spoke of Britain as 'insular and maritime'. 'Her nature, her structure, her economic position differ profoundly from those of the continentals.' His words were widely interpreted at the time as a tremendous snub, a slap in the face to Britain. In fact they were based on shrewd instinct. They penetrated below the surface to a deeper reality. Truly the British should have taken them as a great compliment.

But Britain's 'rejection' by Europe only helped to exacerbate still further that growing sense of national inferiority. As the world moved on, her old overseas ties were diminishing anyway. She was increasingly alone, a country beset with problems, a poor little island marooned off a continent which economically was still forging ahead. In 1967 a second attempt was made to join the Common Market by Harold Wilson, also rebuffed by de Gaulle. It was only in 1970, when the Conservatives were re-elected under the most passionate 'European' of them all, Edward Heath, that the tumblers in the lock finally came together. President de Gaulle had gone the previous year, and was replaced by Georges Pompidou, an altogether less lofty, more pragmatic politician. Heath was so possessed by the idea of taking Britain into Europe that nothing would stop him. As the negotiations began, most difficulties were soon overcome, until in the end the only issue outstanding was the ingenious trap the Six had laid over the surrender of Britain's fishing waters. But Heath was not going to allow a little matter like that to stand in his way, and on 1 January 1973 Britain was in. For fear of being isolated by Britain's entry into the club, Denmark and Ireland also joined, so the original Six had now become the Nine.

Not quite what we thought

When the British entered the Common Market the impression they were above all given was that they were joining in a trading venture, a free trade area which would give them much greater opportunities to sell their goods. Britain already conducted a large part of her trade with her nearest geographical neighbours. Indeed she sold more goods and services each year to the six Common Market countries than they sold to her. But the idea was that, opening up even greater freedom to trade with some of the most prosperous and fast-growing economies in the world, Britain would win a still greater chance to increase her prosperity in line with theirs. The overwhelming message, both when Britain went in and two years later when the 1975 referendum was held to confirm her membership, was that the chief result of joining the club would be that the people of Britain would enjoy a host of new economic benefits. Everyone would share in a new prosperity.

The one concern the committed 'Marketeers' were most anxious to allay was that Britain's membership might entail some diminishing of her political independence. As Edward Heath told the nation on television in 1973, 'There are some in this country who fear that in going into Europe we shall in some way sacrifice independence and sovereignty.' He went on, 'These fears, I need hardly say, are completely unjustified.' The 1971 White Paper, sent to every household in Britain, had gone out of its way to emphasise that there was 'no question of Britain losing essential sovereignty'. 'No nation' in the new club could 'override another'. Britain's 'vital interests' would be guaranteed. She would keep her own parliament, courts and legal systems (except that 'there will be certain changes under the treaties concerning economic and commercial matters'). In every significant respect we would keep 'our own way of life', our distinctive national institutions, our national identity.

Hardly were the often heated debates on the European Communities Act which expressed Parliament's agreement to British entry concluded, however, than word arrived from Paris that President Pompidou was proposing that Member States should make a solemn commitment to 'move irrevocably to economic and monetary union by 1980'. This made a complete mockery of all the assurances given both to the British people and to parliament that the 'market' was just a trading arrangement between independent states. In a BBC documentary history of Britain's involvement with Europe, 'The Poisoned Chalice', in 1996, a former Foreign Office official, Sir Roy Denman, recalled how Foreign Secretary Sir Alec Douglas-Home had looked askance at the news. He told Heath, 'The House is not going to like this.' 'But that', Denman remembered Heath replying, 'is what it is all about.' When Heath himself was asked whether he could really have said such a thing in 1973, his only response, after an unsmiling pause, was, 'Well, that's what it was about.' In 1990, when Heath was asked by another television interviewer, Peter Sissons, whether, when he took Britain into Europe, he really had in mind 'a united states of Europe, with a single currency', he replied, 'Of course, yes.'

The truth is that, to a degree which was wholly concealed from the British in 1973, the ultimate objective that the countries of Western Europe, led by France and Germany, would one day form a complete political, as well as economic union has been right at the heart of the development of the Common Market/European Community/European Union ever since it was first conceived in the 1950s. In the writings of Jean Monnet, as in the minds of other visionaries who dreamed of uniting Europe, like the Communist Altieri Spinelli, it is clear that the real aim of the whole enterprise was to build political union. After all, even the Treaty of Rome itself had spoken of moving towards 'ever closer union'. Always the ultimate goal was the emergence of a new European super-state, burying ancient hatreds and rivalries, which could act as a full counterpoise to the superpowers, the USA and the old USSR. This was also, after all, precisely the future vision of Churchill himself. Except, of course, that he did not for a moment envisage Britain becoming directly involved, and in 1962 Field Marshal Montgomery found the old man sitting up in bed, drinking brandy, roundly cursing Macmillan's attempt to get us in.

But it was equally part of this long game that this ultimate objective would have to realised very carefully and discreetly, stage by stage. If the real purpose of the enterprise was advertised too loudly and too soon, the peoples of Europe might take alarm and shy away from it. That was why, from a very early point, the scheme divided people into two classes: the small group of insiders, the chosen elite, wholly committed to work for the cause, who could therefore be trusted to know everything; and the great majority who were not yet ready for such a visionary plan, and therefore had to be kept largely in the dark. In the late 1950s, Richard Body was one of a small group of young Conservative MPs so fired by the idea of this new free trading area opening up in Europe that they became passionate for Britain to join, at a time when this was completely off their Party's agenda. But in 1967 Body was invited to spend several days visiting the Commission in Brussels. Because he was assumed to be very much an 'insider', he was told about the grand plan, the hidden agenda and how the ultimate objective was political union – and also how important it was to the great cause that this should be kept under wraps until the time was right. He was so profoundly shocked by what he heard that it opened his eyes. He began to see the whole enterprise in a totally different light. By the 1980s he had become one of the most outspoken and know-ledgable critics of the madness of the Common Agricultural Policy, and in the 1990s he was one of the leaders of the parliamentary 'Euro-rebels'.

The truth begins to emerge

One reason, of course, why in the 1990s Edward Heath felt free to be so much more open in admitting what he had known in 1973, but at that time had hidden from the British people, was that by this time so much more of the grand plan was out in the open anyway. During the previous 20 years the scheme for economic and political union had already made enormous strides towards its ultimate objective.

That 1972 plan for 'economic and monetary union by 1980' had proved premature. But in 1978 it was revived again by the French President Valery Giscard d'Estaing, the German Chancellor Helmut Schmidt and the British President of the Commission Roy Jenkins, as the European Monetary System. Through the 1980s into the 1990s, successive versions of the EMS, incorporating the ERM, were put into operation. Each in turn crumbled apart, leaving a trail of havoc through the economies of Europe. But always the intention was that these were merely a transitional prelude to that ultimate goal of a single currency and full economic union.

On the political front the next great leap forward did not come until 1985. In 1979 Margaret Thatcher had arrived on the scene, as potentially the most outspoken, out-of-step leader of any Member State since the Common Market began. Her first five years were dominated by her fight against the ridiculous anomaly which made Britain such a disproportionate contributor to the Brussels budget (in 1985 she contributed 25 per cent of all the money paid in). This was because of historical peculiarities in Britain's economic position, not least that she was importing more food from the outside world than anyone else, notably from the Commonwealth, and having to pay levies accordingly. But once this battle was won, in 1985 Mrs Thatcher's free-trad-ing spirit led her to put forward proposals to dismantle all the non-tariff barriers which still remained to free trade within what was now generally known as the European Economic Community. She believed it would be quite possible to achieve this within the existing terms of the Treaty of Rome. After all, liberalisation of trade was supposedly what the Common Market was all about. Nevertheless she was rather surprised when not only was her idea eagerly taken up by other countries, including France and Germany, and by the new President of the Commission, the French Socialist Jacques Delors, but was accompanied by an insistence that the measures could not possibly be realised without a full Inter-Governmental Conference. This would mean drawing up a whole new Treaty, the first since the Treaty of Rome itself. Soon many more proposals were on the table which had very little or nothing to do with liberalising trade at all. These included a major extension of the principle of 'qualified majority voting', which would greatly restrict use of the national veto; a major extension of the EC's 'competences', or rights to legislate over areas of policy such as the environmental and social policy; and the granting of new powers to the European Assembly, shortly to be renamed the European Parliament. The result in 1986 was the Single European Act. The new treaty certainly provided for the setting up of that new 'Single Market' Mrs Thatcher was after. But it also, as its name implied, included many other elements aimed at moving the 'EEC' nearer to a 'Single Europe'.

In the chapter of her memoirs entitled 'The Babel Express', Lady Thatcher records how from this time on, and particularly from the early months of 1988, 'the agenda in Europe began to take an increasingly unwelcome shape'. Partly this was because of the re-emergence of a Franco-German axis between President Mitterand and Chancellor Kohl, pushing more strongly than ever for the ERM to lead to full 'economic and monetary union', and for other moves towards more complete political union. Partly it was because they found in Jacques Delors an ally prepared to go even further than themselves. Not only was he all for pushing towards economic and political union. He also, revealingly, was demanding much greater powers and a much more active role for his own central power base, the bureaucratic anthill of the Commission itself. 'By the summer of 1988' wrote Lady Thatcher, Delors had 'slipped his leash as a fonctionnaire and become a fully-fledged spokesman for federalism'. In July 1988 Delors told an applauding European Parliament, 'we are not going to manage to take all the decisions needed between now and 1995 unless we see the beginnings of European government'. Within ten years, he predicted, the Community would be the source of '80 per cent of our economic legislation and perhaps even our fiscal and social legislation as well'.

Like a river rushing towards a waterfall, the current towards that 'European government' was suddenly speeding up in all directions. This was the time when in Britain the Europhiles, like Foreign Secretary Geoffrey Howe, were constantly conjuring up the image of 'Europe' as advancing into the future like a fast-moving 'train'. It was vital that Britain should 'jump on board' that train, without enquiring too closely as to its destination, or she would 'miss the bus' and the most fearful, unspecified disasters would follow. Mrs Thatcher viewed all this with mounting alarm, from the way Delors' Commission was constantly extending its authority to the newly aggressive way in which the European Court of Justice was now favouring 'dynamic and expansive' interpretations of the treaty in its judgements. She later wrote:

> The more I considered all this the greater my frustration and the deeper my anger became. Were British democracy, parliamentary sovereignty, our traditional sense of fairness, our ability to run our own affairs in our own way to be subordinated to the demands of a European bureaucracy, resting on very different traditions? I had by now heard about as much of the European 'ideal' as I could take.

Furthermore, in the name of this ideal, 'waste, corruption and abuse of power were reaching levels' which no one could conceivably have foreseen. Mrs Thatcher decided she had to speak out, to sound as public a warning as possible. Choosing the opportunity of a speech in Bruges on 20 September 1988, she pointed to the countries of eastern Europe which, as Communism crumbled, were looking west for an example of liberty, democracy, private enterprise, free trade. She reminded her audience that Warsaw, Prague and Budapest were just as much 'great European cities' as those within the often inward-looking western half of the continent. How could western Europe provide them with any model or inspiration when it was so rapidly sliding towards very much the kind of undemocratic, 'tightly centralised, highly regulated', bureaucratic super-state they were all yearning to escape from?

The reaction from the rest of what now called itself 'the European Community' was, as she recorded, one of 'stunned outrage'. From that moment, so far as the Euro-establishment was concerned, including many in her own Government and Party at home, not to mention the officials of the British Foreign Office, Mrs Thatcher's days were numbered, and over the next two years they tried everything to marginalise, ignore, rebuff and trap her.

One particular trap was sprung just before the Madrid summit in June 1989. M. Delors had produced a devastating report, proposing by far the most elaborate plans so far for full 'Economic and Monetary Union', and stating that the changes involved would be so great that it would require a new Inter-Governmental Conference and a new Treaty to adopt them. In the House of Commons on 2 May, Mrs Thatcher gave a withering response. 'We cannot accept the transfer of sovereignty which is implied by the Delors report, she said:

> Economic and monetary union as spelt out in the report would in effect require political union, a United States of Europe. That is not on the agenda now or for the foreseeable future ... the Government do not believe there should be further treaty amendment as proposed by the Delors report.

The Delors proposals were on the agenda for the Madrid Summit, to be held at the end of June. As the time approached, a number of MPs expressed mounting alarm that deliberate steps were apparently being taken to ensure that the House of Commons would not be permitted to debate them. 'If the Government attaches significance to arguments about the sovereignty of parliament,' a committee of MPs protested, 'it ought not to be selective in its attachment to them.' But when the Summit came and went, it was clear that their worst fears had been realised. The communiqué made clear that M. Delors' proposals for a new treaty conference had been adopted. 'Economic and monetary union', and a new 'social charter' would be top of the agenda. When Mrs Thatcher returned to report to MPs on what had happened, she tried valiantly to play down the defeat she had suffered. 'It was a useful Council,' she said. 'No dramatic decisions, but steady progress in important areas.' She had been completely outmanoeuvred. The clock was now ticking away towards to the negotiations for the new treaty, the centrepiece of which would be precisely that 'economic and monetary union' which she said would in effect bring about 'political union, a United States of Europe'. And, with Britain's veto power on treaty changes, she was now the only EC leader standing in the way of that plan being realised.

Not until the autumn of 1990 was the Euro-establishment able to spring its final trap. So great now were the pressures on Mrs Thatcher, not just from the rest of Europe but around her own Cabinet table, that in October 1990, against all her instincts, her new Chancellor John Major, prodded by the most determined Europhile of them all, Foreign Secretary Geoffrey Howe, took Britain into the ERM. No sooner had this happened than, days later, the rest of the EC was able to 'ambush' her at a Rome summit. Not only did they spring on her their plans for a Single Currency, which it seemed Britain would now, as a member of the ERM, be bound to join. M. Delors also unveiled by far the most far-reaching proposals ever drawn up for a politically fully united Europe. The European Parliament would be the Community's 'House of Representatives' and the Council of Ministers the 'Senate'. Meanwhile M. Delors' own Commission, under its President, would be the 'Executive', in effect the new government of a 'United States of Europe'.

'No, no, no, no', as Mrs Thatcher told the House of Commons on her return. But again, within only a matter of days, she was further ambushed by a carefully calculated and feline resignation speech from that most fervently Euro-loyalist member of her Cabinet throughout the 1980s, Geoffrey Howe. She was fatally wounded. Led by Michael Heseltine, who had been waiting for this moment, the 'pro-Europeans' were now in full cry, and within a fortnight she had been brought down. The Euro-establishment at home and abroad had finished her off because, after decades of obfuscating and concealing what they were really up to, they were now ready to come fully out into the open at last. As the only leader left able to call their bluff, she had been the last remaining obstacle to their Grand Plan. And now she was gone.

The high noon of 'European Union'

Looking back, we can now see the period between 1990 and 1992 as a kind of high noon of the European federalists' dash for complete union. Now that Britain was locked into the ERM, all the talk was of the next and final stage, 'Economic and Monetary Union', the Single Currency. This was planned to be the centrepiece of a new Treaty due to be held by the end of 1991. The lawmaking machine in Brussels was now churning out record quantities of directives and regulations to prepare for the Single Market, due in 1993. And amid the euphoria of the federal dream now driving forwards on all sides, the summer of 1991 saw easily the most ambitious experiment so far in carrying out a common 'European' foreign policy, with the EC's attempt to intervene politically in Yugoslavia.

The federated state of Yugoslavia, only held together for forty years by a cruel Serb-dominated Communist dictatorship, was cracking apart. As Communism crumbled, the peoples of Slovenia, Croatia and Bosnia grimly prepared to break loose from the Belgrade government, to set up free, independent, democratic states on what they imagined was the western European model. Nothing better symbolised these yearnings than the rash of EC 'ring of stars' flags which in 1990 and the first half of 1991 were suddenly flying everywhere in Slovenia and Croatia, alongside their new national flags. But slowly a terrible realisation dawned. Far from championing the right of free peoples to assert their own independence, the EC was encouraging the old Communist tyranny in Belgrade to take tough action to hold its federation together. In the summer of 1991 the Italian Foreign Minister Signor de Michelis said the Community 'could not accept the disintegration of Yugoslavia', just as six months earlier, when Soviet tanks had killed 20 people in Lithuania, his prime minister Signor Andreotti had said 'there are times when tanks on the streets are necessary' (both de Michelis and Andreotti were eventually to face serious corruption charges back home). Worse still was when a self-regarding 'troika' of EC politicians, including de Michelis and M. Poos, the foreign minister of Luxembourg, arrived in person in Belgrade, to represent 'European Community' foreign policy in action. Poos greatly pleased the Communist Serb leader Milosevic by saying that it was absurd for little nations like Slovenia to think they could be independent ('the idea of national self-determination is dangerous as the basis for international order'). He was apparently oblivious to the fact that Slovenia's population was six times that of Luxembourg, but presumably M. Poos no longer thought of his own country as independent. Certainly the chilling message of this ill-starred visit was to confirm just how much more at home was the new *nomenklatura* of the Community in talking to the decaying *nomenklaturas* of Communist eastern Europe, standing for bureaucratic control from the centre, than they were in relating to people who wanted to break away into free, non-communist nationhood. Within three months the massed artillery of the federal Serb army was pounding the Croatian towns of Vukovar and Osijek to rubble, as Milosevic did exactly what the EC foreign ministers had advised.

Over the next three years, in fact, nothing was to be a more pitiful reflection of the Community's dream of a 'common foreign policy' than the utter futility of all its efforts to 'intervene' in the Yugoslav catastrophe. The successive Carrington, Owen and Bildt 'peace missions', the 'peace conferences' summoned by EC countries including Britain, the endlessly self-deluded, self-important waffling of every EC 'statesman' involved, the constant appeasement of Milosevic and the Serbs, comprised as dismal and humiliating a chapter in Europe's history as anything since the days of the late 1930s. Amid the most horrendous and one-sided tragedy to have erupted in Europe since 1945, when the people of Bosnia were crying out for the chance to arm and defend themslves against the gangs of Serbs who were turning their little country into a bloodbath, there was perhaps no single remark more chilling in the entire conflict than Douglas Hurd's statement that the EC could not support a lifting of the ban on the Bosnians obtaining weapons, because this would only create 'a level killing field'. What Mr Hurd and the EC preferred, it seemed, was the 'unlevel killing field' which in the summer of 1994 produced the catastrophe of Srebrenice. At the last moment Dutch soldiers walked away from what the desperate inhabitants had been assured was a 'safe haven', leaving 11,000 defenceless men to be marched out of the town and gunned down by Serb gangsters. Even amid all the other horrors of the Yugoslav tragedy, those sunlit fields and woodland glades piled high with the corpses of men betrayed represented the most horrifying single crime in Europe since the aftermath of World War Two. It was an achievement of which those vain and self-regarding little 'statesmen' of the 'European Community' might well be proud.

Indeed this was another curious feature of the ethos of the European Community which the Yugoslav tragedy helped glaringly to underline. This was the way its adherents insisted on talking of 'Europe' as if this consisted only of those countries making up the 'European Community' itself. The true Europe and its true 'community' of peoples were of course infinitely larger. More than half the land area and half the populations of Europe were not included in the little political experiment going on at one end of the continent. But so obssessive and so self-regarding had those caught up in this experiment become, that all those other lands and peoples were consigned to some outer darkness. This was why people like Mr Hurd and M. Santer could cheerfully speak of how the 'EU' had 'brought peace' to Europe for 50 years, at the very moment when hundreds of thousands of their fellow Europeans were dying in by far the worst and cruellest war to have racked their continent in all that time. But from within the narrow little inward-looking world of the Community, those Bosnians and Croats were not really 'Europeans' at all. In the true 'European' sense they were just 'unpersons'.

Even though this unspeakable tragedy was unfolding 'off stage', nothing could disturb the self-importance of the leaders of western Europe as they gathered in the little Dutch town of Maastricht in December 1991 for the final negotiations which were to lead to the signing of 'the Treaty of European Union'. Dominating the scene were Chancellor Kohl, President Mitterand and 'President' Delors, with around them, like the petty princelings of vassal states, the prime ministers and foreign ministers of Spain and Portugal, Greece and Denmark, Belgium and Luxembourg, Ireland and Italy. For the Dutch hosts this was the crowning moment of their turn in the 'Presidency' of the Council of Ministers (nowhere near so important a role, of course, as President of the Commission). And finally there were John Major, Douglas Hurd and Norman Lamont representing Britain.

There could have been no more telling sign of just how Britain was still the odd man out of the Community than the way, at the end of those two days and nights of wearying discussions, Mr Major and his two ministers had at least managed to hold onto some vestiges of independent British discretion as to how far and how fast she could be bundled down the road to a wholly united Europe. One after another the elements of the next great leap forward to political 'union' were unanimously nodded through. The 370 million inhabitants of the Union were all to be granted 'Citizenship of the European Community' . There were to be a whole range of new 'competences', allowing the Community and the officials of the Commission to take over from national governments rights to legislate on education, public health and many other issues. There were to be moves towards locking the countries of the Union into a much more formal common foreign and defence policy. On only two points did Britain put her foot down, insisting that she could not go along with the rest. She would not sign up to the Social Chapter, granting new rights to workers against their employers. And when it came to the supreme prize of all, 'Economic and Monetary Union', Mr Major and his colleagues insisted on reserving for Britain's parliament the right ultimately to decide whether Britain would go in or stay out.

Considering how much else Britain's parliament had been persuaded to give away over the years, often without even being aware of it, this might not in the end amount to much. On the other hand, it might just prove, some years into the future, that this would be the straw which finally broke the camel's back.

18. The Castle of Lies (II) – The Three Great Deceptions

> One has to say that there is very little sign that British thinking, British philosophy, British common sense is having any impact on our partners in the European Community. They have mapped out a path for themselves. They mapped it out in the 1940s. They have stuck to it. They are not going to abandon it. They will be damned rather than abandon it. Economically they will be damned. Politically and socially they will be damned ... At some point we as a nation have to decide whether we are going to go along with this ... madness. Are we going to throw ourselves off the cliff?
>
> Bernard Connolly, lecture at House of Commons, 30 April 1996

We have seen how the first of the Three Great Deceptions implicit in the evolution of the 'European Union' came gradually to be exposed, and that it was always intended, from its inception, to lead ultimately to a fully integrated super-state. However there was also a rather deeper deception involved in this particular piece of trickery. This concerned the real nature of the new state the once-independent nations of western Europe were being led towards.

Deception no. 1 – the real nature of the System

One impression the shapers of the new state had always been particularly careful to convey was that this new System of government was essentially democratic. In theory it always remained under the ultimate control of politicians elected to express the wishes of their peoples. Nominally at the head of the whole System, as its guarantee of democratic legitimacy, was the Council of Ministers, representing the elected governments of every Member State. Without their agreement, no significant piece of legislation could be issued, certainly no Treaty could be agreed. Yet in practice, as we have seen, the power and influence of the Council of Ministers was very largely a fiction, just another example of the world of mirrors. The real power in the System was generated collectively by that vast unseen army of officials, acting through Brussels as their nexus. To a very great extent the role of the politicians was merely to act as a rubber stamp to decisions already arrived at; but their really important function was then to act as the System's 'front men', at press conferences, in television interviews, in front of their own parliaments, to preserve the illusion that it was they who were in charge.

An even emptier fiction intended to convey the impression that democracy had some part to play in the System was the role played by that very curious institution, the European Parliament. Originally just a nominated 'Assembly', the Parliament had gradually been developed over two decades deliberately to promote the illusion that the peoples of Europe could be directly represented in the System. But in reality this institution was nothing more than an absurd, if very expensive joke. By 1996 each of the 581 Members of the European Parliament cost the taxpayers of the 'Union' just over £1 million a year, far more than the cost of a national MP in any of the Member States. This was partly because of their astonishingly lavish expenses, and partly because of the ludicrous arrangements which had to be made to keep the Parliament in operation. Since it met partly in Strasbourg and partly in Brussels, this meant that every month 58 pantechnicons had to move mountains of parliamentary papers between one city and the other, then back again. Meanwhile the Parliament's library, costing £6 million a year, was for some reason maintained in Luxembourg, 100 miles from either city, which rendered it so much of a white elephant that in 1994 only 126 books were taken out, at an average cost of £46,500 per volume.

The real farce of the European Parliament was that it was no more than a talking shop. Its members indulged in endless debates and committee meetings, of stupefying boredom and irrelevance. They traipsed off round the world on costly, expenses-paid trips. But they had virtually no powers. In April 1994, on one of the very rare occcasions when they were given the chance to vote down a Commission directive which threatened to impose draconian regulations on Europe's motorcyclists, the vote went 252 to 28 against the Commission. But it then emerged that, to be successful, it would have been necessary under the Parliament's arcane rules to muster 260 votes. So, despite their defeat in the vote by almost 10 to 1, the Commission officials won the day. The real purpose of the MEPs was again simply to act as a democratic 'front' for the System: to get their names in the local media, to lobby for grants from Brussels, but above all to act as propagandists for the EU. In this sense their function bore uncanny parallels to the members of another fiction intended to simulate the outward form of democracy without any of the reality, the Chamber of Deputies in the old Soviet Union.*

Behind these outward façades, the real nature of the European state was wholly different, as may again be seen by comparing the emerging constitution of the European Union to one of its supposed models and inspirations, that of the United States of America. The essence of the American constitution, carefully constructed after open and lofty debates between some of the most acute political thinkers in history, is that to preserve liberty and democracy against the encroachments of tyranny, the whole structure must rest at every point on the separation of powers. Each is there to provide checks and balances against the powers of the others. At its heart is the troika made up

---

* In 1995 the new European Transport Commissioner Neil Kinnock visited the European Parliament to tell MEPs about his £70,000 million Trans European Network programme, a plan to link every part of the 'Union' more closely with new autobahns. Kinnock was appalled when he arrived to be told that, under the rules of the Parliament, he would only be allowed to speak for three minutes. On past form, this would scarcely give time enough for Mr Kinnock to complete his first sentence. Rather more significantly, however, it was an appropriate comment on the role of the MEPs that they should only be prepared to devote three minutes to hearing about the most costly single project the EC had ever set in train.

of the executive, under an elected President, chivvied or kept in check by the Congress, the wholly independent legislature; with the ring held by the Supreme Court, the judiciary, to ensure that no one acts against the Constitution, the bedrock of liberty. But the astonishing thing about the emerging constitution of the European Union is that there are no such checks and balances. There is no real separation of powers. The legislature is an hollow sham, dedicated only to serving the propaganda purposes of the System. The Court is likewise only an arm of the System, dedicated to upholding and extending its powers. And in the centre, running the System, is the over-mighty executive, the Commission, a body of unelected officials, with only vestigial restraint from the Member State governments, acting partly on its own behalf and partly as the nexus joining together all the government bureaucracies of the Union.

The European Union is thus in no meaningful sense democratic. It is one of the supreme examples the world has seen of a state run not by democracy but by a centralised bureaucracy. And what makes this particularly significant is not just that it has so little democratic restraint on its actions, but that it falls into the ways and the mind-sets of bureaucracy in everything it does. Its perceptions of problems are bureaucratic. The solutions it proposes to those problems are bureaucratic. And this provides us with the real explanation of why it behaves as it does. Because the essence of bureaucratic thinking is that it so easily becomes an end in itself. It develops its own momentum, operating only within its own frame of reference, concerned only with its own complex and cumbersome procedures. It loses any contact with the real world in which human beings live. And that is why, in almost everything it touches, we find this new System of government going so crazily, unimaginably wrong.

Deception no. 2 – the delusion that the System can work

The second of the Great Deceptions implicit in this System is the delusion that it can actually achieve any of the purposes it sets out to achieve. This is because, even if they are worth aiming for at all, it invariably sets out to achieve them in entirely the wrong, bureaucratic fashion.

We have seen dozens, if not hundreds of examples of this in this book, and to cite one which might stand as a model for them all, let us recall the way in which the officials of the European Commission set out to 'conserve European fish stocks'. They do this primarily by instructing fishermen, through the quota system, precisely which species of fish and how many they are permitted to land. It is a perfect example of what might seem on paper, to the bureaucratic mind, the perfect solution to a problem. The officials can sit in DG XIV in Brussels, just as their predecessors must have sat in offices in Moscow, working out in advance just how many fish of each species can be caught in a year, so that the stocks are 'scientifically controlled' and are not exhausted. But quite apart from the fact that the scientific information as to how many fish there are is also supplied by officials, and frequently bears no relation to what is actually happening in the unpredictable world of nature out at sea, the whole system is based on a flaw so fundamental and so simple that it could only have been dreamed up by bureaucrats who had never been on a fishing boat in their lives. Species of fish do not swim neatly separated from each other. They live all mixed together in the same piece of ocean. So a fisherman cannot necessarily put down his net to catch the species the officials allow him to catch, without catching species which the officials have made it a criminal offence to land, because he hasn't got the piece of paper giving him the necessary quota. He therefore has to discard his non-quota catch and dump the fish dead back into the sea. As even the Commission admits, this amounts to hundreds of millions of tonnes of them every year. The only result of the bureaucratic solution to the problem of diminishing fish stocks is to ensure that billions of fish are wantonly destroyed, to no purpose at all.

Again and again in this book we have seen examples of how the bureaucratic grand plans originating in Brussels end up achieving results which are the very opposite of those intended. We have seen how symbiotically the bureaucracy lives with the 'play safe culture' of our time. Anything which can conceivably be dressed up as putting people 'at risk', which raises the shibboleths of safety or hygiene or concern for the 'environment', is at once regarded as a cue for the officials to roar into action with directives and regulations, trying to impose a prescriptive set of rules, however cumbersome, however costly, which will prevent such things ever happening again. Again and again, precisely because they are setting about it in exactly the wrong way, they end up taking a mighty sledgehammer to miss the nut. Perfectly safe, efficient abattoirs are closed down wholesale, because they do not comply with hygiene rules which have nothing to do with hygiene; meanwhile the very system the officials are imposing might almost deliberately be designed to spread contamination. A highly-efficient private enterprise system for collecting almost worthless old car batteries is destroyed because, in the name of protecting the environment, the officials cannot resist trying to regulate it, at a cost which means hundreds of thousands of batteries simply being chucked away over hedges.

So keen are the noses of these officials for anything which might endanger people's safety or the environment that there is almost no scare or piece of bogus science they won't respond to. We have already seen many examples, whisky, Emtryl, rosin, listeria in cheese, nitrates in lettuces. But in 1996 another instance emerged from the Commission which almost put the rest in the shade.

It became fashionable in the 'green' 1980s to see lead in petrol as one of the most noxious pollutants of our age. Not only did it harm the environment, it inflicted terrible damage on human brains, particularly those of children. If ever there was a case for the regulators to move in and impose the strictest possible controls, this was it. Sure enough, on 19 June 1996, to a mighty fanfare, no fewer than three different Brussels Commissioners came before the media to announce two new directives on the way, to impose much tighter pollution standards on both vehicles and fuel. These would reduce polluting emissions in the EU by 70 per cent within 14 years, while the greatest evil of all, leaded petrol, was to be entirely banned in the EU by the year 2000. There would of course be a small price to be paid. Even the Commission officials conceded that all this would cost 'consumers' £4.8 billion a year, raise the price of a new car by up to £600 and force oil refineries into £70 billion-worth of investment. But surely such an environmental Great Leap Forward was worth every last 'euro'?

The only problem was that the idea there is anything harmful about adding minute amounts of lead to petrol (which makes it so much more economical to refine and use) had already been exposed as one of the great scientific fallacies of the age. The theory that it could damage children, based on one eccentric American study in 1979, had been completely exploded. Lead levels in humans actually fell sharply throughout the time use of leaded petrol was at its height, and any lead damage derived from other sources. In fact the really dangerous stuff, it turned out, was that supposedly virtuous unleaded petrol. Half this is made up not of petrol at all but of oil-derived aromatics like benzene which are both highly carcinogenic and seriously polluting. Of course the theory runs that all these nasty pollutants can be burned up by catalytic converters, which cannot run with leaded petrol. Environmentally, these were supposed to bring about the ultimate nirvana, which is why the EC had already made their use compulsory in new cars since 1993. The trouble here, however, is that, in practice, catalytic converters are not the dream solution to anything. They do not work properly until they are fully warmed up, and meanwhile they chuck out all sorts of filth. They lose efficiency remarkably quickly, often needing replacement after only 30,000 miles, as huge numbers of motorists now find each year to their cost. All of which means that the majority of older catalysts are already emitting nasty pollutants long before they are replaced. And since, even at best, one of their chief functions is to convert carbon monoxide to the supposed 'greenhouse gas' carbon dioxide, it was typical of those Commission officials on the one hand to compel their use, while on the other proposing a 'carbon tax' to reduce emissions of CO_2.

The irony was that use of lead petrol has prevented the discharge of an estimated 3 billion tonnes of CO_2 worldwide since the 1920s, while a complete switch to unleaded would increase emissions in the EU alone by 17 million tonnes a year. Not to mention, of course, that since unleaded is so much less efficient, to achieve the same results means depleting the world's crude oil reserves at a 20 per cent faster rate. Environmentally, in short, the compulsory switch to unleaded petrol would be a disaster. Yet again the officials had fallen for a piece of utterly bogus science and responded by proposing an enormously costly regulatory engine, to achieve results exactly the opposite of those intended.

So deeply does this kind of thinking pervade almost everything the System sets out to do that one can only look for an example which might be considered just about as remote from the regulation of petrol as could be imagined. What was the most ambitious scheme of all dreamed up by those Commission officials? No project had obsessed them more for nearly 20 years than their endless efforts to impose rigid controls on the fluctuations in currencies, as a prelude to the ultimate dream of that Single Currency, described by Belgian Prime Minister Jean-Luc Daehaene as 'the motor of European integration'. Yet those bureaucratic visionaries could no more impose their will on the movements of money, delicately reflecting the economic performances of whole nations, than they could impose their inflexible little plans on the fishes swimming in the sea. Again and again their European Monetary dreams had come crashing to the ground, as country after country had fallen out of the ERM, usually leaving a trail of devastation behind. And now as they moved nearer to that ultimate Holy Grail of the Single Currency itself, which would bring all these unpredictable, uncontrollable, messy fluctuations to an end, when money in Europe would finally arrive at the state of perfect stasis, they could look round at all the misery and unemployment spreading through those countries which were squeezing their public spending and their economies into the straitjacket necessary to achieve the 'Maastricht convergence criteria'; and they could say, 'This pain and misery is just the necessary prelude to salvation. One cannot enjoy heavenly bliss without first a death.' The one thing they would never ask was 'are we really sure we are doing the right thing?' Because the one thing of which they could be certain about the System whose will they represented was that the System was never wrong.

*

As one surveyed the continent in 1996 in fact the one thing that was certain about the great experiment known as the 'European Union', wherever one looked, was that it was not realising its declared aims. The contrast with the optimism of those far-off days of the 1950s and 1960s when the German 'economic miracle' was a wonder of the world, and the booming economies of the original 'Six' were not far behind, was total. In those days it had been widely assumed that a major reason why they were enjoying such enviable prosperity was that this was one of the benefits of the Market. Now it was tempting to reflect in retrospect that perhaps they would have enjoyed that success anyway. But certainly a major factor now in their rising unemployment, their stagnating, over-regulated, high labour cost economies and the general air of depression and gloom, was the way those brave dreams of the 'new Europe' had gone so strangely sour.

Although there was no country which was not suffering this wave of disillusionment, a particularly interesting example was what was happening in two of the last countries to join. In 1994 both Sweden and Austria had voted in referendums to join the European Union by small but decisive majorities. In each case the political and big business elite had been deeply committed to the 'European' cause, and had held out the usual promises of a new age of prosperity, once they were free to trade in the wonderful Single Market. But in each case, as usual, theory and practice had turned out to be two very different things. A year after entry, as their economies shared the general EU recession, as they experienced the reality of all those new regulations and restrictions on their economic freedom, opinion polls showed both Swedes and the Austrians regretting their decision to join by overwhelming majorities. In each case only those elites within the System clung on grimly to what remained of the lost dream.

What was also interesting were some of the individual reasons why the tide of opinion was now turning against the EU. In by no means every country was its unpopularity expressed in the same way. It would have been hard, for instance, to find a country whose experience of the System was more different from Britain's than Greece. Far from being a net contributor to the

Brussels budget, the Greeks enjoyed one of the highest returns in subsidies per household of any country in the Community. In 1994 each Greek household had on paper been given £933 from the EU. Only Luxembourg with £1,311 and Ireland with £1,318 had received more. Again, although one of the chief reasons for the EU's unpopularity in Britain was the endless deluge of oppressive directives and regulations, in Greece, where such things were treated with a much lighter hand, this scarcely counted. Nevertheless it did not take long in conversation with ordinary people in Greece to discover that the reason why so many of them detested the the 'EOK' (Greek for EEC) was that so much of that tidal wave of money from Brussels ended up in the hands of a comparatively small number of politicians, officials, businessmen and farmers who were turning the flow of subsidies into an colossal racket; and what was worse, this then reinforced their power to bully and coerce the rest of the population, who saw very little tangible benefit from the EU.

One of the maddest symbols of the EU anywhere in Europe is on a mountain top in the Peloponnese where, looking down towards the central plain of Arcadia a thousand or so feet below, there stands the grey limestone Temple of Apollo at Vassae. Built by the architect who designed the Parthenon, it was until recently the best preserved Greek temple of them all. But the days are gone when this was one of the most haunting sites to visit in all the classical world. Today its crumbling columns stand shrouded in a huge, ugly plastic tent, part paid for by the EU. The nominal explanation is that it is 'under repair'. But the real explanation can be seen on the plains of Arcadia far below, which are now dominated by two huge, Soviet-type power stations belching out filthy plumes of sulphur-rich smoke from soft brown coal. These factories too were built with the aid of EU funds; and it is their acid smoke, carried by the prevailing wind 20 miles to the north, which is so corroding the limestone columns that the temple must be kept permanently protected beneath its plastic shroud.

When we reported this it provoked a sad letter from someone who lives in that part of Greece. She recited a whole list of other disasters which had been inflicted on places around where she lived by the misuse of EC funds, from the bulldozing of 'many wonderful old Turkish' buildings, as a way of diverting funds into the pocket of a local mayor and local contractor; to the way a new slaughterhouse, built with EC money, had then been allowed to establish a monopoly over a wide area, grossly overcharging local shepherds whose livelihood was already threatened by 'cheap imported meat from the EEC'.

> When we came to live here ten years ago, the villages around were some of the most thriving and traditional in rural Greece. But the children are encouraged to leave as soon as they grow up by parents who see no future for them on the land; for if they can make no money from their goats, there is nothing left for them. Their way of life, that has existed here since long before classical times, and on which invasions of Franks, Slavs, Venetians, Albanians and Turks have had little impact, seems certain to disappear over the next twenty years. It is the machinery of the EEC that will finally drive the shepherds and their flocks from the mountains of Arcadia.

*

18. The Castle of Lies (II) – The Three Great Deceptions

What this Greek story yet again highlighted was the astonishing way in which, behind all its apparent idealism, this immense new bureaucratic System with its tentacles all across Europe, and its mountains of taxpayers' money to hand out, could so easily and so routinely be corrupted. The fact that billions of pounds of EU money each year disappeared in countless scams and rackets had long been familiar. Almost more depressing was the insouciance with which the System accepted there was virtually nothing which could be done about it, except for the comparatively few token cases which hit the news each year, when some particular racket became so glaring that it was stopped. In 1996 we heard from David Behar, an experienced business consultant who for months had been trying to alert both the European Commission and the British Foreign Office to the quite open and flagrant corruption which was responsible for the disappearance of millions of pounds a year in EU aid to the small West African country of Sierra Leone. Eventually, for his efforts, he was arrested in July 1996 at his Freetown hotel by the local police and deported back to England. But the officials of DG VIII in Brussels, responsible for the EU's overseas aid programme, showed not the slightest concern, any more than did those of the Foreign Office and their minister Lady Chalker.

Another very widespread, if rather subtler form of corruption to which this new System lent itself was the way in which, by applying the right kind of pressure in the right places in Brussels, the legislative system itself could be bent by particular interests to their own purposes. We have seen a few examples in this book, as in the case of the southern European lettuce growers who gave such enthusiastic support to the regulation on nitrates in vegetables, because this would have the effect of driving their northern competitors out of business; or the continental bus manufacturers who were so keen to see their British competitors damaged by the bus harmonisation directive; or the continental art dealers who lobbied so effectively for their system of paying royalties on modern works of art to be enforced on the British art market. The very rules which, it was loftily claimed, were intended to 'liberalise the market', 'promote competition' and establish the 'level playing field' were so often used by lobbyists behind the scenes to rig the market, to crush competition and ensure that the playing field was as bumpy as possible.

But in this respect, as in so many others, the way this System operated in practice, as opposed to the high-flown ideals it proclaimed in theory, went right back to the earliest days of the whole story. No one is more revered in the pantheon of heroes of the 'European construction' than Jean Monnet, the French visionary who launched it all on its way. In his memoirs he movingly described how he conceived his vision in the years immediately after the war, when he was wandering round the steelmaking and coal-mining areas of eastern France. It was then he had his dream that, if the terrible catastrophe of another war between France and Germany was to be avoided, then a supra-national authority should be set up, to bind the coal and steel industries of the two countries so closely together that neither of them could ever independently be used to forge the weapons of war again. Such was the genesis of the Coal and Steel Community, which set the whole mighty adventure on its way, inspired by the noblest dream of them all, of peace in a united Europe which would last for ever. But just before he gets on to these

223

shining visions, Monnet confesses to a rather more ignoble thought. As he looks at the decaying steel works and rundown mines of the French rust-belt, he imagines the time a few years in the future when their German competitors might take advantage of the fact that their factories had been flattened by the war to reconstruct with the most modern equipment. Then the future for the French industries would truly be bleak. How much better if a supra-national authority could be set up to control the market, and to ensure that the Germans would never be in a position to compete 'unfairly' in this way. The way the loftiest of ideals could be used as a cloak for the desire to rig a market went right back to the moment when that European dream was first conceived.

Deception no. 3 – the need to insist that the System is working even when it has failed

The final Great Deception is the compulsion to insist that, whenever the System fails, as it must, it is in fact working more successfully than ever. This again was a principle only too familiar to observers of the Soviet system.

Nothing might have been better calculated to arouse scepticism about the Euro-system in the mid-1990s (the word 'sceptic' comes from the Greek *skeptikos*, meaning 'thoughtful') than the increasingly reckless methods its spokesmen used to defend it. During that long initial period when most debate about Britain and Europe was conducted in abstract, theoretical terms, its supporters could rest their case for the System on how wonderfully it was going to work in the future. The sceptics could be dismissed as just nit-pickers who did not understand, were stuck in the past or lacked 'vision'. But now in the mid-1990s the whole balance of the argument had shifted. It was now possible in every direction to see how the System was actually working, or not working, in practice. At this point the abstract arguments, based on wishful thinking about the future, lost their force with dramatic speed. And suddenly the champions of the System were woefully at sea, bereft of any rational arguments for defending it.

One technique used by officials and their ministers, as in those tens of thousands of letters churned out each year to defend some specific action of the System, was simply to prevaricate round the point, either by not answering it at all, or by trying to produce an answer which managed to give a wholly misleading impression without actually telling a direct untruth. Just occasionally, however, so tight was the corner the spokesman was boxed into, that untruth was the only way out. A tiny instance was when in 1996 a junior agriculture minister, Angela Browning, was being angrily attacked in the House of Commons on the numbers of slaughterhouses which had been closed down, following the introduction of the new meat hygiene regulations in 1993. Not once, but twice, she tried to demolish her opponents' arguments by stating that the total of closures over three years was much smaller than they were claiming, only '51'. Only after the debate was it pointed out that the true figure was '151', confirming precisely the point MPs were making. The minister disarmingly explained that what of course she had meant was that 51 was a 'yearly average'.

A rather more general argument which arose in 1995 was that over the amount of legislation coming out of Brussels. In what was obviously a concerted move, spokesmen for the System, such as Foreign Secretary Douglas Hurd and the Commission Vice-President Sir Leon Brittan, had been claiming that there was a significant reduction in EU legislation. As Sir Leon had put it, 'Britain and her partners have limited the flow of regulation considerably.' Yet the Commission's own figures showed that in the previous year, 1994, the total number of directives and regulations emerging from Brussels had in fact risen quite sharply, from 1,602 to 1,800.

Another sensitive point for the System was the amount of money the British people contributed to the Brussels budget. For most of the first 20 years of her membership, Britain and Germany were the only net contributors to the budget. Every other country received back more money in grants and subsidies from the System than it put in. Admittedly in the 1990s, as the Brussels budget soared by anything up to 15 per cent or more a year, this had changed. By 1994 there were many more net contributors, and indeed the country which now paid proportionately more than any, measured in contributions per household, was not Germany, as everyone assumed, but Holland. Each Dutch household in 1994 made a net contribution of £534, whereas the German equivalent was only £470.

The means used by the System to allay British concern on this score was curious indeed. In June 1996 David Williamson, as Director General of the European Commission the top civil servant in Brussels other than the Commissioners themselves, made a speech in York in which he claimed that the contribution by 'each Briton' to the budget was only '2p a week'. It was a measure of the level at which such matters were commonly reported in the British press that the *Observer* immediately translated this into a statement that 'British budget payments now amount to just 2p per head per year'. In fact the more one looked into Mr Williamson's startling figure the odder it became. For a start he was obviously relying on the System's favourite trick of talking only of 'net contributions' to the budget, rather than the gross contributions which were the sum taxpayers actually paid in. This in itself of course was highly misleading because, while everyone pays in to the gross contribution, the 'benefits' which come back are only received by a tiny minority of the population, such as those 13 'barley barons' who each collect over £500,000 a year in subsidies. Mr Williamson's next trick, it appeared, was very carefully to base his calculations on the year 1994, when for technical reasons Britain's contribution was much lower than usual. In fact, even in his own terms, his figure of '2p' was still wildly inaccurate. But if he had wished to make his point in a more open and straightforward fashion, he should have taken the latest figures available, those for 1995, when Britain's contribution returned to a more normal level, at £7,733 million (of which £4 billion was returned in grants and subsidies). This amounted to an average contribution per household of £345, or £132 a head, which worked out at £2.54 per week. Yet this was what Mr Williamson had managed to turn into a claim that the contribution by 'each Briton' was only '2p a week', dutifully converted by the *Observer* into '2p a year'. The statement by the EC's senior permanent civil servant was in fact inaccurate by a factor of 12,700 per cent (and the *Observer*'s version by 660,000 per cent).

It was perhaps appropriate that an increasingly favourite buzzword in the

System in 1995 was 'transparency', seeking to convey that everything about the workings of the Commission and the System was transparently easy to understand. The 'Reflections Group' paper drawn up by Member State governments in preparation for the new treaty discussions in 1996 was full of references to 'transparency', which was needed 'to ensure that European construction becomes a venture to which its citizens can relate'. In a letter in November 1996 explaining how efficient was the EC's control of its budget, Sir Leon Brittan wrote 'the EC has a very transparent budgetary system with stringent monitoring and control carried out by the European Court of Auditors', ending 'I am aware of no other public finance system which is as transparent and rigorous'. Yet only three weeks earlier the President of the Court of Auditors had said he could not approve the EC's previous year's accounts because £4.2 billion of expenditure was 'not properly accounted for'. Budgetary planning was 'poor', and huge sums had obviously vanished in fraud although no one could say how much. Yet this was the public finance system more 'transparent and rigorous' than any Sir Leon had seen. Not for nothing did the phrase 'Reflections Group' conjure up the image of a world of mirrors.

A very different but telling illustration of the increasingly wild methods the System's supporters were having to employ was the curious way in which they tried to enlist Britain's greatest 20th-century statesman, Winston Churchill, as an early fellow traveller with their cause. As all the historical evidence showed, Churchill had supported the idea of a 'United States of Europe', but one quite specifically excluding Britain, and when Britain applied to join the Common Market he had viewed this as a fatal blunder. This did not prevent Michael Heseltine writing an article in the *Sunday Times* in 1995 headed 'Britain Must March Behind Churchill Into Europe', citing Churchill's 'Zurich speech' in 1946 in which he spoke of 'a United Europe in which our country must play a decisive part'. In Heseltine's article the quotation of these words immediately ran on with a call to 'all responsible statesmen' to 'shape and fashion the structure'. It took historian Andrew Roberts to note a telltale row of dots in the middle of the quotation, and to check what Churchill had actually said. The passage was in fact from an Albert Hall speech in 1947, and the passage Heseltine so carefully omitted was that which spoke of Britain and her 'Empire and Commonwealth' being quite separate from the 'United Europe'.

A year later, on the 50th anniversary of Churchill's Zurich speech, this did not prevent other spokesmen for the System, such as Edward Heath, Douglas Hurd, Sir Leon Brittan and Geoffrey Howe, continuing to cite Churchill as a supporter of Britain's involvement in a 'United Europe'. It was by now just about the only emotive argument for their cause they had left to fall back on (apart from the parrot cry that any criticism of their System was just 'xenophobia') – even if, as usual, it came only from that same old world of mirrors.

The final inversion – Britain's trading benefits

The real reason why Britain had joined 'Europe' in the first place was very simple. The central argument put by Edward Heath in the early 1970s was the one which dominated his 1971 White Paper and the subsequent debates on the Treaty in the House of Commons. It had gone on to dominate the national referendum campaign in 1975. And in one way or another it had continued to dominate the debate ever since. This argument was that Britain needed to be part of the new Europe because she would benefit by it economically. Not only, the theory ran, would she be able to share in the prosperity of those fast-growing economies on the Continent. She would have the chance greatly to expand her trade by selling to the rest of the Community in this vast new 'domestic' market.

One reason why this central argument came under increasing scrutiny in the mid-1990s was that, like everything else about the new System, it had not worked out in practice quite as the theory promised. At the time Britain joined the Common Market in 1973, she had been selling more goods and services to the other Six than they sold to her. And it was certainly true that, over the next 20 years, Britain did increase her exports to the rest of the Community very substantially. But the other countries increased their exports to Britain over the same period by a much greater margin. By 1995 that original modest trade surplus had turned into a very substantial yearly deficit. In 1994, Britain's deficit on visible and invisible trade with the EC was £6.79 billion. And by 1995, on visible exports alone, the cumulative deficit over the first 22 years of Britain's time in Europe had reached a staggering £100 billion. By any accounting, therefore, the rest of the Community had done much better out of trading with Britain than she done from selling to them (quite apart from the further £100 billion Britain had by 1995 contributed to the EC budget, of which only £70 million had been 'returned' in grants and subsidies).

But this was not the end of the story. For in many ways, particularly since the dramatic changes to Britain's economy during the Thatcher years of the 1980s, Britain's underlying economic performance had been dramatically improving. The chief reasons for this were nothing to do with her membership of the EC, but sprang from purely domestic factors. These ranged from the breaking of the restrictive stranglehold of the trade unions and the dramatic changes brought about in over-subsidised dinosaur state industries to the emergence of a remarkable new spirit of enterprise. This showed in fields ranging from electronics to the way the City of London had transformed itself into one of the three leading financial markets in the world.

Britain's trade with the rest of the world, in fact, particularly after she had escaped from the suffocating clutches of the ERM, was expanding in a remarkable way. In 1994 those same figures from the Central Office of Statistics which showed Britain's trade deficit with Europe at £6.79 billion, showed that with the rest of the world Britain was running a surplus of £5.1 billion. In fact the only continent in the world where Britain was now trading at a deficit was Europe. And what made this still more significant was that Britain was doing more of her trade outside Europe than inside it. According to those same CSO figures in the 1995 'Pink Book', only 44.6 per cent of Britain's visible and invisible exports were to the EC. 56.4 per cent were to the rest of the world.

Precisely because these highly revealing figures were beginning to show the whole of Britain's economic involvement with Europe in such a questionable light, the supporters of the System began to make enormous play in 1995 with the claim that, thanks to the wonders of the Single Market, Britain now did 'most her trade' with her new European 'partners' (they were never of course referred to as 'competitors'). It became tremendously important to them to show that the greater part of Britain's exports were now to Europe, and it was remarkable how consistently this point now came up in speeches, letters and other propaganda from supporters of the Euro-system. But what was most striking of all was how wildly the figures they cited varied from one another.

According to then-latest official figures, it must be recalled, Britain's exports to Europe, visible and invisible, accounted for only 44.6 per cent of the total. But in 1995, the Director-General of the CBI claimed that '53 per cent' of Britain's exports now went to the EC. Michael Heseltine, when still President of the Board of Trade, gave the figure as '55 per cent'. Labour's Robin Cook said '56 per cent'. Stewart Steven, a fanatically pro-EU columnist in the *Mail on Sunday*, gave it, with an interesting mathematical twist, as '57 per cent of our exports – coming up to two-thirds of the total'. Former Foreign Office official Sir Roy Denman gave '58 per cent'. Ex-Cabinet minister David Hunt on television, curiously precisely, gave '58.6 per cent'. A Lib Dem spokesman, Malcolm Bruce, said '60 per cent'. Sir Martin Jacomb, a respected City figure, wrote 'more than 60 per cent of all our exports'. And a backbench Tory MP, Keith Hampson, topped the bill, again with curious precision, insisting the EU now accounted for '61.3 per cent'.

No doubt some of these figures might in part have been accounted for by a failure to include figures for invisible trade, and it was true that subsequently the CSO rather strangely issued revised figures, to show Britain's exports to Europe at 48 per cent rather than the earlier 44.6. But this scarcely affected the point at issue.

A much more significant point, however, which none of these Euro-enthusiasts mentioned at all, was the fact that, in Britain's trade with Europe, the advantage now lay very much with her continental competitors. And this was a point which became of increasingly crucial significance, because it meant that, if ever Britain found herself having to leave the EU altogether, the other countries would lose much more than Britain from any attempt to restrict trade between them. The remarkable fact was that Britain was now gaining so much more advantage from trading with the outside world than she was from her trade with the EC. It could scarcely have been a more striking reversal of that vision which had been held out to the British people in 1973.

In fact it would have been hard to find a more graphic example of the way the Euro-system's supporters were increasingly having to turn everything upside down in their efforts to maintain their case than a reply sent by Sir Edward Heath early in 1995 to one of our readers who had suggested to him, somewhat provocatively, that Britain might prosper if she left the EU. Such a suggestion, of course, was the wildest heresy. But it was typical of Heath's courtesy that he should have taken the trouble for a reply to be sent. 'Sir Edward', wrote an aide, 'believes this is nonsense. One only need look at Norway to see why.' Citing a recent report suggesting that Norway's economy was now in 'sharp decline', Sir Edward had suggested this was entirely due to 'Norway's 1994 decision to reject EU membership'.

18. The Castle of Lies (II) – The Three Great Deceptions

It was true that in 1994 Norway had, in a referendum, become the only country in Europe to decide twice not to join the European club. As on the first occasion in 1972, one of the chief reasons for this was that, having seen the horrendous example set by Britain, she did not wish to hand over her rich and efficiently conserved fish resources to the lunacy of the Common Fisheries Policy. But the truly remarkable thing was the way Sir Edward seemed to be looking at Norway down the wrong end of a very long telescope. Her economy in 1995 was not in 'sharp decline' at all. It was true that her growth rate was predicted to fall during the year from 5.7 per cent in 1994 to just over 4 per cent. But the main reason for this was simply that the economies of her two main trading partners, Germany and Sweden, were now in such deep trouble that those countries would have given their eye teeth for Norway's rate of growth. Norway outside the EU was in fact still doing outstandingly well. Her only problems came from the stagnation and general economic malaise prevailing inside the EU – which was why since that 1994 referendum, the number of Norwegians opposed to membership had soared from 52 per cent to 65 per cent.

What was particularly conspicuous about the way the Euro-enthusiasts put their case was not just the extent to which they so often had to turn the facts upside down, but how much of the true picture of what was happening they had to omit altogether, because it did not suit their argument. And there was no more dramatic instance of this than the way they managed to ignore just how well Britain was now doing economically, either in spite of the EU or for reasons which had nothing to do with the EU at all. One of the most remarkable features of the 1980s and and early 1990s – apart from the disastrous interlude of her two years in the ERM – was how Britain had re-established herself on the world stage as a global trader. Her exports of goods and services to America, the Middle East and above all to the fast-growing economies of the Far East were rising at dramatic speed. In telecommunications, oil, civil engineering, above all financial services, she was a world leader. As a financial centre the City of London stood alongside New York and Tokyo, dwarfing anything else in Europe. Britain's income from overseas investments, many of them made in the boom years of the 1980s, were yielding record dividends.

To all this picture of confident, outward-looking expansion, there was just one increasingly dubious exception. It was certainly true that Britain did a very substantial amount of her trade with Europe, and there was no way that could cease. But increasingly 'Europe', as it plunged further and further into this strange psychological labyrinth of the EU, with its ever-multiplying mountains of regulation, its ever-growing thickets of 'politically correct' social legislation, its ever more grandiose economic schemes and monetary experiments – and with the threat of much worse to come – was becoming an ever darker and more depressing place to contemplate.

Had the time not come to consider very seriously the possibility of extricating Britain from this mess altogether – and returning to the wider stage of the real world?

Epilogue

What Then Must Be Done?

Europe is yesterday's idea.
> Norman Lamont, Today programme, BBC Radio 4, 8 June 1995

The key to the question lies in psychology, in that unconscious mindset which can shape how we look at the world without our being aware of it.

The mindset we must consider began to take shape more than a generation ago, when the people of Britain first began contemplating the enormous step of entry into the Common Market.

Having 'lost an empire and not yet found a role', Britain at that time was confused, depressed, suffering from a profound loss of national self-esteem. It seemed she was no longer good at any of the things she used to be good at.

The countries of western Europe on the other hand seemed to have found themselves. After their miraculous recovery from the war, they were prosperous, successful, full of optimism, and nothing symbolised this more than the imaginative, idealistic adventure they had together embarked on, of moving together in ever closer economic and political co-operation.

It seemed like an idea which represented the future. And if Britain could join in, she might share in their prosperity, their efficiency and their idealism. Furthermore, instead of just remaining claustrophobically isolated, shrunk in on herself, as an unsuccessful, inefficient little island, Britain would now have the chance to play a leading role on a new and larger stage.

Europe, in short, was not just the future. It was the opening of a door out of a prison, the liberation of stepping out into a wider world.

Then we entered. And for a long time nothing very much seemed to happen. British politics seemed to carry on in their same old way, centre stage. 'Europe' in the political sense was little more than 'noises off', still something remote which did not really touch our lives, experienced largely in terms of occasional glimpses on television, half way down the news, of our leaders posing at 'summit' conferences with groups of foreign politicians in suits.

For nearly twenty years 'Europe' remained rather a puzzle. Occasionally there were flashes of drama, as 'Maggie' staged some showdown over 'the budget'. Occasionally absurdities wafted into the news, like some silly directive making out that a carrot was a fruit. Mostly it was just a bore, incomprehensible, distant from our real everyday lives, remote.

But then those noises-off grew louder. Brussels was being mentioned in our news programmes much more frequently. M. Delors, with his tight, unsmiling little bureaucrat's face, became the first top, non-British official in Europe whose name and appearance were instantly recognisable.

Suddenly 'Europe' was becoming a major influence on our own domestic political drama, as a whole succession of senior Cabinet ministers and finally our Prime Minister herself were brought down by it.

Then, from 1992 onwards, the whole thing suddenly came in at us with a rush. Suddenly we were being confronted with the reality of what we had become involved in, on every side, the regulations, the bureaucracy, the extent to which Europe had quietly stolen away our democracy.

We found that over all those years when we were not really noticing it, we had been imperceptibly stumbling further and further into a great impenetrable thicket, which now surrounded us on almost every side.

Suddenly, in every direction, there were problems, enormously convoluted, enormously messy problems, which were having a direct impact on people's daily lives. The vast bureaucratic labyrinth of the Common Agricultural Policy. The crazy disaster of the Common Fisheries Policy. Regulations snaring more and more industries and businesses into their suffocating grip. Bills shooting up for all sorts of mundane, everyday household needs, from the water in our taps to the medicine we required from the vet for our cat, all just because of 'EC regulations'. The irritations and hidden snags of the forced jump into metrication, and worse still, the implications of the way this was forced on us.

More important than anything, in fact, was the effect 'Europe' was having on the whole of our political system, the realisation that, without our being aware of it, we had simply given away many of the powers of our parliament and our courts, and our rights as a people to govern ourselves. We had become just a comparatively small part of some huge, amorphous and sinister new entity, over which we had very little influence; which was ultimately run by an army of anonymous, unelected bureaucrats in another country; and which was always, ceaselessly, trying to move onwards; to seize more power; to develop more tentacles; to impose even more control over our money, our economy and our lives.

What made this most disturbing of all was the growing realisation that our own Government, our own ministers, our own civil servants, were no longer on 'our side', speaking and acting for the British people. Although they continued to sit in London, still preserving the outward semblance of being a 'British Government', they had in fact become merely the representatives of this vast alien System with its centre of power elsewhere. In a fundamental sense, as countless examples in this book have shown, these people no more spoke and acted on behalf of the interests and wishes of their fellow-countrymen than the Vichy government had acted for the people of wartime France. Again and again, as in the betrayal over fisheries, it was profoundly shocking to have to recognise just how far and how repeatedly since 1971 our ministers and officials had become practised in sacrificing the interests of their own people; and to recognise the lengths to which they would go to hide what they were really up to, until evasion and distortion of the truth had become almost the chief end of their Government. So much the prisoners of that alien System had they become that, in its Service, there was almost no humiliation to their country that they would not accept.

What really helped to bring home the plight we were in was that, whenever one tried to look seriously at any of the host of specific problems created by this system, trying to work out what could be done to solve them, it soon became clear that we were in a complete cul de sac. The absurdities of the CAP, the criminal insanity of the CFP, that endless, burgeoning maze of regulations: it was quite easy to suggest what should or might be done to make radical improvements to all these things, to knock some sense back into them, to make them work honestly and efficiently. But this was completely out of the question, because this was the system. And not just the system, but the System, with a capital S. There was nothing we could do to change these things at all. We were locked in. And the only prospect for the future seemed to be that the System would get worse. More constricting. More suffocating. More claustrophobic. We were trapped.

*

There was one thing we could do, however. We could learn how to look at this extraordinary situation we had reached in an entirely new way. We could retrace our steps and analyse just how and why we had come to this impasse. And once we consider all the evidence, clearly and dispassionately, once we understand the real nature of the problem, as we have tried to present it in this book, there is only one rational conclusion we can come to.

We must get out. We must leave. Or, in the language which was more and more coming to be heard in senior political circles in 1996, we must 'renegotiate an entirely new relationship with the European Union'. Which is just a polite, responsible way of saying the same thing.

But the vital thing is that this must be done in the right spirit and in the right way. It must not be done in any demeaning spirit of petulance, such as we saw flashes of in Mr Major's 'beef war' in the summer of 1996. It must not be done in a tide of silly nationalism or 'xenophobia', to use the Europhiles' favourite and almost only term of abuse for those rather more thoughtful about these matters than themselves. The argument here is not in any way 'against foreigners'. It is an argument against a new, ill-conceived, practically unworkable, potentially catastrophic System of government, which has been progressively foisted on the peoples of western Europe without their proper consent and without their being democratically consulted, and of which they are just as much the victims and potential victims as anyone in Britain.

When Britain leaves the European Union she must do so in an entirely dignified, self-possessed fashion and she must explain to her former 'partners' precisely why she feels impelled to do so. She must explain that she does this in no spirit of reproach. Despite our constant nagging reservations, we have been just as much a party to the evolution of this System in the past 20 years as anyone else.

Above all, Britain must face this historic transition in our national story in a spirit of complete self-confidence. We entered on this adventure 25 years ago at a time when our national morale was at one of its lowest ebbs in history. It was precisely because we had lost confidence in ourselves and in our capacities as a nation – and not without reason – that we were prepared to make such a bold, even reckless leap into a wholly new adventure, which marked a break with almost everything our national character and traditions had stood for over the centuries.

That was the time when we could look on joining this new, fast evolving experiment launched by our neighbours across the Channel as an exciting step into an unknown future, a moment when we could shake off the oppressive, accumulated inheritance of a past which belonged to history, and find an entirely new identity for ourselves with friends who had taken the same brave step into the unknown.

But at deeper levels of our national psyche, we never really made that break with the past, in the way some politicians would like to think. What happened instead was that, beneath the superficial trappings of our new role in the world, we went on evolving as a nation in entirely our own way. We survived that depressing, introverted decade of the 1970s, when British life was overshadowed by the power of the unions and the dispiriting sight of huge, unwieldy state-owned industries draining away billions of pounds a year in subsidies. In the 1980s we fought back. We saw the union dragon slain. We saw those dinosaur industries, like steel, go through a dramatic transformation. And in all sorts of ways we saw a rebirth of that old imaginative spirit which for centuries had marked out the British as one of the most enterprising, innovative trading peoples in the world. Instead of looking across the Channel for our future, to Germany and France, we found it was right here at home, for example in that dazzling explosion of skill and energy which established London as the leading financial centre of the world. More recently we have found it in the extraordinary success so many British businesses have had in selling to the booming economies of the Far East. That is where the future lies, out on the true world stage, where Britain has been winning her place once again as a global trader; not in the stagnating, stifling, sad, over-regulated backyard of Europe.

That is why in the mid-1990s we look back on that dream of 'Britain's future in Europe' held out to us in those far-off days of the early 1970s, and we now see it like so many other fashions of that time, as something which very much belonged to a particular moment in history, from which we have now moved on.

We must not underestimate the immense scale of the task which will confront us as we embark on the process of disengagement from the European Union. It will require two things above all: first, a real understanding of what needs to be done and how: and secondly, a titanic act of political will, requiring leadership of the highest order, to ensure that the whole operation is properly, effectively and thoroughly carried through.

The simplest thing will be to make clear to our European friends that we expect to continue trading with them in exactly the way that we have been doing. Since they benefit much more from that trade than we do, we can be confident that they will not wish to erect any obstacles to that trade. We shall continue to import their goods and to export ours to them, just as Norway and Switzerland do from outside the EU, and both of whom conduct a much higher proportion of their trade with the EU than we do.

As for that 'inward investment' from countries outside Europe which has provided such a further boost to Britain's economic growth in recent years, most of this has been directed here primarily for reasons unconnected with the EU, such as our lower labour costs and our English language. Goods from Britain will continue to gain access to the Single Market, not only for the reasons outlined above but also because of the general drastic lowering of trariffs and trade barriers through the GATT reforms.

A much more complicated challenge will be presented by the task of unravelling the huge quantity of legislation which has been passed into British law in recent years to meet the requirements of Brussels. It will be one thing to repeal the European Communities Act 1972 which provides the mechanism whereby most EC legislation is automatically put into UK law. But that is just turning off the tap for the future. What will involve a far more laborious operation will be to sift through all the legislation already in force, most of it in the form of regulations, to assess how much of it can simply be repealed and how much contains elements which can sensibly be retained. It will of course be essential that this exercise is not carried out primarily by civil servants, who are so imbued with the ethos these regulations represent that their judgement as to what was genuinely necessary could not be relied on.

But this in turn only raises the further challenge of what we are to do about that regulatory ethos itself, which has so taken over our own civil service in recent years that many of our most absurd and damaging examples of misplaced regulation have come about not directly at the instigation of Europe at all. Our involvement with Europe has certainly played a very influential part in encouraging the attitudes which we identify with that ethos. The whole style of the Brussels system of government, as with any quasi-totalitarian system, is top down, centre outwards. Laws are to be made by officials and handed down from the centre, through the System and without consultation, until they are enforced on the ground, by officials who expect their will to be obeyed without question. Such has increasingly been the style of much of our domestic government in recent years and the task of rooting that out will involve a culture change affecting every part of the public service. Once again it is a task which will require, first, a real understanding and analysis of the problem; and, secondly, genuine leadership from the top, with the will to push the transformation through.

A quite specific challenge that must be very high on the list of priorities will be the need to call a halt as soon as is practicable to the multiple insanities of the Common Fisheries Policy. This is a matter of the highest urgency, not just in the interests of Britain but of every country in Europe. If the current policy were to be allowed to continue, particularly after the year 2002 when the CFP is due to take its final form, and that vast, predatory Spanish fleet is unleashed to enjoy 'equal access' to every drop of water, right up to Southend pier, then we really should have a disaster on our hands. Europe's fish stocks might genuinely be destroyed beyond recovery. Certainly this can only be avoided by dismantling the CFP in its entirety, and starting again from scratch on very much the basis which has already been so effectively pioneered in the fishing waters off Norway, Canada and Namibia. A genuinely effective, scientifically-based, properly enforced conservation policy can only be administered by one sovereign country, acting in full control over its own waters. That is why the first action will be to give notice that we are intending to phase out all the regulations made under the Fisheries Limits

Act 1976 which allow the fishermen of all other EU countries to enter Britain's 200 mile limit, for the purposes of fishing (those countries, incidentally, include Luxembourg and Austria). This will not of course mean excluding the boats of other nations from British waters. But a series of bilateral deals will be negotiated with each of those countries, except possibly Luxembourg and Austria, permitting their fishermen to enter, but only on strictly defined terms. These will embody all the types of condition now so successfully enforced in Norwegian waters, including the technical measures which enable catches to be much more precisely targeted, and also a total ban on the discarding of catches. The startling fact is that, although this policy would be run primarily to ensure a sustainable future for Britain's own fishing industry, it would also allow fishermen from other countries to catch as many fish in British waters as they do now. But because they would do so on a rational basis, without the present holocaust of discarding, the present immense conservation disaster directly engineered by Brussels would be brought to a halt. A policy which would serve Britain's interests would also, ironically, serve the interests of every other fishing nation in Europe.

We come finally to what could prove to be the two greatest prizes of all from our leaving the European Union. The first is the effect it could have on our political life in general and on the psychology of our politicians in particular.

Few things have been more dispiriting about our country in recent years than to see our politicians turned into grey ghosts, as they have to preserve the outward show of still being in charge of the country, when in fact they have merely become the creatures and puppets of a System almost wholly out of their control. They have continued to act out the shadow play, appearing at the despatch box of the House of Commons, turning up to be interviewed on the Today programme, signing the letters drafted by their officials, signing the latest batch of statutory instruments drafted by their officials, trotting off to Brussels for a Council of Ministers to rubber stamp a whole series of decisions already arrived at by the officials of Coreper. But in reality all but the outward show has departed, which is the real underlying reason why our political life has become so thin and sterile and unreal.

Give them the chance to take control of our country again, on our behalf, and to take back some of that immense power which has passed to the armies of officialdom, and what a transformation we might see in our politicians. Even in the very task of disentangling our laws and political structures from Europe, they would once again find a challenge which would give them the chance once again to address real problems; to use their capacity for independent thought; to act once again like real men and women, instead of just as the overworked, dispirited servants of a huge, emasculating machine. They would once again have the chance to use their imaginations, to exercise their ingenuity in working out genuine solutions to real problems instead of just meekly having to execute the non-solutions to bogus problems passed down from Brussels. They would be freed to have vision again, vision for the future of their country, instead of being permanently imprisoned in the evasions, weasel words and concealments required to sidestep the political embarrassment of stepping an inch out of line on the Single Currency or the Common

Fisheries Policy. They could step out of that world of mirrors into the real world. And what a miracle that might perform for their self-respect.

Finally, the greatest prize will be that to be won by the British people themselves. It is not just the politicians who have found their self-esteem subtly eroded in recent years, as we have come to wake up to the plight our country is in. The greatest prize as we disentangle from the European Union will be the sense that we are free to stand on our own two feet again, to decide our own destiny as a people, to play to our strengths instead of always having to look over our shoulders to watch the response of our shadowy 'partners'.

We shall have once again a political system which is answerable to our own needs as a nation, no longer hamstrung by the constant need to defer. Recall that pretty blonde Norwegian girl, looking into the camera in December 1994, overjoyed that her side had won in the referendum and would not be forced into the EU? 'It is the lack of democracy in your system we don't like,' she said. And it is still something of a shock to realise that when she said 'your system' she did not mean something 'over there', somewhere else, but the System we ourselves now live under.

We shall be able to act again in our own character, instead of constantly acting out the charade that we are jointly part of some shadow pseudo-nation, with its own flag, its own passport, its own anthem debased by its hi-jacking from one of the greatest pieces of religious music ever written – a ramshackle, bureaucratic sham of a nation with which we feel no moral or spiritual identity whatever. There were few spectacles more chilling in recent years than the sight of those three self-important, shabby little politicians, one soon to be disgraced and gaoled for fraud, wandering round Belgrade in 1991 urging a Serb bully to take the strongest possible line against the Slovenes and the Croats, to save the unity of another bogus bureaucratic federation; and then to realise that, when they presented themselves as representing the 'European Community', they were there representing us, the British, as well.

When we finally summon up the courage and the will to leave this growing catastrophe, this failed mess of a sentimental dream which, by its own self-contradictions, is inevitably doomed to fall apart in catastrophe, we shall find that it is a truly liberating moment. We may even find it timely to rephrase those immortal words of William Pitt the Younger after Trafalgar: if Britain can save herself by her exertions, she may yet save Europe by her example. Along with our recovered self-respect, it will release a great charge of national energy. We shall once again be able to walk tall and free. It will be the finest thing this country has done since we helped lead Europe through to victory over tyranny in 1945.

Index